Pharmaceutical Sales Data 101

The client Perspective

A

`p·h·i´ Publications

Book

Written by Kosta Tzavaras

National Library of Canada Cataloguing in Publication

Tzavaras, Kosta
    Pharmaceutical sales data 101 : the client perspective / Kosta Tzavaras.
Includes index.
ISBN 1-4120-0270-2
    1. Selling—Drugs. I. Title.
HF5439.D75T92 2003   615'.1'0688   C2003-902424-5

TRAFFORD

This book was published *on-demand* **in cooperation with Trafford Publishing.** On-demand publishing is a unique process and service of making a book available for retail sale to the public taking advantage of on-demand manufacturing and Internet marketing. **On-demand publishing** includes promotions, retail sales, manufacturing, order fulfilment, accounting and collecting royalties on behalf of the author.

Suite 6E, 2333 Government St., Victoria, B.C. V8T 4P4, CANADA
Phone   250-383-6864   Toll-free   1-888-232-4444 (Canada & US)
Fax   250-383-6804   E-mail   sales@trafford.com
Web site   www.trafford.com   TRAFFORD PUBLISHING IS A DIVISION OF TRAFFORD HOLDINGS LTD.
Trafford Catalogue #03-0639   www.trafford.com/robots/03-0639.html

10   9   8   7   6   5

Table of Contents

Table of Figures

Preface

The book is intended for the pharmaceutical and Biotechnology sales and marketing professional with interest in sales data. That includes professional sales reps, sales and finance analysts, sales administration and information technology professionals and consultants providing data management and analysis services.

For those just entering the industry, the goal is to accelerate their learning and training process by introducing them to some general concepts about the industry and the data. For those already in the industry, the goal is to clarify some concepts, 'connect the dots' and provide the reasoning behind certain processes, and deepen the understanding of the data.

This knowledge prepares the sales administration staff to successfully handle field requests, sales analysts and consultants to support the decision making process with insightful analysis, and information technology staff to manage data better. Specifically for the sales reps, for which the data has some financial implications, the book is intended to broaden their understanding of the data and reinforce their confidence in it. This book is not intended for teaching sales analysis methods.

The book is written to reflect the client's perspective and complement but not replace product information provided by data vendors. Equally important perspectives both, their differences lie between the vendor's product-centric approach and his often generalized, perceived customer need, and the customer's solution-driven approach and his specific, actual need. The client perspective is derived from industry common practices and not necessarily best practices. The author does not have conclusive evidence that the industry practices are indeed best practices and not merely common practices.

The book uses a top-down approach introducing the market, the customer, the product and finally the data. That is because a lot of the complexities of the data can be better understood by first understanding the market mechanisms, the customer interactions and the properties of the product. Some of the methods and techniques discussed in the book require considerable levels of staffing and funding. The user should use his discretion in choosing the alternative best suited for his company.

The key idea of the book is that you can derive maximum value from the data only by thoroughly understanding its limitations. That is because the strengths of the data are effortlessly identifiable and can be easily exploited by everyone. Incremental value can be derived by exploiting alternative solutions where data becomes a limiting factor. An effort is made to highlight wherever possible the implications of the data limitations to core applications like quota, compensation, targeting, alignment, forecasting, etc.

Chapter 1
The Market

THE MARKET

The U.S. pharmaceutical market is based on the four-tier structure of manufacturer-wholesaler-retailer-consumer. This structure allows the manufacturer to focus on product research, development and marketing, the wholesaler to provide the economies of scale to operate an efficient logistical infrastructure, the retailer to contribute the value-add services, and ultimately the consumer to get the best, most comprehensive product package deal.

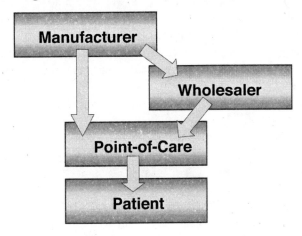

Figure 1. Pharmaceutical market tiers

To further define this model, the first tier belongs to the pharmaceutical manufacturer. This tier represents the supply side. For the purpose of this discussion the term pharmaceutical manufacturer refers to manufacturers of both pharmaceutical and biotechnology products. Even though the science and technology for discovering, producing and delivering pharmaceutical and biological products vary substantially, the marketing and sales techniques, and data to support them are virtually indistinguishable. Additionally, many of which would be considered traditional pharmaceutical manufacturers have interests in biotech ventures. With that trend likely to continue in the future the distinction between the two terms will be less meaningful, at least in the area of sales and marketing.

Furthermore, the discussion will be limited to prescription branded and generic products only. Although pharmaceutical manufacturers produce and market over-the-counter (OTC) medications, the marketing techniques and data to support them are quite different from those of prescription drugs, skewed heavily towards direct-to-consumer (DTC) methods.

The pharmaceutical distributor comes in the form of drug wholesaler supplying the various outlets at the next lower tier, chain warehouses supplying their own outlets and re-packers of the original product into consumer-ready packages serving niche markets. This tier's purpose is to maintain a well-optimized distribution web for end-to-end movement of product rapidly and inexpensively.

The retailer tier, or more appropriately the point-of-care (POC) tier, is where supply meets demand and the end-user comes in contact with the product. In this tier, outlets sharing the same characteristics are grouped and classified in the following general categories: pharmacies, clinics, hospitals, healthcare plan facilities, long-term care facilities, purchasing agents and various government sites.

The last tier of the market belongs exclusively to the patient and it represents true demand. The diagram below shows the market tiers tailored to the pharmaceutical market.

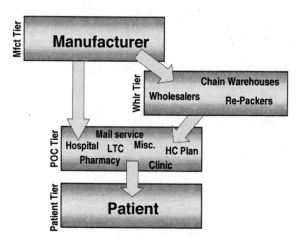

Figure 2. Pharmaceutical market tiers expanded

The entities in these four tiers, through a series of transactions, physically handle the product passing it from one to the other until it reaches the patient. A number of regulatory and economic reasons make the existence of a fifth tier necessary in this market. This tier, however, does not physically handle the product and will be discussed in a later chapter.

THE MANUFACTURER

The pharmaceutical industry is a large, high profile, research-intensive industry with annual sales of more than $200 billion, growing at a steady pace.

The industry derives its high profile from the importance of therapeutics to humans and the controversial issues surrounding healthcare, such as managed care, Medicare drug coverage, drug importation, cost of drugs, etc. The very costly and lengthy process for bringing new drugs to market has ranked the industry as the top research industry in the United States.

There are more that 300 companies currently producing drugs in the United States. A number of them engage in the discovery, development and marketing of new drugs while others produce and market generic versions of drugs whose patents have expired. The industry has achieved tremendous growth in recent decades going from 650 drugs in 1960 to more than 10,000 at the end of the century. The driver behind this growth was the replacement of surgical procedures with the use of medicines.

To survive the competitive environment, the manufacturer must develop new drugs and market them aggressively. For that, he must invest continuously in research and development to maintain a pipeline with potential new drugs. The process is long and expensive. According to one estimate, it takes more than 10 years and a cost in excess of $800 million to develop a new drug. Only 5% of the thousands of compounds researchers test make it to pre-clinical testing and the failure of drugs having entered clinical trials is approximately 80%.

The Food and Drug Administration (FDA) regulates the manufacture and sale of drugs. The FDA is part of the Public Health Services of the US Department of Human and Health Services. The agency's objective with respect to drugs is to assure that drugs are safe and effective for their intended uses. The uses of drugs that contain controlled substances are further regulated by the Drug Enforcement Agency (DEA) to assure that they are not prescribed and used illegally. The DEA is part of the US Justice Department.

Once a compound is tested and believed to have therapeutic value it must go through a rigorous testing process for safety and effectiveness (efficacy) before it becomes a commercially available drug. The figure below outlines that process.

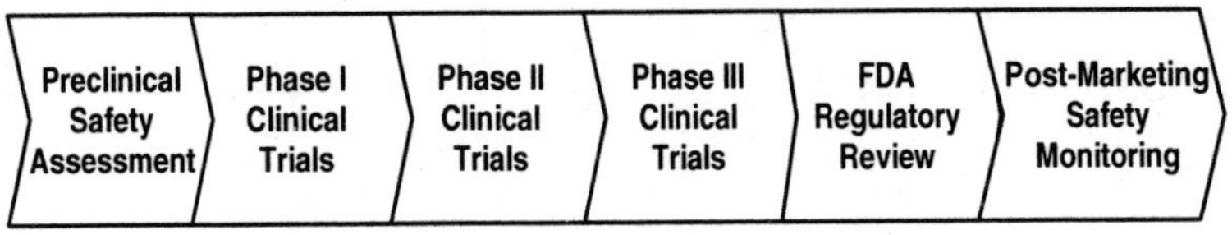

Preclinical Safety Assessment	Phase I Clinical Trials	Phase II Clinical Trials	Phase III Clinical Trials	FDA Regulatory Review	Post-Marketing Safety Monitoring

Figure 3. Regulatory process for drug development

The first step in the process, the preclinical safety assessment, determines the biologic effect of the compound on the disease from tests performed on animals and in laboratories. It also studies the toxic effects of increased doses of the compound on animals. Compounds that do not pose a risk to humans to the satisfaction of the FDA advance to the clinical trial phase.

Phase I trials test the safety of the drug on a small number of less than 100 healthy humans with single and if safe with multiple doses. In Phase II clinical trials the drug is tested on 100-300 patient volunteers to determine its safety and efficacy on the patient population it is intended to treat. These are double-blinded studies where some of the patients are given the actual drug and some are given an inactive compound, or placebo. To ensure that the results are not influenced in any way neither the investigators nor the patients know who is receiving the drug. Phase III are large trials involving typically between 1,000-5,000 humans. These trials determine the effects from different drug doses, drug interactions and side effects, results by gender, etc.

The FDA regulatory review phase begins with the manufacturer submitting a New Drug Application (NDA) to the FDA. The filing includes reports on the results of the clinical trials and any pertinent information available on the safety and efficacy of the drug. The FDA regulatory review takes between 12 and 18 months to complete and the manufacturer may start marketing the drug immediately following approval.

The post-marketing safety-monitoring phase begins when the drug becomes commercially available and it is intended to monitor on an on-going basis the drug's safety. This phase may include phase IV clinical trials at the request of the FDA as a condition for product approval or may be voluntarily conducted by the manufacturer. Phase IV trials may be undertaken to further investigate reported adverse reactions or to demonstrate improved health outcomes and cost effectiveness (pharmacoeconomic studies). The results from phase IV trials are used extensively by manufacturers as product promotion tools.

The biggest threat to the manufacturer's business is patent expiration and generic intrusion. The patent life of a drug is 17 years from discovery. Pharmaceutical manufacturers may be granted an additional 6-month of marketing exclusivity as an incentive to conduct studies of drugs in children when requested by the FDA. Accounting for the product development and approval processes it leaves on average about 12 years of effective patent life for the manufacturer to recover its investment and make a profit.

To bring a generic drug in the market the generic manufacturer must file an Abbreviated New Drug Application (ANDA) with the FDA. If the application challenges a patent and the brand manufacturer responds within 45 days with a lawsuit, a 30-month stay may extend the patent protection to allow time to litigate patent disputes between the innovator company and the generic manufacturer. The first generic manufacturer to challenge a patent with a paragraph IV certification in their ANDA receives six month market exclusivity. No other generic can enter the market during this period.

The manufacturer commonly attempts to introduce a newer, improved version of the drug before the patent expires and switch the use to the new product as a defense to generic intrusion. Another defense mechanism for products with exceptional safety record is to attempt to obtain OTC status for the drug. In other cases the manufacturer finds it beneficial to enter into an authorized-generic deal with a generic manufacturer.

The Orphan Drug Act of 1983 provides manufacturers incentives to develop drugs for less viable, small markets of diseases with fewer than 200,000 patients. The incentives include seven years of market exclusivity from approval and 50% tax credit for certain clinical research expenses. Orphan diseases number approximately 5,000 and since the legislation was enacted more than 200 drugs have been developed.

Despite the cost of developing new drugs the industry has continued to innovate mainly due to tax incentives companies receive when they increase R&D spend above a certain amount. As a result pharmaceutical research in the United States increased significantly in recent years to surpass the level of R&D in Europe.

Marketing is another area where manufacturers place a lot importance. The success of a product is not guaranteed and for that the manufacturer must make sure to capture enough market share. Pharmaceutical manufacturers implement a variety of marketing techniques for the promotion of their products backed primarily by big investments in sophisticated market research and data. Commonly used promotional programs include the use of large sales forces, e-detailing, publishing of post-marketing clinical studies, medical journal ads, direct mail and phone campaigns, sponsoring meetings and speaker programs, media promotion including TV, radio, print and internet ads, etc.

Perhaps the most critical issue for the manufacturer is reimbursement, primarily from third party payers, Medicaid and going forward Medicare. This is the area where successful companies differentiate themselves from the rest. The manufacturer must overcome any reimbursement obstacles in order to clear the way for the success of its marketing programs.

THE WHOLESALER

This layer of the market consists of drug wholesaler warehouses and pharmacy chain warehouses. The wholesaler is an integral part of the healthcare industry in general and a very important partner of the pharmaceutical manufacturer. His main role is the distribution of prescription and OTC pharmaceuticals, herbal, health and beauty aids, medical supplies and equipment, hospital supplies, medical and home health care items. Not a small task considering the economic impact to the healthcare industry if each of the 650 manufacturers had to distribute their products directly to the 140 thousand point-of-care outlets.

Wholesalers solve the logistical problem by providing one stop shopping for these outlets for all of their needs, reducing the number of transactions between manufacturers and care providers. By bringing their warehouses closer to their clients they are able to rapidly supply them, often more than once daily, thus, satisfying the manufacturer's need for market coverage and rapid delivery.

The low profit margin forced the drug wholesalers to consolidate heavily through mergers and acquisitions in recent years. Today, the three top wholesalers account for approximately 90% of the sales with each of them having roughly equal share of the market. The Healthcare Distribution Management Association (HDMA), formerly known as National Wholesale Druggist Association (NWDA), is the industry's main association with more than 70 distributors operating approximately 240 warehouses. HDMA member sales account for 50% of all wholesale volume, non-HDMA for 8% and chain warehouses accounting for 25%.

National wholesalers build distribution networks covering broad geographic areas across the country, while regional wholesalers concentrate in local and niche markets. How does the wholesaler meet their objectives of providing full market coverage, in a timely and cost effective manner?

First, by strategically positioning their warehouses close to their markets. When an area is not covered sufficiently by a national wholesaler, a regional one fills in the un-met need. In the end, all of the 140 thousand outlets in the market have sufficient access to the product. Enough to keep their inventories low, relying on just in time stocking.

Positioning of the warehouses allows wholesalers to meet their second objective of rapid delivery. Being close to their customers, they are able to deliver product more than once a day, fill emergency orders and respond to disaster situations.

The third and perhaps most important objective of cost effective delivery is met primarily by reducing the overall number of transactions between manufacturers and point-of-care outlets. A wholesaler can fill a pharmacy order for ten items made by ten different manufacturers in a single transaction, whereas, it takes ten shipments to have the order filled directly by the ten manufacturers. Using the middleman there are fewer dots to connect between the 650 market suppliers and the 140 thousand POC outlets in the marketplace.

By outsourcing the distribution to the wholesaler, the manufacturer needs only a small logistical operation to handle mostly bulk shipments to wholesalers. In fact, according to the HDMA the industry is able to reduce the more than four billion potential transactions between manufacturers and POC outlets to just a few tens of millions of transactions.

To survive the competitive pressure and enhance their profitability wholesalers depend on state-of-the-art automation of their facilities to increase their operating efficiencies. This means large capital expenditures in computer and automated order filling equipment. Very frequently they engage in speculative buying, purchasing large quantities of product in anticipation of price increases based on historical norms. Additionally, they have ventured out to offer their partners and clients a number of value-added services, mainly in information management and technology, marketing and training. Information systems include order entry and inventory control, prescription processing, sales analysis reports, decision support for inventory levels and purchasing. Part of their revenue is also derived from the sale of transaction, inventory and other data.

Manufacturers push overall 85% of their sales through wholesalers. They ship the remaining 15% directly to healthcare providers. The level of direct sales varies by manufacturer and so does their strategy, which might be product or customer specific. Typically the product or customer profile determines the distribution method.

Specialty products, prescribed by smaller number of physicians for use in clinics and hospitals, are better suited for direct distribution. More common drugs, such as broadly used antibiotics, require distribution to thousands of retail accounts making them unattractive for direct distribution. Companies may choose to ship directly to certain accounts regardless of the product profile. These accounts are considered important enough to require the attention of the manufacturer or cannot be adequately serviced by their supplier.

Manufacturers can afford to outsource distribution because keeping control of it does not offer them a strategic competitive advantage. The manufacturer must focus on product development and marketing. Building a large distribution capability, when they can leverage the wholesaler, is counter-productive because it ties capital to the wrong operation. That is where wholesale distribution comes in. It allows the manufacturer to keep his logistical operation small and his investment in it low.

The savings from the economies of scale brought in by the wholesaler would have otherwise been costs that the manufacturer and the patient would have to absorb, thus making healthcare even costlier. Distribution costs are not limited just to shipping charges, but extend to inventory costs, billing, bookkeeping, bad debt collection, etc. Wholesalers provide a buffer for that. Much of the inventory costs are transferred to the wholesalers and along with that the credit extension to retail accounts and risk of bad debt and collection. Wholesalers also use their large networks to recall products efficiently when the need arises.

Another very important service provided by wholesalers relates to the contract pricing granted by the manufacturers to certain healthcare providers. It is particularly interesting from the data perspective because it helps solve certain problems that will be discussed in a later chapter. Pricing contracts allow accounts to purchase product below the wholesaler's cost. Recognizing that, the wholesaler charges his client the contract price plus his service fee and in turn submits a rebate claim back to the manufacturer for the difference between the contract price and the wholesaler acquisition cost. This claim is called a "charge back".

Charge Back = Wholesaler Acquisition Price - Contract Price

The manufacturer supplies the wholesaler with the contract pricing by account. Accounts are identified by their DEA (Drug Enforcement Agency) number. DEA numbers are assigned to all sites authorized to possess prescription drugs. The wholesaler loads the contract information into their computer system. When filling an order for a contracted product to a contracted account, the computer overrides the wholesaler's price with the contract price and generates a charge back to the manufacturer.

Contract pricing is product and customer specific. Manufacturers ordinarily grant contracts to customers for some but not all products in their portfolio. Similarly, they may grant contract pricing for a product to a market segment, but not grant any contract pricing to another segment. All accounts within a segment must have access to the same pricing. Exempt from this rule are any non-profit accounts. Contract pricing is granted to provide accounts the economic incentive to increase product use which leads to market share growth, participation in outcomes studies and clinical trials, and other special circumstances.

Wholesalers cannot create demand and have little power to switch market share, and therefore, have little leverage with the manufacturer. They often acquire product at list price minus a few percentage points from the payment terms offered by the manufacturer. Markups and service fees charged to their customers are low as well. Occasionally they are able to charge manufacturers a service charge for services they extend to their clients.

With very thin profit margins, the wholesaler looks to the manufacturer for operating efficiencies, better payment terms and just-in-time delivery for better inventory management.

THE POINT-OF-CARE (POC) OUTLETS

The point-of-care tier is made up by the healthcare providers. This is where the patient gets his preventive care, diagnosis, and treatment and fills his prescriptions. The outlets in this tier are numerous and one or more of them are conveniently located in or near every neighborhood across the country. They vary in size and in scope of services they provide.

The larger of these entities are centrally located serving a greater area and perform the most complex and costliest medical operations. Smaller entities are more abundant, often found in clusters competing for the same customer. These outlets serve smaller areas, performing simpler medical procedures or simply fill prescriptions and consult patients. The entities in this tier are hospitals, healthcare plan facilities, clinics, pharmacies, Long-Term Care facilities and various government sites.

This tier is very important to the manufacturer. Because of that he concentrates a large amount of resources in this tier through which he hopes to reach the patient. The following section discusses the different types of outlets in the POC tier.

The Hospital

Hospitals are the largest and most complex entities in this category. They treat patients requiring acute care, emergency room, intensive care and inpatient surgery. They also treat patients in their outpatient departments. Hospitals make large investments in state-of-the-art diagnostic, lab testing and medical equipment and facilities.

Hospitalization is by far the most expensive care provided to patients and it is in the best interest of insurers to minimize the inpatient days. This is good news for manufacturers with drugs that help reduce hospital days.

There are more than 6,000 hospitals throughout the country. Hospitals are commonly classified into federal, community, Long-Term Care and institutional hospital units. Federal hospitals are owned by the Veteran's Administration (VA) and the Department of Defense (DoD). The VA and DoD, with approximately 250 hospitals and centralized purchasing are attractive targets for pharmaceutical manufacturers.

The largest category, with approximately 5,000 units, is that of community hospitals and it consists of non-government not-for-profit hospitals, investor-owned for-profit and state and local government hospitals. Its number of beds, the utilization rate and the number of admissions determines the size of a hospital. Data vendors such as Verispan and IMS provide complete profiles of hospitals.

Of particular interest to pharmaceutical companies are the academic medical centers and teaching hospitals. These hospitals are important because they are usually large medical centers on the cutting edge of medical advancement, treating large numbers of patients and using state-of-the-art procedures. It is there that many of the key influencers and opinion leaders can be found. Piers follow the practices of these physicians widely, shaping their way of thinking. Manufacturers have also the opportunity to expose interns and residents early on to their products.

The inpatient pharmacy manages the hospital's medicinal needs. It is a closed-wall pharmacy serving only the needs of the patients admitted to receive inpatient care. An outpatient pharmacy at the hospital serves the needs of discharged patients or patients of the outpatient clinics. Outpatient pharmacies are either owned by the hospital or are independently owned.

The hospital's medical staffs include physicians, interns and residents meeting their educational requirements, physician assistants, nurse practitioners, etc. Hospital based physicians are salaried employees of the hospital. A hospital profile should include an accurate affiliation list of medical staff that can be used for targeting. Office-based physicians may have admitting privileges at the hospital, which allows them to admit and treat their patients.

The vast difference between acute hospital care and outpatient care has resulted in a class of drugs used almost exclusively in the hospitals during the course of the treatment. Strong antibiotics fall in this category. Similarly, because some diseases almost never require hospitalization, there exists a class of non-hospital drugs, commonly referred to as retail drugs. Allergy drugs fall in this category. Retail drugs are sometimes used in hospitals when the patient besides his acute condition suffers from a concomitant disease requiring treatment with these drugs. Other drugs have more balanced use between hospital and non-hospital settings.

The distinction between hospital and retail drugs has certain implication for the manufacturer who must adopt a suitable strategy for the environment he will be promoting these drugs. Hospitals are more complex than physician offices and require a higher level of sophistication dealing with them. The maze of departments, the numerous medical staff and decision makers are more difficult to navigate. To deal with these complexities, manufacturers often put together dedicated specialty hospital sales forces to promote their drugs to hospitals.

Hospitals are often part of a larger organization called a system that manages, owns, leases or sponsors a number of hospitals. This model is referred to as a multi-hospital system. Alternatively, through a membership arrangement three or more freestanding hospitals including at least 25% of their non-hospital healthcare organizations may form a diversified single-hospital system. A hospital may participate in a network of healthcare providers including physicians, clinics, managed care organizations, pharmacies, etc, offering total patient care. The hospital's affiliation with a system does not preclude it from participating in a network. The association of a hospital with a system or network implies some degree of influence from these entities on the hospital.

The manufacturer needs to be aware of these affiliations and have a strategy of dealing with hospitals that acknowledges these relationships. Hospital data comes in the form of inpatient and outpatient pharmacy purchases, outpatient clinic purchases and prescription outflow at the physician or the hospital.

The Clinic

A clinic is usually the place where the patient gets diagnosed and treated when his condition does not require hospitalization. Clinics vary a lot more amongst them than hospitals do. The simplest form of a clinic is defined as a practicing physician's office. To share overhead administration costs physicians of same specialty often share office space to form a single-specialty clinic; or they share space with physicians from different specialties to provide a wider array of services, forming a multi-specialty clinic. These types of clinics have limited investment in medical and diagnostic equipment. They employ nurses and administrative staff for maintaining appointments, billing and filing reimbursement claims.

The next type of clinic is a specialty type of clinic that performs more complex and specialized procedures. Procedures performed in these clinics can last much longer than the typical office visit. These clinics have considerable investments in diagnostic and lab equipment and appropriately setup space for advanced drug administration, diagnostic testing and surgical procedures. Clinics in this category include oncology, radiology, urology, nephrology, imaging, hemodialysis, orthopedic, urgent care and birth control.

A higher tier of clinics includes outpatient clinics belonging to hospitals, usually on hospital grounds, VA outpatient clinics and outpatient surgical centers. These are likely to be the largest and best-equipped clinics, performing the most complex outpatient procedures. The size of these clinics and the type of ownership distinguishes them from other clinics.

Clinics make up the majority category of healthcare providers diagnosing and treating patients. It is the provider that is most accessible to the patient and the place the patient will most likely visit before he is hospitalized if his condition requires it. Clinics are where most of the one million physicians in the country are found, and where the most common diseases are treated on an ordinary day. All of these are important facts for the manufacturer, whose drugs are most often prescribed here. Realizing their importance, the manufacturers employ collectively tens of thousands of sales reps to establish a presence in the clinics to promote their products and provide support to the physician and his staff.

Ordinarily, the patient receives a prescription from the physician, which he fills in a retail pharmacy for consumption at home. Some drugs, requiring a certain type of administration such as IV injections, are given at the clinic. These drugs are stocked by the clinic or supplied by an outside pharmacy. The dispensing and administration of drugs provide additional revenue sources for the clinic in a tough managed care environment.

The manufacturer must choose from the thousands of clinics where to deliver his message. He must make the connection between the disease his drug is designed to treat, the physician specialties treating the disease and physicians within those specialties active in the treatment of the disease. Broadly used drugs or large physician specialties such as GPs are a challenge and require additional criteria that will be discussed in a later chapter. Data for clinics comes in the form of purchases and dispensed prescriptions by physician.

The Pharmacy

The pharmacy is the only healthcare provider in the POC tier that does not diagnose and treat patients. The role of the pharmacy is to fill prescriptions at the order of the physician and consult the patient on the use of prescribed drugs, potential side affects and drug interactions. Nevertheless, enough of them must stock the drug for it to be available in all geographic areas so that the patient has easy access to it. And that will be the manufacturer's main concern with these types of accounts.

Retail pharmacies are found near almost every neighborhood as stand alone entities or part of another business, typically a food store or a mass merchandiser. Stand-alone pharmacies are either part of a chain or privately owned independent pharmacies. Another type of pharmacy, less known to the general public, is the mail service pharmacy. Unless the mail service pharmacy has a retail component, it is not accessible to the patient for walk-in business.

Pharmacies can also be found inside the sites of these healthcare providers: hospitals, HMO sites, clinics, long-term care facilities and institutions. We will consider those as closed-wall, not open to the public pharmacies, part of the entities they belong. In fact, when we talk about sales to these entities we really mean sales to their pharmacies. Closed-wall model pharmacies can also exist as stand-alone serving more than one of the above type of care providers or even have partly walk-in business. The following discussion focuses on the types of pharmacies.

Retail Pharmacy

Independent Pharmacies - The generally accepted definition of an independent pharmacy is a privately owned pharmacy business with up to a maximum of three locations. In recent years the number of independent pharmacies has declined steadily, however, their total sales volume has been growing, doing more business with fewer stores. Still, with more than 18,000 stores out of the almost 55,000 of retail pharmacies independents are significant in number. Because of the small number of stores they represent as a business compared to pharmacy chains, their biggest disadvantage is the lack of economies of scale to improve operational efficiencies and bargaining power; an important consideration for contracting with managed care, suppliers and drug manufacturers.

Often they must focus on niche markets to survive the intense competition with chain pharmacies. Because of their limited resources they are more likely to utilize value-added services from wholesalers and consequently pay higher premiums for these services. Drug manufacturers often will extend special programs only to the highest volume independents because of the difficulty of managing the programs with the numerous pharmacies in this category. By contrast, chain pharmacies can take full advantage of these programs with central administration by the corporate office.

Chain Pharmacies - Chain pharmacies make up the largest group of pharmacies and they account roughly for 35% of the total retail pharmacies. Industry consolidation in recent years has resulted in the domination of this category by a few large chains. Chains run retail stores and enhance their revenue from sales of other general merchandise. Chains are best positioned to compete with the other retail pharmacies because of the resources at their disposal, purchasing power, operational efficiencies, economies of scale, ability to attract resources, breadth of products, expertise, access to suppliers and manufacturers, etc.

Food store and Mass Merchandiser Pharmacies - Food stores and mass merchandisers have tried to capitalize on the opportunity of having the customer in the store for other shopping needs. Together they account for a little less than 30% of the retail pharmacies. Food stores have grown in number of stores and sales in recent years. Food store and mass merchandiser pharmacy chains are likely to carry fewer classes of drugs, offer fewer services, engage in fewer programs, etc., than pure play pharmacy chains.

Mail service Pharmacy

Mail service pharmacies are pharmacies that fill prescriptions remotely. The physician typically faxes the prescription and the drug is shipped to the patient via a national courier service such as the post office. Because of the method of distribution these pharmacies practically are able to serve patients in almost every part of the country. Although few in number compared to other types of pharmacies, a little over 300, they account for almost an equal level of sales as the independent pharmacies. While the average retail store-sales for prescription drugs are roughly $2 million, mail service pharmacies have average store sales of more than $75 million.

Because of their high volume of business and low overhead expenses not having to operate retail stores, they are able to discount drugs. That makes mail service pharmacies particularly attractive to patients with chronic diseases, or patients requiring expensive drugs. Patients treated for acute conditions, such as infections requiring antibiotics, are not likely to use mail service pharmacies to fill their prescriptions. First, because they need the drug right away and the best mail service pharmacies have to offer is overnight delivery. Second, because mail service prescriptions are economically viable only for larger quantities and when shipping costs are low. For acute diseases, larger quantity would mean longer treatment than the physician recommended and low shipping costs would mean starting the treatment late. On the other hand, this suits perfectly chronic disease patients that need continued supplies of medicines and can time their orders so that the next shipment arrives before their supply runs out.

The ability of mail service pharmacies to reduce healthcare costs has not gone unnoticed by the cost-conscious managed care who is becoming increasingly interested in working with these pharmacies.

Depot Pharmacy

The depot pharmacy is a type of independent pharmacy. It is a wholesale pharmacy supplying other local stores and sometimes a hybrid of wholesale and retail pharmacy handling walk-in store traffic as well. The number of depot pharmacies is insignificant.

Nuclear Pharmacy

The nuclear pharmacy is a closed-wall pharmacy that dispenses radiopharmaceuticals for diagnostic and therapeutic use by nuclear medicine departments in hospitals and outpatient clinics. The drug is prepared in unit-doses, delivered and ready to administer. Nuclear pharmacies are located either inside the hospital and clinic or centrally located serving multiple hospitals and clinics. They are very specialized pharmacies and distribute only certain classes of drugs, therefore, not potential customers for many manufacturers. There are approximately 350 nuclear pharmacies.

Consultant Pharmacy

Consultant pharmacies serve nursing homes, sub-acute care centers, assisted living facilities, home health patients, psychiatric hospitals and correctional facilities. This category includes pharmacies also known as long-term care and home-care provider pharmacies.

These pharmacies specialize in unit dose dispensing of drugs. Unit dose dispensing is the practice of packaging drugs in quantities equal to a single dose and is more appropriate for incapacitated people. Additionally, they offer consultative services, hence the term, for the review of drug regiments of patients, administrative services for establishing policies and procedures for medication use, and management of the regulatory compliance activities of nursing homes.

Consultant pharmacies are mostly closed-wall pharmacies with few of them handling walk-in traffic from retail customers. They are either located inside the facility they serve or centrally located serving multiple facilities in a large radius. Consultant pharmacies specialize in geriatric pharmacotherapy due to the fact that they serve to a great degree the elder population in nursing homes and assisted living facilities.

Specialty Pharmacy

Specialty pharmacies are by definition pharmacies that have a high percent of their business concentrated in just few therapeutic areas serving chronic disease patients. The therapeutic areas include those of complex health conditions and high cost therapies such as HIV, oncology, hepatitis C, infertility, hemophilia, rheumatoid arthritis, multiple sclerosis, growth hormone deficiency, crohn's disease, transplant, prostate cancer, cystic fibrosis, etc.

Specialty pharmacies are very diverse and do not constitute a separate class by IMS' pharmacy definitions. Instead they are found in other classes of pharmacies such as retail, mail service, nuclear and home health. These pharmacies sometimes have separate departments for their specialty drug business and the traditional higher-volume, lower-cost drug business.

Specialty pharmacies do more than just fill prescriptions. They contract with managed care and manufacturers to provide value-added patient and disease management services. These services include patient consultation, drug administration training, side effect monitoring, disease information and patient education material, drug regiment compliance monitoring and intervention, etc. In exchange, the pharmacies may receive for these services administration fees, manufacturer product discounts and increased business volume from managed care. Specialty pharmacies can be of tremendous importance to certain manufacturers.

The Healthcare Plan

The discussion in this section applies only to healthcare plans that own and operate facilities that provide direct care to patients. This category includes staff-model Health Maintenance Organization (HMO) sites, physician network pharmacies, union shop and workman's compensation clinics, and other payer care sites.

Healthcare plans have drastically different business models and as a result the scopes of services they provide differ equally as well. At one end of the spectrum are those plans whose role is reduced to that of the payer, not providing direct care to the patients. Instead they contract all the patient services to healthcare providers. At the other end are plans whose role includes that of the provider and are self-sufficient, owning almost all of the services the patients may require. Kaiser is perhaps the best example of a self-sufficient plan. This distinction is important because without the care facilities to operate a pharmacy, the plans are not directly involved in any transaction with the manufacturer or the wholesaler, and therefore, do not have a place in the POC tier.

The staff-model HMO is one such plan that operates its own hospitals, clinics, pharmacies and ancillary facilities. These sites are closed to the general public and their services are available to members only. Staff-model HMOs hire their own salaried physicians, pharmacists, medical, administrative and other staff. Some of them operate supply warehouses for the needs of their facilities.

This type of HMO is very efficient in controlling costs, performing its own utilization reviews and managing its daily operations. Patient access to care is controlled by the HMO and coordinated between the specialty departments of the organization with referrals. Most importantly for the manufacturer, staff-model HMOs operate their pharmacies, have very tight control of the drugs they use and make extensive use of generics. This segment accounts for a mere 1% of the pharmaceutical sales in the POC tier.

Long-Term Care (LTC)

The Long-Term Care outlets include nursing homes, assisted living facilities, home health care services, hospice sites and the pharmacies that serve the needs of these facilities. It is overall the second smallest segment of healthcare providers in the POC tier after healthcare plans; however, a segment with the potential of high growth given the population aging statistics. It is also the most complex and least understood of all other outlet categories. It is by far also the most challenging in terms of data.

From the manufacturer's perspective, the key player in this segment is the consultant pharmacy that contracts to provide services to these outlets. The consultant pharmacies in most cases determine the list of approved drugs (formulary) to use and they can influence the sales of a particular drug affecting its market share. The segment is dominated by a few chains. The following section discusses the types of outlets in this segment.

Nursing Homes

Nursing homes are facilities that provide short stay (less than 6 months) to people admitted for rehabilitation or convalescence and those admitted for terminal care at the late stages of their disease, and long stay for people with chronic medical problems requiring long-term nursing care. The long stay resident is typically an older person, cognitively impaired by mental disorders, and functionally dependent. The goal of the nursing home is to restore and maintain the patient's physical abilities, mental state and social well being and in the case of terminally ill to allow them to die in a dignified way. The services they provide include medical, pharmacy, nursing, dietary and activity. Nursing homes can be classified in the following categories:

- **Skilled Nursing Facility -** Also known as convalescent hospital, it is a nursing home that must have on duty a licensed or registered nurse on 24-hour basis. It caters mostly to people with reduced physical and mental capacities that require help with even the most basic aspects of life like walking, eating, bathing and dressing.

- **Intermediate Care Facility –** It is a nursing facility that must provide 8-hours of nursing supervision per day and care for people that are ambulatory, needing less supervision and care. Its main difference with the Skilled Nursing Facility is the level of nursing care provided.

- **Skilled Nursing Facility for Special Disabilities -** A facility that provides care to the mentally ill that can be a threat to themselves and to others. These facilities have specially modified areas for the security and protection of the patient and others.

The nursing home business is regulated by state and federal agencies. Nursing homes are licensed by the state they operate in and inspected at least annually to determine compliance with certain standards. The federal government introduced the Omnibus Budget and Reconciliation act of 1987, known as OBRA 87, in an effort to improve the quality of care in nursing homes. The regulations include provisions for periodic comprehensive assessments of the residents, the reduction of use of physical restraints and drugs to control the physical activity and behavior of the patient, personnel training and quality standards definitions. The regulations also require the presence of a medical director. Non-compliance with the regulations can result in penalties and ineligibility for Medicare and Medicaid reimbursement.

Non-profit nursing home corporations are sponsored by charitable organizations or run by federal, state or local agencies. For-profit nursing homes are owned by individuals or corporations with the majority of them belonging to a nursing home chain. The cost of nursing home care is covered by the resident's own assets, Medicare, Medicaid and any supplemental insurance such as Medigap or catastrophic insurance.

The facility's medical director overwhelmingly provides medical care to patients in the nursing home. Other attending physicians specializing in geriatric care who also have private practices in the community may provide care. The pharmacy services are provided on an exclusive basis by an in-house or outside consultant pharmacy. The pharmacist conducts drug regimen reviews on all patients at least once a month for the appropriateness of the drug therapy and monitoring of the patient's response to the medication, according to federal requirements. The pharmacist performs also some administrative duties such as defining procedures for medication acquisition, storage, administration and disposition.

Assisted Living Facilities

Assisted living facilities are long-term care facilities providing care to people needing assistance with every day activities but to a much lesser degree than nursing home residents. The average age of the residents is high; consequently, residents suffer from many chronic diseases. Assisted living facilities are licensed by the state but they are not regulated by OBRA like nursing homes. They offer 24-hour supervision and a range of services to promote the quality of life of the residents. However, assisted living nursing and other staff do not have the level of training of nursing home staff. Residents, long-term care insurance and in some states Medicaid cover the cost of assisted living.

Home Health Care (HHC)

Home health care providers offer services to patients at their residences. Services include nursing, provision of medical supplies and equipment, respiratory services and home infusion. The infusion therapy is intended for the administration of drugs or nutrition directly into the stomach or intravenous. Home health care providers operate out of central locations and dispatch staff to the patient's residence to deliver care. Medicaid covers much of the cost for this type of care. Medical care is provided by a visiting doctor.

Hospice Facilities

Hospice care is provided to patients in the last few months of their lives. It is intended to relieve pain and symptoms of the disease and manage the patient's emotional and psychological state. Other care offered includes dietary, physical therapy, counseling, etc. Treatment of the disease typically ceases during this period. Hospice care is provided in the patient's home, nursing homes, hospitals and hospice centers. Medicare, Medicaid and private insurance cover the cost for hospice care with physician certification that the treatment of the disease is discontinued. Indigent patient programs also provide care to uninsured and unqualified patients. Consultant pharmacies provide pharmacy services for this segment as well.

Other Miscellaneous Outlets

A number of other outlets types in the POC tier that do not fit the above categories engage in pharmaceutical sales transactions. These outlets include export companies, jails and detention centers, veterinarian facilities, pharmaceutical manufacturers, and select school, college and university sites. Individually each of these types of outlets has rather insignificant sales; however, collectively they account for a little more than 4% of the sales in the POC tier.

THE PATIENT

The patient is the consumer of the pharmaceutical market. His role in this market is a very interesting one. Unlike the consumer in other markets who might be subjected to different influences but makes his own final decisions, the patient does not get to choose his own product. The decision on which prescription drugs to take is made for him entirely by his physician. Only recently the patient became more engaged in the process and often asks his physician for specific treatments and drugs. The number of these patients is still low but growing.

This change is brought about by the proliferation of the manufacturer sponsored direct-to-consumer (DTC) campaigns and the Internet. TV commercials, printed and other medium ads serve as the trigger for the patient's interest, while the massive information available through the manufacturer and independent medical sites on the Internet becomes the source of information for the patient. It is this process that raised the patient's level of awareness about his disease.

The manufacturer, understanding the patient's desire to get more involved will continue to attempt to reach the patient though DTC programs and the internet. The interaction between the manufacturer and the patient is limited by strict guidelines set by HIPAA, out of concern of the protection of the patient's privacy. HIPAA guidelines limit the use and sharing of patient information by the players in the market, particularly when it comes to marketing programs. The manufacturer must observe these rules with every activity that brings him close to the patient.

One area where the patient is very much in control is his portion of the cost of the medication. Cost-sensitive and cash-paying patients will affect the physician's decision on the drug therapy, often choosing lower cost or lower co-pay drugs. The physician cannot ignore his patient's ability to pay for the medication and will prescribe drugs accordingly. Manufacturers need not only to get the drug in the plan formularies but to secure also a high reimbursement rate with low co-pay.

Healthcare plans offer two-tier, three-tier and in some cases four and five-tier co-payment systems. Co-pay tiers are set so that generic drugs fall in the least expensive tier with more expensive, novel therapies in increasingly more expensive tiers. Cost is only one of the criteria used in developing the tiered system. Cost factors are overridden when higher prices are offset by better clinical outcomes.

Chapter 2
The Customer

THE CUSTOMER

The customer is a key dimension of the sales transaction and therefore, ever present in sales data. Sales data is meaningful only in reference to the customer or one of its attributes such as its relative geographic position. You can form an understanding of sales data and draw sound conclusions only after you first understand your customer.

Customers can be found in any of the four market tiers including the manufacturer tier, where manufacturers sometimes buy another company's products for research purposes. Within each tier there exist one or more types of customers with unique characteristics. Some customers qualify as members of more than one type definitions. A hospital, for example, is a customer type by itself, and may be part of a system at the same time it is a member of a group purchasing organization (GPO). The customer definition in all three cases is overlapping. Overlapping customer definitions cause data duplication. As a data user you must be able to identify the customer types and recognize overlapping relationships.

WHO IS THE CUSTOMER?

It was mentioned earlier that the drug manufacturer sells his products through the wholesalers or directly to select healthcare providers. One way to define the customer is as an entity that engages directly in sales transactions with the manufacturer. However, limiting the definition to that assumes that the customer is equally interested as the manufacturer in making sure that the product reaches the consumer, the patient in this case. That is hardly the case because the reseller of your products has a number of other products to choose from and will likely take the path of least resistance to the market, potentially leaving your product on the shelf which he can later return as expired inventory. Therefore, the definition of the customer as a direct account is not adequate.

Taking a broader look at the market, the realization is that beyond that first sale by the manufacturer, the product gets re-sold a number of times before it eventually reaches the patient. The customer definition should be expanded to include those accounts indirectly involved in the sales transactions. Additionally, there are a number of outlets that are not currently buying the product but meet certain qualifications and have the potential of buying the product in the future. Those potential customers should be included in the definition as well.

And then, there are those entities in the market that do not ever participate in any product sales transactions but have the power to influence the purchasing decisions of those that do. We will call this group the 'influencers'. In fact, this group will make up our fifth market tier in the definition of the pharmaceutical market between the POC tier and the patient as shown in figure 4.

In summary, our definition of the customer will include anyone who engages, has the potential of engaging or can influence those who engage in sales transactions directly or indirectly with the manufacturer.

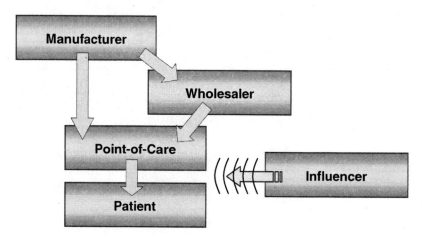

Figure 4. The influencer market-tier

The roles of the different types of customers in the market are unique and cannot be confused with other roles. The physician, for example, diagnoses and treats the patient's symptoms, while the pharmacist consults him on the medication use. Their interactions with other customer types in the market will be unique to them as well. Wholesalers, for example, will engage the clinic for the sale of pharmaceuticals and supplies while the healthcare plan to contract for the provision of healthcare services to its members. The customers' wants and needs drive the types of interactions with the other customer types.

From the manufacturer's perspective, understanding the roles and interactions of the customer is critical because it allows him to evaluate the customer and his importance. The manufacturer is interested in customers that can create product demand or shift demand from one product to another. The discussion in this chapter will center on the customer types, roles, interactions and importance of the customer. The later part of the chapter will focus on the process of evaluating customers within customer types and general activities that allow for better management of the customer out in the field.

THE PHYSICIAN

The physician is the ultimate decision maker in this market and the only one with broad and unlimited authority to prescribe ethical drugs. In the end, the physician has the power to prescribe the drug he deems most appropriate for the treatment of his patient even though the healthcare plan may refuse reimbursement and the patient chooses not to consume it.

Of course, in the real world, he will make a balanced decision that is closer to a win-win situation for everyone. But it was not always that way. Before the patient became more sophisticated and educated about his medical condition and long before managed care, the physician was the sole decision maker. With the ascent of managed care to power, the need to reduce healthcare costs and the advent of the Internet and increased exposure of the patient to DTC ads, it was inevitable that the physician had to share enough power with other decision makers to reach equilibrium. In fact, the equilibrium continues to shape with more players wanting to join. If the physician is practicing at a hospital his decision must consider the hospital's formulary, which might be influenced by a GPO, a hospital system or a network. If he is practicing in a group he may have to consider the treatment protocols and formulary of a physician practice management (PPM) organization or the contracted managed care organization (MCO).

The physician is caught between two opposing forces. On one end is his need to freely perform his professional duties and the market economics on the other. To satisfy his first need he would like to be in a position to prescribe the most appropriate available treatment; however, to remain in business he will need to compromise in order to earn the business of the plans. One thing is clear, that the physician will continue to fight to rid himself from influences he thinks interfere with his duty to provide good care to patients.

Pharmaceutical manufacturers fully understand the important role of the physician. That became apparent at the time when the physician's influence seemed to be declining they continued to add more reps to their sales forces, increasing their capacity to deliver messages. For the manufacturer to succeed, the physician must remain his main focus. Physicians are larger in number than any other customer type besides the patient, therefore, requiring the most resources. Sales forces that call on physicians and their support staff are far larger than any other sales force in the organization covering other customer types. Technically, an organization can have a hospital sales force but not have a physician sales force. However, a hospital sales force manages, again, mostly physician relationships but in a hospital setting.

Because every ethical drug requires a prescription, the physician will be important one hundred percent of the times. Every time the physicians identifies the symptoms of a disease and treats them using a drug he generates new demand. When he switches from one drug to another he affects the drug's market share. These are the two key material elements the manufacturer is looking for.

Not every physician, however, will be important and with more than a million physicians the manufacturer must identify the potential prescribers through a series of activities. These will be the physicians that the sales force will be delivering the marketing messages, provide educational material, clinical and pharmacoeconomic information, samples, share information and collect competitive intelligence, invite to meetings and events, recruit as opinion leaders and speaker program presenters, assist them with treatment protocols, support with CME programs and use as investigators in clinical trial programs.

For drugs with significant retail sales, physician data is the most important sales data. Physician data comes in the form of filled prescriptions and measures both new and total scripts.

PHYSICIAN MEDICAL GROUP

Physicians join medical groups to take advantage of economies of scale. In group practices physicians manage their costs by sharing office space, nursing and administrative staff and medical records. Group practices are classified as single, multi-specialty or primary care. Single specialty groups benefit from referrals to specialists but because they cover only one aspect of the patient's care they are usually offered contracts by MCOs on discounted fee-for-service basis. Multi-specialty groups have the potential of covering most of the patient's needs, and they contract with MCOs typically on a capitated or fixed per month per patient cost basis. Family practice groups are typically offered capitated contracts for a number of lives.

Medical groups are subject to utilization reviews from managed care, which forces the groups to follow prescription drug guidelines and treatment protocols. These reviews measure prescription drug usage and care from referrals. The medical group carries some cost risks from excessive prescription activity and use of referrals and can suffer penalties imposed by the MCO. For that reason many of them take a conservative approach limiting their activity to MCO guidelines. Groups rely on utilization software to track their activity.

Physicians in medical group practices are called by the sales rep. The sales rep must be aware of the group's associations with MCOs and work together with the corporate account managers to secure favorable status with the MCO formularies. Sales for group practices are captured in the form of purchases by the practice or in the form of filled prescriptions by physician.

THE PHYSICIAN ASSISTANT (PA) & NURSE PRACTITIONER (NP)

PAs and NPs are among the few other professionals with some but limited prescribing authority. PAs are licensed healthcare professionals providing care to patients under the supervision of a physician. In general, they diagnose, treat and prescribe drugs subject to certain limitations imposed by the state they practice in. The idea behind their practice is that they deal with routine patients, freeing the physician's time for more difficult cases. PAs provide primary care or specialize in a particular area.

PAs receive their education at accredited medical schools and must pass a national certification exam without having to complete an internship or residency program. PAs can be found in group practices, clinics, hospitals and other medical facilities. The presence of a supervising physician is not required in order for them to practice. They are found very commonly in rural areas where care is sparse and the population density does not support the presence of a physician.

NPs diagnose and treat common illnesses and focus mostly in family care, women's and reproductive health. NPs can prescribe drugs but only after entering into a protocol with a physician. The scope of services they provide may vary depending on state regulations. NPs need not to attend medical school, but must be licensed by a state nursing board.

Physician Assistants and Nurse Practitioners are gaining importance fast with pharmaceutical companies due to the fact that they have some prescribing capabilities, even if under a physician's guidelines, and due to their growing numbers. But it is really economics that has put them in the spotlight. Employers of NPs and PAs like them because they can substitute part of the physicians work at a lower cost. The government likes them as well because Medicare reimburses them at lower rates than physicians.

Pharmaceutical reps encounter them more and more in just about every setting. Even though they may not rank high up on the sales rep's target list, they are definitely in many target lists. As more states allow them more privileges the number of PAs and NPs will grow, and so will their prescribing activity.

The drug manufacturers will need to decide what kind of promotional activities are appropriate for these groups. Sampling may not be appropriate, for example, because generally PAs and NPs cannot sample patients. Other roles such as opinion leader and speaker are best suited for physicians. Regardless, with nearly 140,000 PAs and NPs and 7% of the total prescription volume, this group cannot be ignored.

PA and NP data comes in the form of filled prescriptions and when reported to the manufacturer it is integrated with the physician data in which the PAs and NPs appear as regular prescribers.

THE NURSE

Although the role of the nurse is clear, the importance of the nurse to the pharmaceutical company is not always recognized and it is often shadowed by the physician's importance. Nurses have the task of "caring for or nurturing the patient" according to one definition. Nurses must have formal education and training and must be licensed. Professional nurses have bachelor degrees and Technical nurses associate degrees. Technical nurses work under the supervision of professional nurses.

Nurses that complete a bachelor or associate degree program may become Registered Nurses (RNs) after passing the state exam. RNs help the physician during examinations, treatment and surgery. They monitor, evaluate and chart the vital signs and symptoms of patients and administer diagnostic tests and medication. Licensed practical nurses, under the supervision of an RN or a physician, may provide basic care for patients.

One particular group of nurses, the Advance practice nurses (APNs), is highly specialized nurses. NPs discussed earlier, Certified Nurse-Midwives (CNMs) in gynecological and obstetrical care, Clinical Nurse Specialists (CNSs) in physical and mental health and Certified Nurse Specialists (CRNAs) in surgical anesthesia are examples of APNs.

The nurse is particularly important to the manufacturer of drugs with complex administrative procedures like IV. The nurse must be trained in the proper administration of the drug. The manufacturer addresses that need with in-service presentations. These are targeted training sessions with a practical focus. The sales rep typically coordinates these sessions with expert nurses the manufacturer employs. The manufacturer has a vested interest to see that the product is administered properly; otherwise, he runs the risk of suffering the consequences of improper use of the drug and unfavorable feedback from the nurse to the physician.

In general, the nurse can serve as an excellent source of information for the sales rep and often as a way to access the physician. The nurse is ever present and an indispensable, critical part of healthcare. Since nurses do not have prescribing authority, with the exception of NPs, there is no data linked directly to nurses. The sales reps can evaluate the nurse's importance empirically.

THE PHARMACIST

The basic role of the pharmacist is to compound and dispense drugs and to provide counseling and education on medication use. This role gets increasingly more complex with the level of responsibility and the setting in which the pharmacist operates. Pharmacists have also limited prescribing authority in some states. In the previous chapter we discussed the retail and closed-wall pharmacies in hospitals, HMO's home-health care and long-term care. The following section discusses the various pharmacist roles.

The Ambulatory Care Pharmacist works in retail pharmacies and he interacts with the patient and the prescribing physician. He dispenses and counsels patients in the proper use of the prescribed drugs. He also makes sure that the dispensed drugs do not interact with adverse reactions with other drugs the patient may be taking. One key task of the ambulatory care pharmacist is the adjudication of the prescription. He must make sure that the insurer approves the drug and determine the patient's co-pay. If the drug is not covered by the plan or the co-pay is too high for the patient, he may switch it with a generic or call the physician to have the drug changed.

The pharmacist can replace a branded prescribed drug with a generic without approval from the physician unless otherwise noted by the physician on the prescription; however, he cannot replace a drug with a therapeutic equivalent without the doctor's approval. Healthcare plans try to capitalize on the pharmacist's ability to substitute a drug with a generic and offer pharmacies incentives for increased generic substitution. The manufacturer on the other hand tries to capitalize on the pharmacist's key position and offers pharmacies rebates to improve the drug's market share through therapeutic substitution. These programs are commonly known as interventions.

Pharmacists are assisted by pharmacy technicians who perform certain tasks that do not require the professional judgment of the pharmacist. The practice manager or chief pharmacist manages the budget and personnel productivity and determines which therapies are most effective. Sales reps visit ambulatory pharmacists rather infrequently. Manufacturers usually reach them through trade magazines and direct mail to announce new drugs or new indications of drugs. One subject of interaction between the sales rep and the pharmacist involves the stocking of a drug when it is not locally available for the convenience of the patient. The sales rep will need to work with the practice manager to stock the drug and the physician to refer the patient to the pharmacy.

The bigger stocking issues, especially during a product launch, are handled at the corporate level with retail pharmacies. Stocking issues are more critical to manufacturers of expensive drugs and drugs that require special handling. Fewer than normal pharmacies tend to carry those drugs, or have the storage appliances to house enough of them. The manufacturer's corporate accounts team often has people dedicated to this market segment. This is a specialty sales force responsible for the sales contracts and special programs with the corporate offices of pharmacies.

Perhaps the most important area of collaboration for both the manufacturer and the pharmacist is the compliance and persistency programs for chronic disease patients. Compliance refers to the patient taking the right dose of his medication at the right frequency while persistency refers to re-filling the prescription on time and continuing of the therapy without lapses. Both compliance and persistency result in better health outcomes and maximize the usage of the drug by the patient, and therefore, both mean more revenue for the manufacturer and the pharmacy. The pharmacist is in the perfect position to execute these programs because he has access to the patient. This is done either via telemarketing or direct mail in the form of reminders. The pharmacy is compensated either by rebates for higher volume, a service fee per patient, etc.

Retail pharmacies actively seek contracts to fill prescriptions for managed care organizations to increase their store sales. The independent pharmacies will continue to be a challenge for the manufacturer because he has to deal individually with a large number of them. Currently the most effective way to deal with them is through telemarketing and mass mailing programs, focusing more on those with high sales volume or those whose location is important to the patients.

The Acute Care Pharmacist works in the closed-wall pharmacy of the hospital. He is part of a team of healthcare professionals who ensure that the patient is given the proper drug therapies. Unlike the retail pharmacist, he dispenses medication one dose at the time for the hospitalized patient. The medication is administered by the nurses and recorded on the patient's chart. His responsibilities include dispensing the proper medication, monitoring drug dosage and response, timing, and preventing drug interactions and adverse reactions. The practice manager has similar responsibilities in the hospital setting as in retail pharmacies. The hospital pharmacy is likely to use a formulary, which might be managed by the hospital itself, the system that may be part of, the GPO or the health network. The hospital pharmacist is one of the staff members that pharmaceutical reps call on but not at the same frequency as the physician. There is no specific sales data for the acute care pharmacist. His importance among other acute care pharmacists will be determined by the hospital's sales.

The Managed Care Pharmacist works in the closed-wall pharmacy of an HMO and has similar tasks as the retail pharmacist filling prescriptions and counseling the patient. In general, however, the managed care pharmacist has a lot of administrative duties that include the monitoring of patient outcomes to determine which therapies are most effective, and the design and management of pharmacy benefits for healthcare plans. Perhaps, his most critical task, from the manufacturer's perspective, is his role in pharmacy and therapeutic committees that determine the list of drugs to be used or reimbursed by his organization, commonly known as the formulary. Formulary restrictions impact the manufacturer's ability to realize his sales goals. The corporate accounts team handles formulary issues with MCOs while the sales rep calls on HMO care sites.

The Long-term and Chronic Care Pharmacist, also known as consultant pharmacist, works in closed-wall pharmacies serving nursing home, assisted living and hospice facilities. The long-term care pharmacist dispenses single dose prescriptions or re-packages drugs in multiple single doses. That is because the majority of the patients they serve have some kind of cognitive impairment. Pharmacists that serve nursing homes must perform extra administrative duties to meet certain state requirements.

Long-term care pharmacies are increasingly using formularies, which they manage aggressively. They are sensitive to cost due to heavy reimbursement by Medicaid and Medicare at certain low rates. The consultant pharmacist has a role in that, looking for cost effective therapies with good outcomes. The consultant pharmacist intervenes perhaps more often in the drug therapy recommended by the prescriber than in any other setting.

The manufacturer seeks contracts and good formulary standing with chains of long-term care pharmacies through its corporate accounts team. The sales reps, calling on nursing home medical directors and physicians treating long-term care patients as well as the consultant pharmacists, manage the pull-through.

There is overall lack of comprehensive data in the long-term care segment, which makes it difficult for the manufacturer to deal effectively with it. The consultant pharmacist's importance will be measured by the sales to his pharmacy.

The Home Care Pharmacist is also a consultant pharmacist that works in closed-wall pharmacies that provide services to patients at their home or outpatient clinics. Home care pharmacists specialize in intravenous drug therapies and nutrition. They use formularies like long-term care pharmacies and interestingly enough they enter into exclusive distribution deals for certain drugs with manufacturers.

PHYSICIAN PRACTICE MANAGEMENT (PPM)

A PPM is a company whose business model seeks membership from physician offices and group practices to which it provide business management and purchasing services. This model guarantees members cost-effective management of their business, favorable reimbursement rates with MCOs and better drug and medical supply deals with manufacturers. In one respect then, the PPM is a group purchasing organization for physicians.

There are two types of PPM models. Under the membership model, members pay an annual fee to participate in the network and enjoy its benefits. Under the equity model, the PPM organization has part ownership in member practices. Members in this model pay an annual fee and a portion of their revenue to the PPM. Physicians wanting more freedom from outside influences are finding this model less attractive.

PPM organizations derive their revenue from contracts they negotiate with drug manufacturers, fees paid by companies to conduct clinical trials at the network sites, MCO contracts for covered lives, outcomes and sales data sold to manufacturers, and member management-services fees.

Better pricing for labs, diagnostics and drugs and access to managed care are the most important benefits for members. Through the PPM, the physician or group can contract care to MCOs. These contracts are sometimes hard to get without the leverage of the PPM. Members have also access to a number of other value-added services. PPMs provide members guidance with treatment protocols and disease management. Treatment protocols describe the procedures for treating a disease. Disease management looks into the patient's overall health to improve the quality of life and prevent acute episodes. Because of their large membership pool, PPMs are sought after by manufacturers to participate in clinical trials, which generate increased revenue for them and their members. PPMs also organize Continued Medical Education (CME) certification programs for member physicians to maintain their credentials.

The PPM model allows the physician to focus on providing care while the PPM can focus on business management. The PPM provides the software systems to automate the business functions such as appointment handling, billing and reimbursement claims.

The manufacturer must determine which PPMs are important to him. The criteria include the compatibility of a drug's therapeutic area and the specialty of the PPM, the size of the PPM's membership pool, the patient lives under contract with MCOs and most importantly the influence of the PPM on its members to drive compliance with treatment guidelines. If the PPM lacks the ability to influence the compliance of its members with drug therapy guidelines, the manufacturer must focus on the individual physician instead.

Once the importance of a PPM is established, the manufacturer must focus on getting the drug on its formulary. The manufacturer's corporate accounts team again handles formulary issues. PPMs may or may not allow competing drugs in their formulary. PPMs can get deeper discounts by limiting competition but ultimately the physician must comply with the formulary. For maximum results and better compliance the sales rep from the physician side and the national accounts manager from the PPM side must coordinate their efforts. The manufacturers provide PPMs with a number of value-added services that include sponsorships for symposiums, speaker programs, meetings, web ads, CME certification programs, etc.

PPMs negotiate contracts on the behalf of their members but are not directly involved in sales transactions. PPMs are evaluated based on the aggregate sales and prescription activity of their members. The aggregation requires an accurate mapping of the PPM and its members.

GROUP PURCHASING ORGANIZATION (GPO)

GPOs are companies representing hospitals and hospital systems in negotiations for medical supplies and drugs with manufacturers. GPOs use as leverage the buying power of the hospitals they represent to secure the best possible price. In exchange, the manufacturer benefits from higher sales volumes, primarily from gaining a greater market share from competitors. Manufacturers are particularly interested in GPOs that can influence the market share of their drugs.

GPOs do not participate in the actual sales transactions or physically handle the product. Hospitals place their orders through their supplier who grants them the contract pricing. The supplier then claims a rebate from the manufacturer. The manufacturer's corporate account managers negotiate GPO contracts.

GPO sales are calculated as the aggregate of the sales of the individual member hospitals. The aggregation requires an accurate mapping of hospitals to their GPOs.

MANAGED CARE ORGANIZATION (MCO)

Managed care, as the term implies, is the overall initiative of controlling healthcare costs. It came to replace the inefficiencies of traditional indemnity plans whose freedom of choice led to high premiums for the consumer. MCOs are able to deliver more care to patients for a lower premium but leave patients with fewer choices. Patients must often choose their physicians from approved lists, fill their prescriptions at certain pharmacies, be prescribed certain drugs only, and assume the extra cost when they deviate from the plan's covered care.

The MCO's main role is that of the payer of health care. The type of care MCOs reimburse for is detailed in the plan the enrollee participates in. MCOs may offer a number of plans. There are typically two components to the coverage; the medical benefit covering physician visits, hospitalization and lab tests and the drug benefit covering the patient's medication needs.

Types of MCOs

There are many types of Managed Care Organizations and include HMOs, Managed Indemnity, Preferred Provider Organizations (PPO) and Point of Service plans (POS). The staff-model HMO discussed in the precious chapter is just one type of HMOs. Other types include group, IPA and network model HMOs. Following is a brief discussion of the different types of MCOs.

- **Group Model HMOs** do not employee their own physicians but rather contract with independent physician groups on an exclusive basis. The group is compensated a fixed amount for every patient enrolled with the group regardless of the number of times the patient visits his physician.

- **Independent Practice Association (IPA) model HMOs** contract for the medical care of their patients with solo physician or group practices. These physicians may contract with other HMOs or treat patients on fee-for-service basis. IPAs offer a great degree of freedom and for this reason they are popular with physicians. IPAs are the most preferred type of HMO with patients because they provide the most of freedom of choice. IPAs have no investment in medical facilities. Physicians are compensated either on discounted fee-for-service or capitated basis. To assure the compliance of physicians with IPA protocols, IPAs often withhold a portion of the physician's fees. The withheld amounts are applied against budgetary overruns and are intended as penalties for non-compliance.

- **Network Model HMOs** contract with multiple physician groups to cover large geographic areas. Member physicians can maintain their own practice at the same time they offer their services to the HMO. Network model HMOs do not invest in their own medical facilities. Patients select their primary care physician within a group and fill prescriptions at a local network pharmacy. Physicians are compensated on a capitated basis for each member enrolled in the group.

- **Preferred Provider Organizations** (PPOs) negotiate discounted services with physicians, hospitals, clinics, dentists, ancillary facilities, etc. The provider bills the PPO for each service rendered based on the negotiated fee schedule and does not share any risk with the PPO. Patients select their healthcare provider from a preferred list distributed by the PPO. The patient may seek care outside these providers but has to assume the additional cost above set rates. Both enrollees and providers enjoy a high degree of freedom with PPOs. PPOs are the most preferred managed care plan.

- **Managed Indemnity** plans are traditional indemnity plans incorporating managed care features. The patient has the flexibility to select his provider and the physician has the freedom to treat the patient without having to follow some treatment protocol designed by the plan. The disadvantage with these plans is that enrollees must file reimbursement claims. Additionally, enrollees have limited ability to negotiate the cost of care with the provider.

- **Point of Service Plans** combine aspects of traditional indemnity plans and HMOs or PPOs. The enrollee may choose his provider from a network of providers or outside the network. The benefits for care provided through the network are the same as if the enrollee was an HMO or PPO member; however, for out-of-network care, the enrollee assumes the responsibility of paying the cost of care and submits a claim for reimbursement to the plan. The cost of out-of-network care to the enrollee includes the deductible and a fixed percent of the charges.

MCOs belong in the 'payer' customer category in the influencer tier. With 70% of the drug benefits to patients paid by MCOs from premiums collected from employers, government sponsored memberships, employee contributions and self-insured, they have become the major force in healthcare. The mission of these organizations is to provide quality care and bring healthcare costs under control. To accomplish this they employ a variety of tools discussed below.

- **Contracting** - With the exception of the staff-model HMO, that owns its facilities and employs its medical staff, MCOs contract for patient services with healthcare providers. The most common types of contracts are the capitated and discounted fee-for-service contracts.

  - **Capitated contracts** offer the provider a fixed fee per month per enrolled patient regardless of the amount of care received by the patient, thus, limiting the MCO's exposure. These contracts are typically offered to multi-specialty groups and primary care physicians. Capitated contracts make sense for them because in the first case the patient can receive almost complete care from the group while in the case of the primary care physician the patient can potentially make more than one visit a month. Acute and specialty care is provided by referral as needed. Capitated contracts may include drug risk in which case the provider incurs drug utilization costs above the compensated amount per patient.

  - **Discounted fee-for-service contracts** are more appropriate for specialists, which the patients see only on as-needed basis. The physician earns the fee only if the patient visits. MCOs negotiate rates also on this basis for hospital care, lab tests, x-rays, diagnostic image testing, etc.

- **Formularies** are used by MCOs to control the use of certain drugs. 'Open' formularies promote the use of generic and approved drugs but also allow the use of non-listed drugs with certain cost implications often to the patient. 'Closed' formularies reimburse only listed drugs. Non-formulary drugs are reimbursed only through prior authorization or the patient must bear the entire cost.

- **Tiered co-pays** are designed to manage the MCOs exposure to the cost of drugs and affect the drug manufacturer directly. With tiered co-pays the patient contributes increasing amounts of money for more expensive drugs. In a two-tier system the choice is between generic and branded products, with very low tier-one co-pays for generics. In the most popular three-tier system, tier-one is reserved for generics, tier-two for preferred drugs while the third tier, with a significantly higher co-payment, for all other drugs. Some MCOs use even more tiers with even higher co-pays.

- **Prior authorizations** are used by MCOs both for medical procedures and drugs and are intended as a way to review the appropriateness of the more expensive care. Prior authorizations have a deterrent effect sometimes on patients and providers.

- **Reference pricing** burdens the manufacturer to provide evidence that the drug is more effective than other drugs for the higher price.

- **Treatment protocols** are used to assure that cost effective treatments are preferred over other procedures and to control excessive care from referrals. Treatment protocols are established based on good, cost effective outcomes. In some cases treatment protocols are designed to delay care and referrals or at least not to perform certain procedures too early.

- **Disease Management Programs** is one way for managing high-risk patients in certain chronic disease areas. The idea behind these programs is to improve and keep the overall health of the patient stable to avoid costly hospitalization.

- **Utilization reviews** are systematic reviews used by MCOs to assure provider compliance with protocols and rationing of care. Utilization reviews apply to both medical procedures and prescription drugs. They are often tied to monetary incentives for achieving objectives and penalties for non-compliance. They are proven to restrain the physician's prescribing habits to avoid penalties.

The manufacturer's success in the marketplace depends on his effectiveness of dealing with managed care. The manufacturer must address the concerns of the MCO in order for the MCO to endorse his products. The manufacturer's corporate accounts and reimbursement groups dealing with payers has the responsibility of negotiating the inclusion of drugs in the plan formularies. The manufacturer must demonstrate the cost benefits of using its drugs. Especially for very costly drugs, he must provide evidence that the drug will reduce other aspects of care such as hospitalization. MCOs are often willing to put these high cost drugs in low co-pay tiers if they clearly demonstrate better, more cost effective patient outcomes.

The manufacturer must make sure that the drug is used appropriately and his involvement in protocol designs is critical. Disease management programs are of interest to both the MCO, because it reduces his exposure to a high-risk patient population, but also to the manufacturer who benefits from these programs because they promote patient compliance with the drug treatment. Life-style enhancing drug classes are likely to escape the managed care influence; however, they face steep obstacles because they are usually not reimbursed or are in high co-pay tiers.

The manufacturer must determine which payers of services and which of their plans have significant influence on its business. This must be done at the national, regional and local levels since some payers and plans operate only locally or regionally. The manufacturer must also determine where the formulary decisions are made and focus his efforts in that part of the organization. The key MCO decision makers are the medical director in charge of treatment protocol design, the disease management director, and the pharmacy director in charge of the formulary design.

MCOs assign the responsibility of managing the patient drug benefit to their own pharmacy benefit management (PBM) department or outsource it to one or more third party PBMs. The PBM services may include prescription adjudication, reimbursement management and formulary design. The manufacturer must determine whether the MCO or PBM has the formulary influence and act accordingly. PBMs are likely to use extensively mail service and specialty pharmacies or operate their own for cost control in chronic disease cases.

Data for MCOs comes in the form of filled prescriptions at the plan level by prescribing physician. Payer level data is derived from the sum of its plans' activities. PBM data can also be derived from plan data through the PBM-to-plan affiliations, also in the same form.

MEDICARE AND MEDICAID

Medicare is a federal program that provides access to healthcare for seniors over the age of 65, disabled and end-stage-renal-disease (ESRD) patients. The program is administered by the Centers for Medicare & Medicaid Services (CMS), formerly the Health Care Financing Administration (HCFA).

The Hospital Insurance Trust Fund or Part A is funded by employee payroll deductions and employer contributions. It covers inpatient hospital, nursing home, home health and hospice care. Through Part B or Supplementary Medical Insurance fund, beneficiaries receive physician services, outpatient services and lab and diagnostic tests. However, those eligible to participate in Part B must pay a monthly premium. Additionally, Medicare beneficiaries may choose to buy supplemental insurance for services not provided by Medicare or to cover Medicare deductibles, etc. These Plans are referred to as Medicare Advantage plans and were previously known as Medicare + Choice plans.

In the inpatient hospital setting, drugs are fully reimbursed under the Diagnostic Related Group (DRG) reimbursement system. In the outpatient hospital setting, select drugs are reimbursed under the Outpatient Prospective Payment System (OPPS) with an Ambulatory Procedure Code (APC). In the physician office, CMS has been reimbursing a select few injectable drugs using an authorization document code ("J" code) or a temporary "Q" code. Everything else Medicare did not cover until January, 2006. Essentially, this reimbursement scheme left the elderly for the longest time without a drug benefit. For this reason, historically Medicare drug coverage has been a major issue for the government, the beneficiaries and the manufacturers.

In 2003 the Medicare Modernization Act (MMA) was voted into law with the intent to improve Medicare benefits. Under this legislation, among other things, Medicare introduced in 2006 for the first time an optional, low-cost drug benefit for the entire Medicare-eligible population. The premium for the plan is about $35 per month with a $250 deductible and covers 75% of the costs between $250 and $2,250 and 95% of the drug costs above $5,100. The patient is fully responsible for costs between $2,250 and $5,100. The plan offers additional provisions for low income beneficiaries and for Medicare beneficiaries with Medicaid eligibility and incomes 100% below the federal poverty level.

From May 2004 and until the new drug benefit went into effect in 2006 beneficiaries were given the choice to use one of many Medicare-approved discount cards. The cards came with annual premium of up to $30 and offered at least 10-25% discounts for approved drugs. Limited income beneficiaries received a $600 credit on the card to pay for prescriptions.

Medicaid is a joint federal and state program that provides access to medical care for low income people. Those may include families with children, pregnant women, aged, blind and disabled people that meet certain financial qualifications. The program is operated by the states within CMS guidelines and it is financed by the federal government and the states. Services include hospital and physician care, nursing home care, lab and diagnostic testing. States may provide other services such as dental, vision, hearing, etc. Needy Medicare recipients can qualify for state Medicaid also to cover the out-of-pocket expenses they incur from coverage limitations, deductibles and premiums.

Medicare and Medicaid along with MCOs and other insurers belong in the same customer category referred to as 'payers' because they reimburse providers for the cost of healthcare benefits. Therefore, they have a vested interest, more than any other player in the market, to curb costs. For that reason they are strong influencers on other players in the market requiring special attention.

Medicare is now a sizable pharmacy benefit payer and although their business is contracted out to third party payers they will always be an influence in the market. Medicaid on the other hand has always paid for a significant portion of the drug costs in the United States and will continue to be a significant payer even though some of their beneficiaries are now moved to Medicare. To manage drug costs Medicaid implements a number of measures including restrictive formularies, prior authorization reviews and limits on number of prescriptions and drugs that would be reimbursed. Further, Medicaid employs mechanisms such as drug utilization reviews and disease state management (DSM) programs to manage costs. Medicaid is particularly interested in disease state management programs due to the high incidence of chronic diseases in the elderly population.

To take advantage of the efficiencies managed care has brought to healthcare, Medicare and Medicaid offer their beneficiaries the option to enroll in managed care plans known as managed Medicare/Medicaid plans. The basic premiums for these plans are covered by Medicare and Medicaid but the enrollee can add more benefits at his own expense.

To qualify for reimbursement, manufacturers must provide rebates on sales of products to the government. For generic drugs the rebates are set at 11% of the respective product's average manufacturer's price (AMP). For branded products the rebate is the greater of the AMP minus the 'best price' or 15.1% of the average manufacturer's price. Best price is defined as the lowest-price charged to a customer for the product net of all rebates and discounts. Excluded from the definition are prices charged for state and federal programs and prices on nominal amounts. Starting with January, 2005, select drugs are reimbursed based on the Average Selling Price (ASP) plus six percent. The ASP for these drugs is calculated and published on quarterly basis.

The manufacturer's reimbursement group manages all Medicare and Medicaid issues. Most manufacturers have some kind of exposure to Medicare and Medicaid and states with high number of elderly, like Florida, are often of particular importance. Medicaid as a payer does not purchase the product but just reimburses for it. The product is purchased by the facilities providing the care to its patients. The providers submit claims to Medicare and Medicaid. Drug utilization data is collected by Medicaid from claims against it. Medicaid provides utilization reports to manufacturers for remission of the rebates.

Vendors capture data for Medicaid reimbursed retail prescriptions at the prescribing physician. Managed Medicaid scripts are also captured, however, because managed care plans serve other types of beneficiaries there is practically no way to separate the Medicaid activity from other third party activity.

VA / DoD

The Veterans Administration (VA) and the Department of Defense (DoD) account for a large portion of medical and pharmaceutical expenditures of the federal government. Together they serve a large number of veterans and active duty personnel with their dependents.

The VA covers those that have served a full tour of duty in the armed forces. VA beneficiaries seek care at hospitals, outpatient clinics, pharmacies and nursing homes owned and operated by the VA. The patient's first prescription is filled at a pharmacy located at care facilities with refills handled through the Consolidated Mail service Pharmacy (CMOP). VA uses a national formulary requiring prior approval for non-formulary drugs. VA care is managed by 21 regional organizations, the VISNs. Each VISN is represented in the national VA formulary committee by its VISN formulary leader.

The DoD covers active duty and retired personnel and their families. The DoD provides care through military treatment facilities (MTFs) located in or near army and air force bases, navy stations and through contracted regional managed care organizations. Care is managed through the DoD's eleven-region Tri-Care system of managed care. The system offers its members HMO, PPO and fee-for-service plan options. Prescriptions for DoD beneficiaries are filled in pharmacies located in military treatment facilities, a network of contracted retail pharmacies and through its National Mail service Pharmacy (NMOP). The DoD uses a core formulary giving preferred status to approved drugs. MTFs may approve drugs in their own formulary beyond those in the core formulary. The formulary of the network pharmacies is set by the DoD.

The VA and DoD are important to the manufacturer because they serve more than 9 million beneficiaries. This segment however, is among the least profitable for the manufacturer because of the big discounts it must provide through the Federal Supply Schedule (FSS) and other programs. The manufacturer must demonstrate the drug's safety, efficacy and cost benefits.

The sales rep typically has the role of managing the pull-through at the care sites keeping in touch with the physician and the pharmacist. The corporate accounts group handles the formulary and contracting issues. VA and DoD data is available in the form of purchases for the care sites and CMOP and as distribution for NMOP.

INTEGRATED HEALTH SYSTEM (IHS)

Integrated Health Systems combine the services of many healthcare entities to form an integrated system of healthcare providers. These entities may include hospitals or hospital systems, physician groups, clinics, pharmacies and health plans with their assets either owned or contracted by the IHS. The IHS model is based on the idea that by owning all components of care the system can better coordinate patient care assuring quality at lower cost.

IHSs come typically in the form of staff-model HMOs or multi-hospital systems. The staff-model HMO type has the payer component fully integrated in it while the hospital system type may offer its own plans or contract with payers for access to its system-wide assets.

IHSs are the most complex healthcare entities because of the number of components they combine. To address the needs of the IHS the manufacturer must assign a team of people to these accounts that include sales reps, clinical specialists, corporate account managers, disease management specialists, etc.

Sales transactions do not involve IHS entities directly but outlets affiliated with the IHS. Therefore, reporting sales at the IHS level requires the aggregation of the sales of the affiliated outlets. Affiliation cross-references are available through IMS' DDDIV™ service and other vendors.

OTHER

The influencers we saw so far fall in three categories: medical staff, parent organizations of entities directly involved in pharmaceutical sales transactions, and payers that include managed care plans and government organizations. There are a number of other influencers that can modify the prescribing habits of a physician; however, being further away from the process, their influences are not as strong as the ones discussed above. Those include consulting companies offering advice in the design of benefit packages, management companies used for outsourcing certain functions related to care and other third party vendors with products targeting healthcare providers.

The further away influencers are from the formulary decision making process and the less power they have to affect a product's sales and market share, the less important they will be for the pharmaceutical manufacturer. The manufacturer from his part will concentrate effort and resources to key influencers and to a lesser degree others. Economies of scale will allow only the larger and most sophisticated marketing organizations to pursue certain types of influencers.

For all of customer types deemed important to the company, the sales and marketing organization will be interested in sales data to measure their performance. The key to managing influencer data will always be accurate customer profile and affiliation information.

MANAGING THE CUSTOMER

Customers can be found in every tier of the market from the manufacturer to the patient. By type, they number anywhere between just a few perhaps in the case of manufacturers, to a few tens in the case of wholesalers, to hundreds of thousands in the case of care providers and several millions in the case of patients. The number of customers increases by tier as you move away from the manufacturer and towards the patient as shown in figure 5.

It is neither economical nor necessary for the manufacturer to deal with each potential customer, and for that the manufacturer must approach the customer selectively. The manufacturer must follow a process to identify the right customers, organize them geographically or otherwise, and assign resources to manage them. The guiding principal in the customer selection process is that the manufacturer in the long run will derive a higher value from the account than the cost of the effort he puts on the account. The following section discusses the process of selecting, organizing and managing the customer.

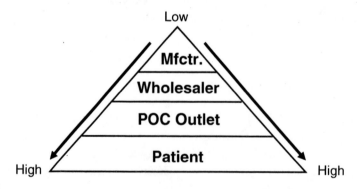

Figure 5. Number of customers by tier

Segmenting the Customer

Segmentation is the process of identifying and grouping customers based on customer types and customer unique characteristics. Segmentation looks further into these defined groups to classify accounts based on their potential. The process of segmenting the customer is not an optional exercise. Without proper segmentation and analysis of each segment's importance the manufacturer can easily miss his target.

The customer's uniqueness translates to unique customer needs. The manufacturer can do a better job understanding the customers' needs by focusing on specific customer types. For each of these types he can now create and deliver custom solutions that will result in better customer satisfaction. To create and deliver these custom solutions the manufacturer will need people with certain skills who understand these customers. Ultimately these efforts will lead to meeting or exceeding the manufacturer's goals.

The first step to segmentation is to identify the potential customer types. The discussion in this and the previous chapter was essentially just that. There we took a look at a cross section of the market where a number of industries interact with each other, among them manufacturing, wholesale, retail, medical and health insurance. In each of those industries we saw one or more customer types.

The next step is to determine the importance of each customer type to a specific product. Overestimating the importance of a customer type will result in a lot of unproductive effort while underestimating its importance will result in lost opportunity. This part of the segmentation exercise must determine how much effort if any should be put in each customer type. Segmentation is a product specific activity because customer types have different degrees of influence on different products. Hospitals, for example, cannot affect sales of retail products. Segmenting customers based on the total product portfolio and implementing the same programs on all of them will not work.

Once the importance of a customer type has been determined the accounts must be further analyzed to estimate their potential. Accounts do perform at different levels. Putting the same level of recourses on every account would result in different return-on-investment (ROI) rates with many of these rates near or below zero. For some accounts the manufacturer would exceed the level of effort it takes to maximize the account's value while for other accounts would not put enough effort. The level of effort should match the account's sales potential to improve its ROI. Sometimes alternative, less expensive efforts might be the answer. Telemarketing programs, for example, lower drastically the cost of the effort compared to sales rep calls. Some accounts, however, are not going to be responsive at any level of effort and putting no effort at all will be the right choice. For instance, regardless of effort urologists will not prescribe cardiology products.

The potential of an account for a given market is often defined as the total sales for the basket of products that make-up the market, adjusted for future growth. In theory you could convert an account to prescribe your product only, adding to your sales those of your competitors, thus, maximizing its value to your product. This brings up a different issue, defining the market correctly. Product inclusions or exclusions from the market definition will overestimate or underestimate the potential of an account. Future market growth is important also, as the ROIs of accounts will change accordingly. In declining markets that would mean accounts moving below a profitability threshold.

A common technique for segmenting accounts within customer type is deciling. Deciling ranks accounts based on sales and groups them into ten buckets based on total volume of sales or number of accounts. Volume deciling puts enough ranked accounts in each bucket so that each decile's total sales are equal to the total sales of every other decile. The number of accounts in each decile varies, with very few accounts in the top decile and too many in the lowest. Volume deciling confirms the 80/20 rule, which translates to 80% of the sales coming out of 20% of the top accounts. The benefit of this type of deciling is that it puts focus on the most productive accounts with high ROI. Count deciling places ranked accounts in buckets so that each decile has equal number of accounts. The total sales volume of each decile, however, varies disproportionally. Quintiling, an alternative to deciling, groups accounts in five buckets. Decile ten is considered typically the highest value decile and decile one the lowest. Figure 6 demonstrates the two types of deciling.

Deciling can be used with almost all types of accounts. The drawback of deciling is that it is a purely quantitative method and does not take into consideration other important attributes of the customer. Qualitative information can be used to refine the deciling by exploring customer attributes. For example, the primary physician specialty prescribing a drug might be such an attribute when deciling physicians. Behavioral characteristics can reveal useful information about a target account. As such, a physician's propensity to switch brands or prescribe a new drug early during a product launch is very important to the company launching a new drug or defending against a new drug. Combining the quantitative and qualitative information the account's relative importance ranking can be adjusted to optimize the list of target accounts.

Volume Deciling			Count Deciling		
Account	Sales	Decile	Account	Sales	Decile
A	100	10	A	100	10
B	80	10	B	80	10
			C	60	10
C	75 ❷	9	D	45	10
D	60	9			
E	45	9	E	40 ❹	9
			F	35	9
F	40	8	G	35	9
G ❶	35	8	H	30	9
H	30	8			
I	25	8	I	30	8
J	20	8	J ❸	25	8
K	15	8	K	15	8
L	15	8	L	10	8
.	.	.	.	.	.
.	.	.	.	.	.

❶ In volume deciling, deciles have un-equal number of accounts
❷ In volume deciling, all deciles have equal amounts of sales
❸ In count deciling, all deciles have equal number of accounts
❹ In count deciling, deciles have un-equal amounts of sales

Figure 6. Volume and count deciling

Reaching the Customer

The next logical step in the process will be to determine the method of targeting accounts, which accounts to target and the frequency by which to reach them. Sales reps usually call physicians and accounts in the POC tier, often with clinical support from nurses. This is where demand is generated and the number of accounts is large; therefore, the manufacturer must match the importance and size of this group of accounts with considerable effort. The wholesalers and non-provider customer types of the influencer tier are typically called by corporate account managers. These tiers have relatively fewer accounts that can be handled by smaller sales forces. They are, however, more complex and they require sales people with considerable experience in the particular area.

Reach and frequency is the coined term for 'which accounts' to call and 'how often'. A sales force is a very expensive resource and the ROI diminishes quickly below a certain decile. Determining what the threshold of profitability is will help you determine which deciles to target with the sales force. The remaining deciles may be targeted using less expensive methods like telemarketing or mailing campaigns. By lowering the cost of the effort and keeping the ROI within an acceptable range the company can continue to allocate resources to cover profitably these accounts.

Companies often use the ABC scheme of classifying accounts in the selected deciles with 'A' being the highest effort accounts and 'C' the lowest ones. The manufacturer will need to call individual accounts as many times as it takes to maximize his opportunity given that by putting too much effort in an account does not compromise his opportunity from other accounts. Generally manufacturers call A list physician accounts every of 4-6 weeks, B accounts every 3-4 months and C accounts twice or three times a year.

The frequency must take into consideration the state of the market, the product and other external factors. For example, trying to create awareness in the market for a newly launched product requires a higher frequency than a mature product. Conversely, products defending from a new launch will need to come out of the maintenance mode, raise the "noise" level to destruct the competitor's message. In a stable market, penetrated accounts could be in maintenance mode and more effort may be put in accounts with untapped potential.

Sales Force Structure

Until now we have segmented the client, selected the target accounts and determined the call frequency. What remains is to decide what type of sales force to use, estimate the number of required sales reps and design the actual territories. The sales force structure decision is subject to a few considerations.

The first consideration has to do with the account mix. When dealing with uniform accounts the choice is obvious. You need a sales force that has the skills to deal with the particular account type. In the case of mixed accounts you can have a sales force that calls on all types of accounts or a separate sales force for each type. You may even have a combination of the two with some sales reps calling on mixed account types and other more specialized sales reps calling on key accounts. For POC tier accounts for example, you could have a sales force calling on physicians, clinics and hospitals or carve out a group of institutional accounts and allocate them to a specialty force.

The second consideration would depend on the total product portfolio the sales reps will be promoting. The product mix may favor one type of sales force or another. The synergies or lack of them should be carefully analyzed. A purely hospital product portfolio requires a different structure and skill set than a retail product portfolio.

Sales Force Size

The principal behind sales force sizing is simple. You must have enough capacity to call the target accounts sufficiently based on the set objectives. Yet, companies often base their decisions on sales force sizing on the actions of their competitors as they compete with other companies for share-of-voice in the marketplace; that is, the amount of exposure they get with the customer vs. their competitors. Companies try to match often the size of a competitor's sales force to maintain their share of voice.

What is the best way to size a sales force? That is a question a number of companies like ZS Associates frequently answer for their clients. Simplistically, the math works like this. You have decided that you want to call on x number of accounts, an average of y number of times per year, for a total of x*y calls. You have determined that a rep can make an average of z number of calls per day and can spend w number of days in the field in a year. A sales rep's calling capacity, therefore, is z*w. To sufficiently cover the x accounts you will need (x*y)/(z*w) reps.

What can complicate this exercise are the account types involved. The duration of the sales calls for different account types are vastly different and that will affect the sales rep's ability to maintain a daily call rate. The call requirements for the account types should be factored in the equation.

Territory Alignment

Alignment is the process of grouping accounts to form territories that will be assigned to sales reps. This can be done through explicit assignments of accounts to territories or geographically by assigning all of the accounts in a certain area to the territory.

In almost every case the alignment has a geographic aspect, at least at the regional level, to minimize travel time. Geographic alignments are very efficient. First, because it is easier to select all the accounts that meet certain geographic criteria than to select them individually one by one. Second, because they provide a safety net for new accounts in the territory. If for instance, a new clinic opens in the territory, the clinic could automatically be aligned to the territory based on its ZIP code. Alternatively, the clinic would need to be aligned by account number manually. The second option requires effort and is prone to data integrity errors. Geographic alignments use attributes like the ZIP code for account assignments to territories. The ZIP code is very efficient because it is always available through the customer's address and is granular enough for fine splits of geography.

Sometimes you will need to override the default geographic territory assignment to create key-account territories or simply to remove certain accounts from the territory. Key-account territories are made up of select accounts with exceptional value to the company usually. These accounts may include leading hospitals in a therapeutic area, high sales volume accounts, etc. You can align these accounts to their exception territories using explicit account-to-territory assignments in a second alignment layer over the geographic. Now the underlying default territory owns all of the accounts except those explicitly assigned to the special territories. All new accounts are assigned by default to the geographic territory.

Some accounts will not need to be aligned to any territory because their performance may not be the result of a rep's efforts. Examples of such accounts include drug manufacturers buying the product for research and exporters. These accounts are normally directed to a dummy territory, commonly named 'unassigned'. As a territory, the 'unassigned' does not have any importance, however, its sales are important for the national aggregate.

For accounts whose activities span over several territories their sales is the result of the efforts of many reps. Those accounts, if aligned, would fall into a single territory making that territory the single owner of the account affecting its performance drastically. These accounts can be directed to special district, regional or even national territories. The performance of these territories can be measured and apportioned back to all contributing territories.

Territory Design

The primary consideration in territory design is the territory workload. Ideally, territories should have equal number of accounts and equal sales potential, however, allowing for the varying distances between accounts, that is not possible. The sales rep will need to divide his time between selling and traveling. Ultimately, travel time reduces his selling capacity. In areas with higher population density the accounts are closer and as a result a sales rep in an urban center will be able to cover more accounts than the sales rep in a rural area. A few square miles in Manhattan, for instance, could have more accounts than several mid-western states collectively. Geographically large territories should be allowed fewer accounts.

The size and complexity of the accounts is another consideration. An institutional account in general is a large account requiring a lot of time and effort. Territories with a higher number of large accounts would require more time to cover them. Reducing the number of accounts in such territories would solve the problem.

Fewer accounts may in turn mean lower total sales. If lower total sales meant lower earning potential for the sales reps that would make certain territories unattractive. This is an issue that can be addressed by the compensation plan. It is, however, important that the territory is large enough to be economically viable. For mature products the territory must have a positive ROI, and for new products it must have the potential for a positive ROI.

The actual design of the geographic territories is done with the aid of specialized computer mapping software. Besides their mapping capabilities, the software can monitor the workload of territories as it changes when adding or removing geographic areas and accounts to a territory. The workload is measured by key variables like the number of accounts, total sales, potential, etc.

High-end territory design systems have the capability of analyzing driving distances and accessibility of accounts taking into consideration transportation routes and natural obstacles like rivers and mountains. These features help optimize the territory design to maximize the sales rep's productivity.

Alignments have the potential of affecting a company's profitability and they should be given a lot of attention. Incidentally, they are not static and they can be affected by changes in the marketplace. The balance of key metrics can be changed resulting in the sales force operating not optimally. For that reason alignments should be examined for their validity periodically or when there is strong evidence of dynamic changes in the marketplace.

Because alignments are very important to so many applications they should be treated as a core function in sales operations with enough dedicated skilled staff to keep them always current. In fact, alignment should be a core competency of a well-functioning sales operations group.

Chapter 3
The Product

THE PRODUCT

The product is one of the dimensions in a sales transaction with the supplier, customer and time of the transaction being the other three. A very important dimension indeed, the product has a few of its attributes always listed on the transaction - the product description, the quantity and the price. The description itself consolidates a few more attributes which may include the brand or generic name, the form, the strength and the volume. All of these attributes must be precisely defined from the clinical aspect for the safety of the patient and from the data aspect for the accuracy of the data. The following sections will define the product and its attributes.

ETHICAL DRUGS

Ethical drugs are drugs that require a prescription for dispensing. OTC drugs, themselves prescription drugs once, on the other hand do not require a prescription and can be found on the shelves of almost every retailer. OTC drugs get the prescription requirement waived after they have demonstrated an excellent safety profile for a prolonged period of time and they are relatively very low risk for self-medicating patients following simple instructions. Manufacturers seek OTC status for their products sometimes as a defense to generics when the drug patent nears expiration. The focus of this book is on ethical drugs.

Drugs are chemical or biological substances used to diagnose, cure and prevent disease or to prolong the life of patients with incurable conditions. The use of drugs in the treatment of patients has replaced excessive use of surgical procedures and reduced hospitalization of patients. The eradication of certain diseases and the extended life expectancy of the population are also attributed to the use of drugs. In third world counties, where drug use is limited, the life expectancy is considerably lower than developed countries and disease epidemics are very common.

DRUG CLASSIFICATION

There are thousands of drugs in the market, which makes it necessary to use some kind of classification for easy reference to them. A common way to classify drugs is by therapeutic area; that is the general medical condition or conditions associated with a particular area of the body. A five-digit coding system, the Uniform System of Classification (USC) was developed by IMS Health and is adopted as the standard of drug classification.

Based on this system a general therapeutic class is assigned a 5-digit code referred to as the USC-2, such that the last three digits are zero. A therapeutic class is broken down into pharmacology classes. A pharmacology class is defined based on the product's mechanism of action. It is assigned a USC-3 code, as shown in the example below, by adding one more significant digit to a USC-2 code and reducing the number of trailing zeros. Further, classes of drugs based on their chemical structure within a pharmacology class can be defined using USC-4 codes. Finally, a USC-5 code may be used to further classify products of the same chemical structure based on form.

USC-2	**51000 – Therapeutic Class**
USC-3	**51100 – Pharmacology Class**
USC-4	**51110 – Chemical Structure**
USC-5	**51111 – Form**

Products are referenced by their brand, chemical or generic name. Most often the drug is called by its brand name. The brand name is given by the manufacturer and while the product is still under patent it can only be found under a single brand name. Products with expired patents may be produced under different brand names by a number of manufacturers. The drug's chemical name describes its molecule structure while its generic name is given by the United States Adopted Name Council.

The therapeutic class of a product is determined based on its approved indication by the FDA. As part of the approval process, the manufacturer performs studies on the effectiveness and safety of a drug treating a particular disease. The affect of the drug on different diseases must be performed separately and the FDA review process must be repeated for each disease. Not every form and strength of a product may be approved for the treatment of a particular disease.

FDA regulations prohibit manufacturers for promoting a drug for a non-approved indication; however, physicians may voluntarily prescribe a drug for non-approved indications when there is evidence of the drug's effectiveness. The evidence often comes from the manufacturer's early clinical trials of approved drugs seeking approval for new indications. The practice is known as off-label drug use.

Direct competitors, drugs indicated to treat same or similar symptoms, share normally pharmacology and chemical structure attributes. These products are typically found within the same USC-4 or USC-3 codes. There are exceptions, however, and that is drugs with multiple indications with entirely different USC codes. Other drugs within the same USC-3 code (a different USC-4) may treat some of the symptoms of a particular disease and could be indirect competitors. It requires a lot of market analysis and savvy to define a product's market and its competitors. As mentioned in the previous chapter, the wrong market definition will impact the account potential estimates with consequences to realized potential and proper deployment of resources.

Below are some major drug categories with a brief description of their medical properties.

- Anticancer drugs prevent the growth and spread of cancer or eliminate some forms of it by preventing cancer cell division or killing cancer cells by altering their DNA.

- Anti-infective drugs fight microorganisms in the body. They are divided into antibacterials or antibiotics for bacterial infections, antiviral for suppressing viruses and antifungal for fungal infections.

- Blood disorder drugs enhance the red blood cells (antianemic), reduce blood-clot formation (anticoangulants) or dissolve blood-clots (thrombolytic).

- Cardiovascular drugs are used to reduce blood pressure (antihypertensives) or regulate the heartbeat (antiarrhythmic).

- Endocrine drugs regulate the production of natural hormones of the body. Examples of endocrine drugs include insulin for the treatment of diabetes, estrogen and progesterone for birth control and hormone replacement therapy.

- Anti-inflammatory drugs reduce inflammation caused by infections and chronic non-infective diseases such as rheumatoid arthritis.

- Central nervous system drugs include antidepressants, antipsychotic, antianxiety, antimanic, antiepileptic, sedatives and stimulatory, narcotic and non-narcotic pain relievers, local and general anesthetics used for surgery.

- Anti-allergic drugs counteract the effects of histamines.

- Muscle relaxants relieve muscle spasms caused by disorders such as backache.

- Gastrointestinal drugs combat the burning sensation of the esophagus.

FORM

The form is an attribute that describes the product's physical characteristics relative to the administration method. During product design, the manufacturer determines the best method of administration for the drug and decides on its form. The method of administration of a drug is important because it can affect the drug's potency. It is possible for the digestive process to destroy a drug that is given orally, for example.

A product may be administered more than one way and for each method of administration there may be more than one form. This is typical for products with single or multiple indications. For example, a product may be administered orally and through inhalation with liquid and solid forms for the oral administration.

Below is a list of administration methods with the associated product forms:

- **Oral administration** of drugs is the most common method and the most preferred by the patients. Oral drugs come in liquid and solid form. Liquid forms include syrups and gels. Solids include caplets, tablets, capsules and powders.

- **Injectables** are administered one of three ways - intravenously, subcutaneously and intramuscularly. Intravenous is the injection through the vain and its properties are quick distribution and rapid affect. Subcutaneous is the injection under the skin for localized action, a common method for delivering local anesthetics. Intramuscularly is the injection into the muscles for absorption through the blood vessels of the muscles. Depot forms of drugs, where the drug is bound on proteins for slow release into the blood, are given intramuscularly. Injectables come in liquid or powder form for solution or packaged in vials, ampoules, pre-filled syringes or IV packs. Vials are mostly used for a single dose (SDV) and less frequently for multiple use or dose (MDV).

- **Inhaled** drugs are administered through the nose or the mouth and deliver their effect to the nasal passage and the lungs. Nose administered drugs come mostly in spray form, drops or gels. For mouth administration, aerosols are very common. Others include aerosolized powder solutions and liquids.

- **Topical** use drugs are administered through the skin and come in liquid or semi-liquid form like oil, ointment, gel, cream, foam, lotion, etc., in aerosol spray form or in the form of a patch.

- **Ophthalmic and optic** administration drugs come mostly in liquid and semi-liquid form of drops, cream, gel and ointments.

- **Vaginal and rectal** administration drugs come mostly in semi-liquid and solid form.

It is important to understand the difference between the drug administration method, the form of the drug and yet one other aspect, the form device. The administration refers to the method through which the drug enters the body, i.e. orally, through inhalation, etc. The form of the drug refers to the drug's physical characteristics. The form device is just a physical object, not part of the drug, used to contain a particular drug form and is designed to aid its administration. The form device, however, cannot change in any way the drug properties. Pre-filled inhalers and syringes, self-injectors, dispensers, etc. include such devices. The form description is often a mix of the administration method, the form of the drug and the form device used.

The administration method of a drug is important because it may limit the drug's potential due to patient preference. Patients prefer oral drugs to injectables, for example. An injectable product with the same efficacy and cost profile as an oral would have a tremendous disadvantage against the oral. In other cases the administration method offers a marketing advantage. Such is the case of drugs that provide the physician with business opportunity and upside revenue potential from administration fees and drug sales. IV drugs in oncology fall in that category.

Similarly, forms offer advantages over others. A form that is easier and cheaper to administer would have an advantage over another form. A wet vial versus a dry vial is an example of that. Devices, such as pre-filled syringes cut down the administration time and can save money even though they may come at a premium.

STRENGTH AND VOLUME

Another attribute of the product is its strength. The strength is the amount of active ingredient or live organisms found in a given volume of the drug. It is often measured in milligrams (mg) or micrograms (mcg) in a tablet, capsule, etc. for solids, or in the specified number of milliliters (ml) for liquids.

For solids, the volume is implied and the strength notation may look like "500mg" instead of "500mg/1 tab." For liquids, however, because the volume of one unit of drug is not always one milliliter the notation may be stated either in terms of the unit of volume or the total volume. For example, a product with a strength of "500mg/2ml" may alternatively be stated as "250mg/ml, 2ml".

Manufacturers often produce drugs in various strengths. That is because when indicated for different diseases, one disease may require a much more potent version for the drug to have an effect. Another reason is the variability of patient weights. Patients require doses of drug proportional to their weight. For some forms of drugs the dose requirement can easily be met by giving the patient multiple lower strength units; two 250mg tabs instead of a 500mg tab, for example. For injectables, however, that would mean injecting higher amounts of the drug into the body, causing discomfort on the patient. Instead, more concentrated versions of the drug are developed for the same or slightly higher volume than the lower strengths.

Same brand and form products with different strengths are not equivalent. This is an important fact when counting sales units for different strengths. Manufacturers often attempt to optimize the forms and strengths or introduce new ones after the initial product launch.

PACK

Manufacturers package products in certain ways to meet the needs of the marketplace. For the pharmacies, requiring smaller quantities, products are packaged in one or multiple dosages. Oral solids like tablets, capsules, etc. are packaged in bottles of 30, 50 or 100 tablets. Injectable vials are packaged in any number, typically up to 10. Ointments, creams, oils, gels, etc. are packaged in single-use tubes. For the wholesale trade requiring larger quantities, the manufacturer provides products packaged in cases or boxes of packs.

Pack units are given their own NDC (National Drug Code) number. For tablets, an NDC number is given by the FDA for every bottle size. For vials, an NDC number is given to the vial itself and a different one for every pack it comes in, if it is packaged different ways. Products of different form or strength per volume cannot be packaged together and each pack unit and pack must have their own NDC number. The pack information is very important for accurate calculation of sales quantities.

In recent years, product kits have gained a lot of popularity. A kit includes more than just the drug; in fact, in some cases it includes more than one drug. The kit also includes everything else the patient may require for the administration. For injectables, the kit may include syringes for the injection, alcohol prep pads, etc. Sometimes kits will include more than one drug as in cases of combination therapies. An example of that is the Rebetron kit, which includes pre-filled syringes of Intron-A and tablets of Rebetol. Calculating units of drugs in kits requires good knowledge of the kit's contents.

DOSE

The dose is the manufacturer recommended quantity of the drug to be administered that produces the best therapeutic response for the majority of patents based on scientific data. The dose and the frequency of administration are based on the drug's half-life. Half-life is the amount of time it takes for the body to reduce the concentration of the drug by 50% from its peak.

Less frequently dosed drugs have an advantage over those dosed on a more frequent basis, in consideration to the patient's convenience. This is particularly true with biologics. Manufacturers understand this well and go to great lengths to develop depot versions of drugs. Depot drugs last longer and are dosed less frequently. These drugs bind on proteins and remain in the blood longer before gradually detach from the proteins and attach onto the tissue to deliver their effect.

PRODUCT DEFINITION

To fully describe the product we must provide five of its key attributes. In fact, the product's full name is synthesized by those attributes as shown below:

Brand + Form + Strength + Volume + Pack Size

PRODUCT PRICE

The price is another attribute of the product. Because the product moves through so many tiers in the market there are several pricing levels. The effect of a tier on the price is to drive price higher as it moves away from the manufacturer tier and towards the patient. The major price types are discussed below:

- **The Wholesaler Acquisition Cost (WAC)** or Wholesaler Acquisition Price (WAP) as it is often referred to, is the list price of a specific form, strength and pack of a drug. It is the basis of calculating other price types and discounts. It is also the price used in most data and sales analysis applications. WAC is suited for these applications because it is a fixed price for every segment and customer and does not include discounts or markups. WAC is very useful for benchmarking performance with competitors who may have considerably different pricing strategies. Pricing strategies for specific products change as well over time, with manufacturers becoming more or less aggressive with discounts and markups. List pricing removes the variability in pricing strategies. WAC, however, is subject to price increases like every other price type.

- **The Average Wholesale Price (AWP)** is the suggested wholesale price of a drug and it is published by pricing data services such as the Red Book and PriceChek. AWP is based on the list price of the drug and is approximately 20%-25% higher than WAC. It is used by the industry and government to set outpatient reimbursement rates for drugs. AWP is seldom used in sales data applications.

- **Contract pricing** is the agreed upon pricing between manufacturers and provider accounts for specific drugs. Contract pricing may include an upfront discount and tiered back-end rebates for different levels of sales volumes. Only the up-front discounts are 'visible' in sales transactions. Contracted accounts are not necessarily supplied directly by the manufacturer but they may maintain their own distributor. The manufacturer's contract department deals extensively with this kind of pricing; otherwise contract pricing has limited uses in sales data applications.

- **Invoice pricing** varies drastically depending on suppliers, customers, segments, etc. The invoice price is not always the final price when there are back-end rebates owed to the customer; however, it is the price type that comes closest to the actual pricing. Rebates are given based on performance and once the account has reached a certain level of sales. They are paid periodically or at the end of a specified period. Discounts on the other hand are granted up front on the invoice. Invoice pricing data is collected by vendors and reported as an average by market segment or channel. Its main application is for competitive pricing strategy analysis.

Prices are specific to product packs and should be qualified by the form and strength. Higher strength products have proportionally higher AWP and WAC prices and products of different form but same strength have similar prices. Depot versions of drugs often have a premium built in the price and so do products that come in special delivery devices such as pre-filled syringes, inhalers, etc.

The importance of price in sales data is in its use to calculate dollar sales from units sold. Dollar sales are not used directly off invoices because of price variability. Dollar sales are the most commonly used metric of performance in an organization and benchmarking with the industry. For these measurements to be valid there must be some consistency in the calculations across markets, competitors, segments and customers. The consistency must hold over time as well, however, price increases pose a challenge. The advantage of using dollars in sales analysis is that the dollar is a common denominator across all products and does not require conversion to a common base.

UNITS OF MEASURE

The strength, volume and pack of a product mentioned earlier are all measurable attributes of the product representing quantity. Quantity is an essential element of the sales transaction; therefore, it is important to define precisely the units of measure and the relationships between them.

Two things became apparent in our previous discussion about brands, forms and strengths. First, talking about units of a brand is not particularly meaningful because brands consist of products with heterogeneous characteristics. Second, there is more than one way to measure the quantity of a product, even when we are talking about a specific form and strength. The following section provides some definitions for measuring quantity and attempts to clarify the relationships that smooth inconsistencies.

Pack Unit

The pack unit is the most intuitive quantity measurement for a product because it can be easily observed. Vials, syringes, bottles of tablets, nasal spray bottles, inhalers, tubes of cream, bottles of ointment are all examples of pack units readily identifiable. The quantity of their contents on the other hand would require some effort to measure. The pack unit is the smallest tradable unit typically from the wholesaler to the pharmacy and is the immediate content of the pack. The pack contains one or more pack units. Pack units are calculated by multiplying the number of packs times the quantity per pack.

Pack Units = # of cases * packs per case * units per pack

The manufacturer sells the product in packs or larger quantities such as cases or boxes. Wholesalers on the other hand often split the case or even the pack and supply their customers with the required number of pack units. Each pack must have an NDC number, but not the case or box. The last two digits of the NDC code are assigned to a specific pack size. To standardize the quantity for packs, cases, boxes, etc. in the transactions data, vendors convert the quantity to its lowest common denominator - the pack unit. The pack unit is the most common unit of quantity used in sales data. Unless there is a good reason to use a different unit type, pack units should be used in most cases for in-house applications and field reports.

Volume Unit

Volume units measure the contents inside the pack unit. For liquid products it is the number of milliliters in the vial or syringe. For solids, it is the number of capsules, tablets, gel caps, etc., in a bottle. Volume units are calculated based the following formula:

Volume Units = pack units * volume per pack unit

Using volume units you can convert different pack sizes of the same product into equivalent units. For example, a 30-capsule bottle and a 100-capsule bottle of

Brand-A have an equal but un-comparable count of 1 pack unit each. In volume units, they translate to unequal but comparable quantities of 30 and 100 capsules respectively for a total of 130 volume units.

It is implied that this works for products of equal strengths. The addition of 30 capsules of 100mg to 30 capsules of 200mg is not valid. Products of different brands are typically un-comparable through this method. The products must have very similar clinical profiles for the conversions to be meaningful, such as in the case of branded and generic products.

Even though volume units aid in the conversion of unequal pack units they are not used very often. Volume units magnify the quantity of oral drugs by a large factor over pack units. In the example above, the two pack units resulted in 130 volume units. Volume units have a three-sided effect on the total quantity of liquid products. When the volume of the pack unit is greater than 1ml, volume units exceed pack units, and when the pack unit volume is less than 1ml, pack units exceed volume units. Products with volume of 1ml have equal pack and volume units. The examples below demonstrate that by converting 10 pack units of products with different volumes. Compare the pack and volume units after the conversion.

Unit Volume = 1 ml

Volume Units = 10pack units * 1ml = 10ml

Unit Volume > 1 ml

Volume Units = 10pack units * 2ml = 20ml

Unit Volume < 1 ml

Volume Units = 10pack units * .5ml = 5ml

For two products of the same brand, same total strengths, but different concentrations, volume units yield odd results. For example, Brand-A, 100mcg/ml, 2ml and Brand-A, 200mcg/ml, 1ml have equal strengths of 200mcg, yet the first has twice as many volume units as the second.

TIP: Volume units are found more often in prescription data because pharmacies record the amount of product dispensed rather than the pack unit count. With sales data in pack units and prescriptions in volume units, caution should be exercised when working with both. Unit reports integrating sales and prescription data should use a common unit type.

Strength Unit

Strength units overcome the limitations of volume units in dealing with products of different strength. Strength units measure the amount of active ingredient in a volume unit. While a tablet of 250mg and a tablet of 500mg for the same Brand-A have equal count of 1 volume unit each, their volume units are un-comparable. The two tables have unequal but comparable strength units of 250mg and 500mg respectively for a total of 750 strength units. Strength units are calculated using the formula below:

Strength Units = volume units * (strength / volume)

For oral products, if you have calculated the volume units to be 500 tablets and each tablet has a strength of 100 mg, the strength units are:

Strength Units = 500tabs x 100mg/tab = 50,000mg

For injectables, if you have calculated the volume units to be 500 ml of a product with a strength of 250mcg/2ml, the strength units are:

Strength Units = 500ml x (250mcg / 2ml) = 62,500mcg

The full conversion formula is shown below:

Strength Units = volume units * (strength / volume)

Strength units are the most versatile of units because they can be applied with most conversions and should be used when other unit types fail the conversion. The drawback is that they are very impractical because they result in very large numbers, and for that reason they are not used very often. Strength unit comparisons are meaningful for products of the same brand and form and some products of other brands with similar clinical profiles.

SALES UNIT CONVERSIONS

Sales unit conversions are very important and are in fact used very frequently in sales data operations. They are used in calculations for unit sales aggregations and in comparisons of intra-brand performance between forms and strengths of a product as well as the performance a brand against its competitors.

Unit comparisons overcome the limitations of price increases in dollar-sales comparisons; however, the incompatibilities between the different types of units make the comparisons difficult at times. Analyst must device techniques for meaningful, easily understood unit comparisons.

There are two levels of complexities with unit comparisons. The lower level involves solving same brand and form product differences including those of cloned generics. These differences can be smoothed out using the volume and strength conversions discussed above.

The higher level of complexity involves comparing same brand but different form units and units in therapeutic areas with a mix of products of dissimilar clinical profiles. In the first case you must determine the unit equivalencies between two forms of the same brand. In simple terms, what quantity from each form would deliver the same therapeutic effect? The ratio of the two quantities would be the basis for conversions. Keep in mind that forms of a product are not necessarily indicated for the same diseases. Only the forms and strengths relevant to a therapeutic area should be aggregated and benchmarked against the market.

In the second case the product formulations are different and therefore, the quantities are not comparable on a unit-to-unit basis neither in terms of volume or strength. In this case you need to look for measures that involve quantities in relation to outcomes. The following section discusses two techniques that deal with unit conversions.

Equivalent-Unit Conversions

From the above discussion you can draw some conclusions. Pack units among all unit types discussed are the least comparable between them. Volume units partly solved the comparability issue and work for products of same strength. Strength units provide the most flexibility. The advantage of pack units is that people can visualize them. Volume and strength units are more abstract and result in large counts.

You can use all of the above to create an alternative, hybrid method of equalizing units. This method is referred to as equivalent unit factoring. It is mostly applicable for intra-brand and generic-to-brand conversions and has the intuitiveness of pack units and the versatility of volume and strength units. This method converts units of products to a 'base', typically the lowest strength pack unit or a virtual pack unit. For example, you may convert the pack units of 150mg, 250mg and 500mg units to pack units of 150mg or a virtual pack unit of 100mg.

The first step in this method is to decide which strength and volume to use as the base of conversion. Then calculate and assign a conversion factor to each product using the formula below:

Conversion Factor = (total pack-unit strength / total base-unit strength)

The pack units of each product are then multiplied by the conversion factor to calculate the equivalent units. The result is in pack units of the base. The example below demonstrates the unit conversion and aggregation of three strengths of the same brand to units of the lowest strength.

Product	Pack Units	Conversion Base	Factor	Equiv. Units
Prod-A 100mg, 60 tabs	40	100mg, 60tabs	1.0	40
Prod-A 300mg, 60 tabs	30	100mg, 60tabs	3.0	90
Prod-A 500mg, 30 tabs	20	100mg, 60tabs	2.5	50
				180*

* In units of 100mg, 60tabs

Figure 7. Equivalent unit factoring

In the above example, we used the strength of 100mg and the volume of 60 as the base with a total of 6,000 strength units. The first product has a conversion factor of 1 because its strength and volume equal that of the base. The second product has a conversion factor of 3 (300*60 / 6,000). The third product has a conversion factor of 2.5 (500*30 / 6,000). In the end, we have converted the 90 pack units of various strengths and volumes to 180 equivalent units of the same strength and volume.

Equivalent Therapy-Unit Conversions

The conversion in the previous example works because the products involved are of the same brand sharing the same clinical profiles. If you have a mix of product brands where Product-A requires twice the daily dosage of Product-B to achieve the same effect and the length of treatment with Product-A is 3 days longer than the treatment with Product-B, this kind of conversion does not work.

To convert pack units of different product brands with same indication to equivalent units requires some knowledge of their therapeutic outcomes. One way to calculate the equivalent units is to divide the total strength units of a brand by the number of strength units required for one full therapy. The formula for calculating the therapy strength units is:

Therapy Units = dosage strength-units * daily dosages * days of therapy

The example below converts pack units of products A, B and C to equivalent units using this method. Prod-A has a total of 240,000 strength units (100 * 60 * 40) and requires 4,200 strength units for one therapy (300 * 2 * 7). In equivalent therapy-units, Prod-A accounts for only 57 units (240,000 / 4,200), even though it has the highest number of pack units, because each therapy requires a high number of strength units.

NOTE: *For chronic diseases, where the days-of-therapy is not a finite number, the number of therapy days should be omitted from the formula.*

Product	Pack Units	Dose	Daily Dosages	Days of Therapy	Therapy Strength Units	Total Strength Units	Equiv. Units
Prod-A 100mg, 60 tabs	40	300mg	2	7	4,200	240,000	57
Prod-B 250mg, 60 tabs	30	250mg	1	10	2,500	450,000	180
Prod-C 500mg, 30 tabs	20	100mg	3	12	3,600	300,000	83
							320*
* In therapy-units							

Figure 8. Equivalent therapy-units factoring

TIP: *Real world situations can get a lot more complicated than this. Complication factors include the number of products, forms, strengths and indications involved. Unit conversions for products in un-related therapeutic areas are meaningless. You should quantify sales for products in diverse therapeutic areas strictly using dollars.*

Chapter 4
The Data

SALES DATA

In the previous chapters we focused on the sellers, the buyers, the payers and the products of the pharmaceutical market. This and the following chapters focus on the sales data. A pharmaceutical product, much like other products, reaches the consumer after a number of successive transactions through the market tiers. The data vendors collecting and reporting sales data must follow the process every step of the way tracking the series of transactions leading from the manufacturer to the patient.

The rest of this chapter discusses some general data principles and concepts. The remaining chapters cover some key industry datasets capturing the sales activity in the POC and the influencer tiers. Although this book focuses on specific datasets, the general concepts discussed here are applicable largely to other available datasets in the market. That is because the methodologies for collecting, processing and reporting data are rather common. The similarities end there, however, and the actual data vary based on the amounts of it collected, size and composition of samples, projections, processes, etc.

WHAT IS SALES DATA?

Sales data is logically organized information about an executed sales transaction. A sales transaction is executed when the order has been filled and the customer has been billed for the product. That is typically done through an invoice. Sales data does not include orders under negotiation, back orders and orders received but not filled yet. Reverse sales transactions also qualify for data capture. Returns are negative sales transactions that should be captured to offset a previous sale.

Sales data starts with three fundamental questions; "who bought", "how much", of "what product" and goes beyond to determine how much of the product was actually consumed vs. what is still 'hanging' out in the market and what the pricing dynamics of the market were. All of these questions have tremendous implications for the manufacturer who tries, among other things, to gauge its present financial condition, predict future performance, manage inventories to meet market demand, identify threats and opportunities in the marketplace, etc. That explains why the manufacturer places so much importance on the data.

Undeniably, there is value in the raw sales data collected from a data source; however, so much more value is added when the sales data is cleansed and enhanced with data attributes brought in from secondary sources either by the data vendor or the data users. The vendor's biggest contribution to the process is in the cleansing of data and as a client the manufacturer should be most demanding in this area.

Sales data is only part of the spectrum of data that a sophisticated pharmaceutical marketing and sales organization requires. To understand the depth of the available data one must look at the depth of the market activities. A market exists because of the presence of certain epidemiologic conditions for which the medical community, physicians and institutions, are engaged in the diagnosis and treatment of these conditions. Meanwhile, an array of R&D, manufacturing and marketing organizations engage to provide solutions, consequently filling the pipeline with product candidates. The shape and form of these organizations is influenced by the political, social and economic environment. To make sense of all the market conditions marketing steps in to investigate and chart a successful promotional strategy. Once a product is brought in the market, the sales organization mobilizes and starts to generate sales, prescribers write scripts and insurers reimburse claims. Market research and business analysis groups come in to take a retrospective look at the program effectiveness and fine-tune the promotional strategy.

To support these activities, vendors have produced a wealth of databases and research reports in the areas of company profiles, politico-economic, product pipeline, epidemiology, diagnosis, promotional spend, sales & prescription, claims & reimbursement, promotional response, etc. Some are more encompassing and others more applicable to specific therapeutic areas. Some are focused on a single topic while others integrate data for various aspects of the business into a single integrated report. Some capture data over time while others are more static.

The term sales data within the context of this book is a rather broad definition going beyond a single database to include a suite of databases all complementing each other and all adding a little more depth to better understand the market. Therefore, if your main sales database is DDD, chargeback and adjustment data fill-in for gaps in DDD, the profile and affiliation databases paint more complete portraits of the customer and inventory and pricing provide snapshots of the market conditions at a point in time. In a prospective fashion, sales data is used to predict performance and retrospectively to validate it. While the sales data provides the supply view, the prescription and plan data provide an alternative view, measuring almost the same thing but from the pull-through side.

DEMAND AND TRUE DEMAND

The typical account buys enough product quantity to meet its customers' demand. For that to happen, the account must carry some inventory to fill new orders. The level of inventory fluctuates and varies between customers; however, with the ability to re-stock within a short period of time the level of inventories is typically kept low. The following formula shows the relationship between an account's purchases, sales and inventories.

Purchases = Sales + Inventories

Demand is an account's sales in which case the formula can be rewritten as follows:

Purchases = Demand + Inventories

Depending where the account is positioned in the market structure, the account's demand may become, at least temporarily, another account's inventory, as in the case of wholesalers and pharmacies. Product inventory is an outstanding liability for the manufacturer with the potential of being returned for credit. Only when the product is consumed demand has materialized. True demand is, therefore, patient demand or sales out of the POC tier outlets.

That is why most of the manufacturer's sales efforts are focused on this tier. The manufacturer is interested in generating true demand that translates to wholesale demand and ultimately manufacturer sales. Consequently, the data value increases for transactions that take place in the lower tiers of the market with POC outlet sellout holding the most value and wholesaler sell-in the least. This is important because tracing some sales all the way to the consumer is not always possible and as a result sales data will include transactions at various levels of detail.

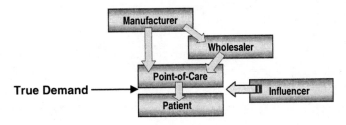

Figure 9. True demand

SELL-IN vs. SELL-OUT

Sell-in and sell-out are technical terms that describe an account's purchases and sales respectively. The manufacturer is involved in transactions as a seller, while the patient only as a buyer. Other accounts are involved both in the purchase and sale of products. An account's purchases of a specific product for a given time period can be summarized in a single transaction. Its sales, however, require a number of transactions to describe them - one for each buyer.

Sell-out transactions, therefore, offer a lot more granularity in the data and are always preferred over sell-in transactions. Sell-in transactions are a compromise and used in cases where the sell-out transactions are not available. In that case, the sell-in transactions serve as a proxy for the missing sell-out transactions. Because of inventories, sell-in and sell-out are not equal but close enough. Sales data sometimes includes a mix of sell-in and sell-out transactions. The higher the content of sell-in transactions the lower is the value of the data. The figure below demonstrates the sell-in and sell-out concept.

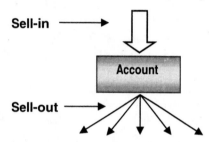

Figure 10. Sell-in vs. sell-out

The successive re-selling of the same product until it reaches the patient results in sales transactions that capture repeatedly the value of the product. If for example, the same physical unit of a product was sold an average of three times before consumed by a patient, by capturing and aggregating every transaction involving the unit we would have overestimated the total value of the product sold by a factor of 3.

To avoid this kind of duplication, sales datasets report transactions of a product unit only once. Based on our previous discussion about true demand, the transaction that better represents true demand will be the one reported in the dataset. That is the last transaction in the chain of transactions. Therefore, a sell-out transaction from the POC tier when available takes precedence over the sell-in of the same tier or any type of transaction from a higher tier.

CENSUS vs. PROJECTED DATA

When vendors attempt to capture sales data they opt for one of two methods - census or projections. The census method tries to capture every sales transaction whenever possible. Sell-out data that cannot be captured is either left out of the dataset or substituted with an alternative source, typically the sell-in. Census data tends to be very accurate but rather incomplete by a few percentage points.

The projection method serves as an alternative to census. The quality of the projected data depends on the quality and size of the data sample. Projections from small samples produce accurate top line numbers, but ultimately, it is projections from very large samples that produce accurate data at lower levels of detail. Projected datasets are complete by virtue of projection but less precise than census data at the account level.

The number of sources the vendor must tap into is a key determinant of which method the vendor pursues. Census data works best when the number of sources reporting the data is rather small and manageable with reasonable effort and cost. For large number of data sources the vendor will likely choose the projection route. The amount of sample data to collect will depend on the ultimate uses of the data. In the end, the product must be marketable and provide the best data quality at a reasonable cost to the client. When that does not happen, you end up with an inexpensive but low quality product or an unreasonably expensive, high quality product. The vendor must strike a balance between two key variables; quality and cost. Quality is ultimately associated with the amount of data to be collected. The cost has two components; the amount paid to suppliers and the overhead cost to cleanse and process the data.

The latter depends very much on the collectability of the data. Information exists in the form of knowledge of an individual, in written or electronic form, etc., random or organized. Unless data is organized, collecting large amounts of it ends up being very expensive. Systematic organization of random data is possible but costly. Disparity in data sources is counterproductive to data cleansing while data adhering to industry standards requires little effort.

COLLECTED vs. REPORTED DATA

A distinction should be drawn between data collected by the vendors and data reported to their clients. One key concern of data reporters is whether they would face a competitive risk if they shared their sales data. Vendors address that concern with the use of confidentiality guidelines. To meet their obligations, vendors at times release to their clients only part of the data they collect so that it does not compromise the competitive position of the data reporters.

In general, vendors collect a lot more information than they are willing to share with their clients bound by the commitments made to their suppliers. For example while you can see who purchased the product you cannot see who supplied it. In that respect, you know the clinic but you do not know its wholesaler, or you know the prescriber but you do not know the pharmacy that filled the script. Under special circumstances the manufacturer can obtain a waiver from a data supplier to access its information in finer detail; however, these are exceptions to the rule.

DATA = COMPETITIVE ADVANTAGE?

One must wonder if merely having data offers companies a competitive advantage. The answer to that is clearly and undisputedly "it does not". The reason for it is that in order for data to put you in a competitive advantage you must have almost exclusive access to it and the pharmaceutical industry is a very data-rich industry with everyone having rather easy access to it. You can, however, make the argument that not having sales data can put you in a competitive disadvantage.

The implication of it is that the manufacturer now must deal with the data issue simply to stay in par with the competition. That by itself is a big hurdle given that some of the competitors are very sophisticated with data analysis methods. In fact, they constantly innovate to stay ahead of the rest. And that is where a small window of opportunity exists for some to get a small competitive advantage by making better use of the data. In the end, however, through learning and imitation the data analysis techniques tend to be shared.

DATA INTEGRITY, COMPLETENESS & VALUE

Both owning and benefiting from data come with the burden of protecting the integrity of the data. The owner of the data must define the rules of engagement and make sure they are adhered to by the data users. As a data user and a beneficiary of it you must make sure to conform to the stated user guidelines. If you have some part in the pharmaceutical market you are part owner of the data and at the same time you are one of its beneficiaries. It is best to think of data as an industry asset with everyone having some responsibility to maintain its integrity.

Most of the datasets available in the market today are quite mature products by now and have rather little room for improvement. They do, however, have tremendous downside risk when it comes to their quality and while incremental improvements have very marginal impact, on the downside the impact has a much greater effect. That is because the relationship of data completeness and value of the data is not a linear one. As the chart in figure 11 shows, the value of the data drops precipitously at progressively lower levels of completeness with almost all of the value diminished in relatively high levels of completeness. Simply, once you reach a level of missing data, the data is unreliable enough to use in an application and it is practically worthless.

The highest risk for data integrity comes from the manufacturer's contact with the data suppliers and the accounts. It is not a coincidence that many of the major data-hostage situations are the result of the interaction between the manufacturer's field staff and their clients. The fact of the matter is that neither the supplier nor the account needs to be told or reminded that their sales data is being shared. That tends to antagonize them and forces them to react with apprehension.

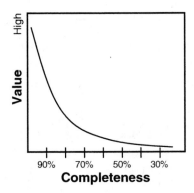

Figure 11. Data value vs. completeness

Another area of risk is the diametrically opposite actions of the data vendors and the manufacturers with regard to data collection. The manufacturers very often will try to negotiate their own private data deals directly with distributors that do not report their data to vendors. This is an incentive not to report for these suppliers and it fully undermines the efforts of the data vendors to improve the completeness of their data. Worse yet, it tempts those already reporting their data to abandon reporting for more "lucrative" direct contracts.

This shortsighted approach of the manufacturers can have serious consequences in the long run. The manufacturer trades off the future state of the data for a small benefit today. Data supplied directly by non-reporters has very limited uses and primarily solves a tactical problem with compensation programs. Besides, considering the actual cost of the data and the processing costs it is an expensive proposition. There are alternative methods to solve the missing data problem and the manufacturer should abandon the practice of rewarding those that created it in the first place.

An equally shortsighted view of the data is that it will only affect you for just a while longer and until you move on from your current position. The best way to describe this is using the popular phrase "you can run from it but you cannot hide". Sales data integrity has far reaching implications both for individuals and the whole sales and marketing department in general. Sales and marketing is all about data at any level of the organization. So, everyone planning a carrier in sales and marketing has a vested interest to see that data is used within the stated guidelines.

WHAT IS PERFECT SALES DATA?

Perfect pharmaceutical sales data is an elusive concept and exactly what most people expect when they are first exposed to it. Those expectations have the potential of becoming quickly disappointment and ultimately despair. Unfortunately, there is no perfect data; therefore, an approach of "how can I get the most out of my imperfect data" is likely to pay off handsomely over the agony of "how can I perfect my data in order to do my job". Besides, efforts to make data perfect are expensive and have mixed results. What is more important is to understand the limitations of the data and implement solutions that minimize the impact on your applications.

While the expectation of perfect data does not help, understanding what would be perfect data does, because it puts in perspective what you have vs. what you ideally need. So what is perfect sales data? In sales data discussions it helps to keep in mind the flow of product through the market tiers. For the wholesaler and POC tiers perfect data would include every manufacturer and re-seller sell-out transaction as well as every sell-in transaction to wholesalers and POC outlets. That would include inventory transfers from one warehouse to another. These transactions would need to be complete with full product information, quantities and their units of measure, the actual prices charged including rebates and the time of the transactions. Sell-in and sell-out data would be comprehensive and would permit you to map all of the supplier-to-customer relationships and calculate stocking and inventories at every tier of the market by outlet. Actual prices and rebates would allow pricing analysis to determine discounting and markups strategies by market segment, customer type, and customer.

For the influencer tier and the payer type accounts perfect data would indicate in all transactions the payer, plan and PBM to determine their influence locally, regionally or nationally, and the prescribing physician of each prescription. It would also include the exact formulary status of each drug together with the co-pay levels, the true number of lives covered by each plan, the healthcare providers associated with each plan and their contracting status. For IDNs, IHNs, PPMs, GPOs, hospital systems and other organizations, perfect data means knowing their affiliations with outlets in any market tier from which to calculate their purchases, sales and true demand from the affiliates.

In the following chapters as we discuss different types of data, you will be able to assess how close a particular data set is to what we would consider perfect data. Again, the focus should be turned away from making the data perfect and placed on understanding the data limitations and developing alternative ways to deal with them.

Chapter 5
DDD Data

DDD™ SALES DATA

DDD is a data collection and reporting system that captures sales transaction data from manufacturers and wholesalers and reports demand at the pharmacies, clinics, hospitals, LTC facilities, HMO sites, government facilities, etc. DDD is a product of IMS HEALTH.

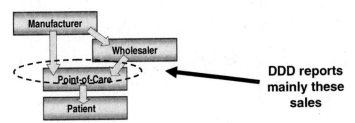

Figure 12. DDD Sales

The Point-of-Care tier is where true demand is generated and therefore, sales data into and out of the outlets in this tier are the most important data for the manufacturer. DDD does not attempt to capture sales out of the POC tier except for mail service pharmacies. Retail and mail service pharmacy sell-out captured in the form of filled prescriptions is reported through a separate product that will be discussed in a later chapter.

The data vendor's objective here is to capture as many of the sales transactions to compile census data as close to 100% as possible. The manufacturer typically desires to see all of that data in its finest detail baring any confidentiality limitations.

What is the Source of DDD Data?

Sales data is about fully executed sales transactions. The sales transaction is finalized and documented by the seller and therefore, it is the entity on the seller-side of the transaction that supplies the data to DDD. That would be the product manufacturers and the wholesaler warehouses.

As discussed earlier, the manufacturer sells his products mostly through the wholesalers with a small portion sold directly to POC outlets. The wholesaler tier is made up of national, regional and niche drug distributors, chain warehouses and re-packers.

There are well over 500 potential data suppliers and the vendor must establish business relationships with as many of these suppliers as possible. The completeness of the data depends on the percent of them supplying their data to

DDD. IMS has been largely successful recruiting data suppliers, however, a number of them choose not to participate. We will use the term 'non-reporter' for any warehouse not cooperating with DDD. As a result of this DDD sales are partly or wholly unavailable for a number of providers in the POC tier.

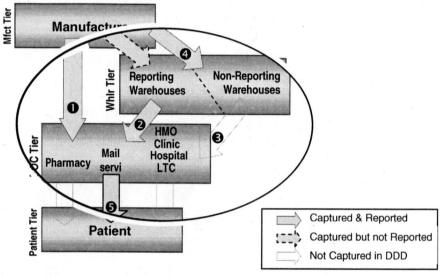

① DDD captures & reports direct sales from reporting manufacturers
② DDD captures & reports sell-out from reporting warehouses
③ Sell-out from non-reporting warehouses is not available in DDD
④ DDD reports sell-in for non-reporting warehouses. For reporting warehouses DDD compares the sell-in and sell-out for data validation
⑤ DDD captures & reports sell-out from reporting Mail service outlets

Figure 13. Channels in DDD

The vendor compensates for a warehouse's unreported sell-out by including its sell-in. The sell-in for non-reporter is reported to DDD by their suppliers, typically the manufacturer or another warehouse. The sell-in is inferior data that lacks the detail of the sell-out and at the same time it includes some level of inventories. At the minimum, the warehouse sell-in assures that total sales at the national level are complete.

A second issue DDD must consider deals with the fact that certain pharmacy types exhibit characteristics of warehouses, contacting business far beyond their immediate geographic area and crossing the boundaries of several territories. Consequently, the sell-in to these outlets reflects demand generated largely in other territories. This is generally a problem for sales force applications because a single territory is credited with the performance of several others. To correct this problem DDD collects distribution data from mail service pharmacies. Unfortunately, DDD does not address this problem for several other types of pharmacies that may also engage in this practice.

In summary, DDD collects data from manufacturers, various types of drug distributors and mail service pharmacies. DDD reports the sell-out for reporting manufacturers, drug warehouses and mail service pharmacies. For non-reporting warehouses and mail service pharmacies DDD reports their sell-in. DDD captures more data than it reports. To avoid double counting, whenever DDD captures both the sell-in and the sell-out for an entity, it reports only the sell-out.

	Manufacturer Tier	Wholesaler Tier	POC Tier	Patient Tier
Supply Sell-out Data to DDD	Most manufacturers	Most wholesalers, chain warehouses & re-packers	Some mail service pharmacies	N/A
Have Outlets With Sell-in Data in DDD	Some manufacturers that buy other company's products for research	All non-reporting warehouses	Most outlets except reporting mail service pharmacies	N/A

Figure 14. Reporting outlets & outlets with data

The Invoice

The DDD data originates in the invoice. The invoice documents a sales transaction and the seller issues it typically after he has fulfilled his obligation of shipping the product to the customer. DDD uses much of the information on the invoice but not all. Invoice data is used in other applications as well such as pricing. Figure 15 demonstrates a sample invoice.

The supplier information is key information on the invoice even though it is not reported in DDD. To protect the confidentiality of suppliers, vendors as a practice exclude the supplier information from the sales record. In DDD, account sales can never be tied back to the reporter of the data. That way, all sales are traceable only back to the manufacturer of the product. Internally, DDD uses the supplier data for quality assurance purposes to make sure that the reported sales into a warehouse approximate the sales out of the warehouse. When that does not happen the warehouse is deemed to have a reporting problem in most cases.

The ship-to information identifies the customer. Entities identified here are represented in the DDD customer master file and linked to a DDD outlet number. The ship-to location of clinics, hospitals, HMOs and LTC facilities are demand points. These entities will make up a rep's target account list. Pharmacies are only proxies for where demand was generated.

The bill-to address is where the invoice is sent and may be different from the ship-to address. From the sales data perspective, the bill-to entity is not significant unless it also receives shipments of drugs. In that case it would be referenced as the ship-to entity in other sales transactions and would have its own DDD outlet number.

ACME Drug Distributors
100 Main St Suite 500A
Uptown, IL 60603
Phone: (999)/999-9999

INVOICE

Invoice No: 1234567
Date: 02/15/2003

Bill To: ABC Pharmacy
200 Washington Rd
Newtown, NY 10001

Ship To: Third Street Apothecary
300 3rd St
Newtown, NY 10001

Qty	Product	Unit Price	Amount
10	AB 123 Ibuprofen, Tabs, 100mg 30	$35.00	$350.00
40	BC 234 Methotrexate, Vial, 25mg/ml, 10	$15.00	$600.00
:	:	:	:

Terms: 2% net 30 days

SUBTOTAL	$950.00
SALES TAX	$71.25
SHIPPING & HANDLING	$20.00
TOTAL	$1,041.25

Figure 15. Sample invoice

The invoice date is the official transaction date. DDD does not report daily sales but it uses the invoice date to aggregate weekly and monthly sales.

Each invoice lists at least one product, which is typically identified by the supplier's product number and a full product name. The item listed could be a pack unit, a pack, a box or a case of a product. DDD converts quantities to pack units by multiplying the quantity by the number of units in the pack, box or case.

The product unit price and dollar amount on the invoice have limited use in DDD and are available in reports for the manufacturer's own direct sales only. DDD dollar sales are typically derived based on invoice quantity and the product's WAC price. The WAC price is not supplied on the invoice. IMS obtains WAC pricing from their clients for products they manufacture and purchase data through DDD. For non-client products, DDD uses several outside sources to obtain the WAC price. Transactions with zero dollar amounts are considered free goods and are not included in DDD. Product returns are subtracted from sales and the net amount is reported in DDD. Invoice terms, ship and handling charges, and tax are not used in DDD.

Actual invoice prices and dollar amounts are captured in other IMS products and have many uses in business applications. One very important IMS product that uses actual invoice pricing is PriceTrak. PriceTrak analyzes the level of off-invoice discounts given by the manufacturer for its products. It provides the average discount for products down to the form and strength level by market segment at different percentiles. The discount at the first percentile gives you a very good idea about the deepest up-front discount given. Discounts for every fifth percentile are also shown on the report.

When using PriceTrak you should be mindful of the sales volume of the product in a given segment as deep discounts in segments with low transaction volume are insignificant. The limitation of PriceTrak is that it does not account for back-end rebates given by the manufacturer. These rebates are often much more significant than off-invoice discounts. Additionally, PriceTrak does not account for invoice terms; a discount given for paying the invoice within a specific timeframe. PriceTrak is available for entire USC classes and has applications in pricing strategy and reimbursement.

In conclusion, the invoice provides the customer, product, quantity and time that define the DDD sales transaction with the invoice price used only selectively in applications.

What is the Importance of DDD?

DDD captures sales into outlets and as such it does not represent true demand. For a given data period, part of these sales become inventories or inventories may be depleted at a faster rate they are replaced. In either case,

DDD runs at best slightly ahead or behind true demand. During a product launch and while outlets are stocking up the product DDD provides a much distorted view of demand. In these cases true demand trails significantly behind stocking. Despite these limitations DDD offers its customers two very significant benefits: visibility into wholesaler sales and access to competitor sales data.

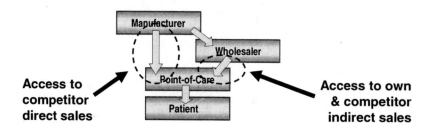

Figure 16. DDD benefits

With a large part of its sales going through wholesalers, the manufacturer's visibility into the sales to providers is compromised. This is a significant setback for the manufacturer because this is where his most important customers are. Without DDD the manufacturer might have to incur higher direct distribution costs to maintain that visibility.

Direct distribution, however, cannot address the lack of competitor sales data. DDD makes that possible by offering the manufacturer the option to purchase competitive sales data. The pharmaceutical industry is very data rich and one of few industries with so much access to a competitor's sales. Pharmaceutical manufacturers can paint a complete picture of the market down to the customer. The data allows them to evaluate opportunity more precisely and launch promotional programs with higher ROI.

Certainly manufacturers and suppliers could do more to restrict competitor access to their sales information. The dilemma is 'does data sharing pose a competitive threat or can one gain more from data sharing'? The industry seems to overwhelmingly agree that data sharing is the more important.

DDD has a significant weakness, however. It reports retail pharmacy sales at the point where prescriptions were filled as opposed to where they were written. Consequently, it does not credit territories creating retail demand accurately. For this reason, DDD is not suitable for territory level data applications for a product's retail pharmacy sales.

DDD COMPLETENESS – ENHANCING DDD

The DDD completeness is a predicament for everyone handling DDD data or being affected by it. Because the reporting status of warehouses changes, the question of completeness perpetuates in time. The fact of the matter is that completeness of the data today is different from yesterday and will likely change tomorrow as more reporters come aboard or others decide to stop reporting. Therefore, for this discussion we will examine the DDD completeness as a snapshot in time. We will define data completeness by:

- the amount of data included in DDD
- the data being reported at the right level of detail

Conceptually, between the sell-in and the sell-out from warehouses and manufacturers DDD should account nationally for 100% of the sales. Operationally, however, a number of factors contribute to reduce the completeness of DDD by at least a few percentage points.

From the manufacturer's perspective, DDD data should lend itself for uses in several applications ranging from top line finance applications to sales force tactical applications. Sell-in data included in DDD is usable in some but not all applications. Therefore, DDD completeness should always be defined with respect to the application the data is used in.

The following section discusses the factors that affect the completeness of DDD and the potential steps that can be implemented to enhance the data. Any attempt to enhance DDD should involve reasonable effort that yields reasonable results and not extreme effort to perfect the data. The commonly used methods in the process yield good results; however, while you can deal effectively with some causes you cannot defend against others and while you can do more for your own products you cannot do as much for your competitors'.

Non-Reporters

Non-reporter data is a case of data not reported at the right level of detail in DDD. DDD captures and reports the sell-in for non-reporters; however, sell-in data does not identify the end-customers and their buying patterns. DDD maintains lists of non-reporters and runs an on-going recruitment program. Outlets in this category include certain warehouses, mail service pharmacies and specialty pharmacies.

In addition to non-reporters, there are a number of other outlet types with drug distribution for which DDD does not attempt to collect data. These outlets have the potential of impacting territory performance and include certain depots, purchasing agents, long-term care providers, home health care providers, nuclear pharmacies, etc.

The table below summarizes by sub-category - IMS' classification of outlets - the types of outlets that could have sales across multiple territories.

Sub-Categories	Description
W2, W4, W5, W6, W8	Warehouse type non-reporting outlets
S4, S5, I5, G7	Depot, mail service and Internet non-reporting pharmacies
N2, N3, N4, P7	LTC provider pharmacies
A3	Nuclear unit-dose pharmacy
V1, V2, V3, V4	Central-fill locations for retail pharmacies
A2, A4, A8, S8	Non-reporting purchasing agents
A5, A6	Non-reporting HMO warehouse or purchasing agents

Figure 17. Non-reporting DDD sub-categories

The above outlets certainly have the potential to impact the manufacturer's business but only when they have enough sales volume. From the warehouse group, the W2 and W4 sub-categories tend to be an issue more often. The mail service sub-category (S5), which incorporates most of the specialty pharmacies, is at the present time the most challenging fuelled by the growth of the segment. Equally important may be the DoD's mail service pharmacy (G7). Internet pharmacies (I5) are still emerging without a significant sales volume at the present time. Large LTC provider outlets specializing in nursing home and home health care, especially those with mail service capabilities, have significant potential to impact data completeness. Nuclear pharmacies (A3) are not going to be always a problem because their business is concentrated in local hospitals and clinics, but when they do, they impact business similarly to mail service pharmacies. Central-fill pharmacies process prescriptions for chain retail stores to relieve their large workload. The first problem with these outlets is that sales are shifted from the retail stores and concentrated into their location. Additionally, they can cause reporting issues when the script is not logged in the computer system of the local pharmacies they support. In the purchasing agent group, Kaiser is the standout; however, its data is blocked and sell-in is not available in DDD except from any manufacturer's direct sales. Otherwise, federal depots and large HMOs may in some cases have the sales volume to impact applications.

Applications that use national level data are not at risk from non-reporters; however, targeting and compensation applications can be impacted. Non-reporters affect sales data only for products they carry and customers they serve. The severity of the problem for a given product depends on the amount of sales of the product going through the non-reporters.

There are two ways to compensate for the missing non-reporter sell-out; using chargebacks or adjustment data. Chargebacks are supplied by the wholesalers to claim rebates for sales to contracted accounts. This method is as good as the percent of contracted business with the warehouse's customers. It yields excellent results for heavily contracted products but it is ineffective for non-contracted ones and does not account for competitor sales. This method cannot be used for mail service and specialty pharmacies.

The second method relies on sell-out data provided by non-reporting warehouses, mail service and specialty pharmacies. This method yields best results when competitor data is supplied as well. Yet, it is a high-risk option because it offers non-reporters an incentive not to report their data to vendors. This option should be reserved only for high volume accounts.

When using these methods, the account's sell-in amount must be reduced by an equal amount for the chargebacks or sell-out data added in; otherwise data will be duplicated.

Unreported Direct Sales

Unreported direct sales are unaccounted for in DDD. Direct sales are reported by the manufacturers. Most but not all manufacturers report their direct sales. Reporting direct sales is a pre-requisite for manufacturers in order to gain access to competitive data through DDD.

Unreported direct sales affect the competing products and markets. Market share and targeting applications for those products are affected. Alignment and deployment can also be impacted when the product with unreported direct sales is dominant in the market. Generally, the severity of the problem depends on the percent of product's sales shipped direct.

TIP: Withholding direct sales is definitely not a strategy that pays often. A manufacturer must have a significant portion of their sales sold direct and market dominance for this strategy to work.

Manufacturers can integrate their unreported direct sales with DDD if they choose to forgo the competitor sales. The sales can be integrated at the account or the ZIP level to allocate credit to sales territories. There is little that can be done about a competitor's unreported direct sales, however. You can estimate the national sales for a competing product through other sources but sub-nationally data will remain a challenge. Market share calculations at the territory and district levels will be inaccurate if not impossible.

Blocked Accounts

Blocked-account data is missing from DDD and involves situations where a group of accounts chooses not to have their data shared by instructing their wholesalers to withhold it from being reported to DDD. For example Kaiser; DDD processes direct sales to Kaiser distribution centers, but because Kaiser refuses to report to DDD and has requested that their wholesaler distribution vendors do not report sales to Kaiser outlets. Therefore, DDD does not cover distribution to the Kaiser facilities (Kaiser owned clinics, hospitals, pharmacies, etc.)

The non-reporter and blocked account data situations are quite distinct. In the first case, the decision not to report is made by the supplier while in the second by the account itself. Blocking can be selective by manufacturer and product or across the board for all products.

Omnicare also belonged in this category until recently when it finally reached an agreement with IMS to report its data. The release of the data, however, is not unconditional and manufacturers can get account level access only for products under contract with Omnicare and their markets. For non-contracted products, access is restricted to territory level or higher.

The motives for blocking data are mostly financial in nature. Data is used as leverage against the manufacturer to secure favorable product pricing. In other situations it is the perception of competitive threat.

Blocked data may or may not affect specific products and markets. US oncology data may have a big affect on oncology products but it may not impact products in other therapeutic areas. Omnicare should not impact non-contracted products with low LTC distribution, and UHC should not be a threat to retail drugs. You must assess the situation of each entity's blocked data individually by product.

The most effective way to deal with contracted blocked accounts is using chargeback data supplied by their wholesalers. For non-contracted accounts, lack of a contract sometimes means low or no sales.

Blocked accounts do not necessarily have zero sell-in in DDD. Direct sales and shipments from secondary suppliers are often reported in DDD. Even the primary supplier may be reporting partial sales because of an incomplete or inaccurate list of accounts. In that case, you might duplicate sales for some accounts by simply adding chargebacks. Before applying chargeback adjustments you should make sure that sales for these accounts are not already captured in DDD. For a given account, the chargeback adjustment should equal its total chargebacks minus the non-direct DDD sales already reported, as shown in the formula below. There are no chargebacks for direct sales and therefore, they should be removed from DDD.

Chargeback Adjustments = Chargebacks - (DDD - Direct Sales)

Ideally, own-product adjustments should be accompanied by competitive product adjustments for market share applications. The contracting relationship will allow manufacturers sometimes to obtain competitive data directly from the blocked accounts.

Late Reporting & Off-System Warehouses

Late reporting may result in missing DDD sales. DDD has a production schedule that it must adhere to in order to deliver data to its clients' expectations. That means, whenever a supplier is late with the delivery of their data, the system must proceed with the production without it.

Missing sales from off-system warehouses is the result of a warehouse's inability to report data for one or more weeks due to certain events. Mergers, warehouse moves and new system implementations all have the potential of impacting reporting. Eventually, the warehouse resumes reporting on regular basis and provides unreported data retroactively. Warehouses off reporting are referred to as temporarily-off (T/O) warehouses.

Late reporter and T/O warehouse situations are dealt with, to a large extend, by the vendor with the use of account level historical data. The historical sales are used as a placeholder for the missing sales until the warehouse resumes reporting. Smaller warehouses, however, are not adjusted for the most recent reporting week. Also, the use of historical data causes the overstatement or understatement of account sales.

The impact from T/O warehouses and late reporting is temporary and in many cases it lasts until the next processing cycle. By then the missing data arrives and gets processed. Late reporting is, however, a recurring problem and one or more new warehouses may be late reporting during the next period. The magnitude of the impact is proportional to the size of the warehouse. Specialty warehouses may have a big impact on certain products.

Most applications use data that spans several months back with little impact from late reporters. Finance and forecasting applications, on the other hand, rely on the most recent data available and have more exposure to late reporting. For these applications sales can be adjusted weekly with estimates provided by the vendor. These adjustments are very temporary and are best made at the national level for a product brand as a single transaction.

For compensation at the end of the incentive period, using sales data that has aged at least a month past the cut-off date corrects most missing sales problems.

Unmatched Data

Unmatched data is a case of missing sales. At any given time, a certain amount of data is held out of DDD in the 'reject bin' because the product or the customer referenced on the invoice cannot be matched to an entry in the product or customer master databases. This is referred to as 'reject data'. Reject data eventually gets matched, 'recycled' through for re-processing and eventually put in DDD. However, fresh reject data, from subsequent data processing cycles, replenishes constantly the reject bin. As a result, an almost constant amount of product sales is excluded from DDD always.

Rejects are the result of warehouses reporting sales for new products or new customers for the first time. The problem with any particular rejecting transaction persists until DDD updates its product or customer master databases with the reporting warehouse's new product and customer numbers.

At the product level, a newly launched product is most at risk as all warehouses carrying it report new product numbers. Product rejects affect sales for all accounts served by the reporting warehouse that purchase the particular product.

At the outlet level, new outlets and accounts that switch suppliers may have their recent data disrupted. Customer rejects affect all of the products supplied by the reporting warehouse to the rejecting outlets. Because of the random nature of the account rejects there should not be a concentration of this type of rejects in any particular area.

Reject data for transactions that failed the customer match can be provided by the vendor down to the ZIP level. Reject data that failed the product match, on the other hand, although it exists, it is unavailable, obviously because the product was not identified.

For top line finance and forecasting applications national level adjustments can be made on weekly basis. The adjustment is typically a single transaction for the product brand for each data week. In theory, there can be rejecting transactions for any week in the last two years. Most of the reject data, however, is concentrated in the recent few months.

For compensation applications, ZIP level adjustments can be made at the end of a compensation period with reject data aligned to territories. Reject data should not be used in regular field reports and is not suitable for market share and targeting applications. Reject data may include warehouse-to-warehouse inventory transfers which have the potential of duplicating data. Large 'suspect' transactions should be excluded from the ZIP data before adjusting.

Product Mismatches

Product mismatches result in missing DDD sales. They affect data completeness by crediting the sales of a certain product to another. As a result, one product's sales are understated while the other product's sales are inflated. The two products often are different forms, strengths or packs of the same brand and in some cases two entirely different products.

Product mismatches impact accounts and territories serviced by the reporting warehouse. The severity of the problem is proportional to the amounts of sales for each of the two products. The amount of missing sales from the correct product and the credited amount to the wrong product can vary depending on the price differential between the two products.

This is a 'silent' kind of data problems and in many cases it goes undetected for a long time. It requires cross referencing to the right product number in order to resolve it. Detecting the problem may come from auditing account level sales.

Monthly Warehouses

The frequency by which warehouses report data to IMS is weekly or monthly. Weekly and monthly reported sales are combined to compile the monthly DDD data; however, the weekly DDD does not include sales for monthly reporting warehouses. This impacts Weekly DDD data for accounts supplied by monthly reporting warehouses. The problem is clustered in the areas surrounding the locations of the monthly reporting warehouses and it is limited to the products supplied by these warehouses.

Because sales from monthly reporting warehouses are rather small compared to that of weekly reporting warehouses, the magnitude of the problem should be overall small. The problem is further mitigated by the fact that the weekly DDD is used as an early warning tool and most applications are based on monthly DDD.

This is one of the reasons why weekly and monthly DDD do not match, with monthly DDD being more complete. However, weekly DDD is updated more frequently and it includes history adjustments not yet reflected in the monthly DDD. Sometimes these adjustments are significant enough to offset the sales of monthly reporting warehouses raising the total amount of weekly DDD sales to that of the monthly and even surpassing it.

Pharmacy & Physician Office Sales

Technically, these are case of sales not reported at the optimal level. DDD does not report sales to retail pharmacies individually but in aggregate at the ZIP level. Similarly, it does not report sales to physician offices located at the same street address individually, but rather aggregated for groups of physician offices based on their medical specialty. This has considerable implications for manufacturers who are left to determine which pharmacies carry the products and which physicians account for the sales at a given location. For more on this subject see 'Level of Data Detail' later in the chapter.

HOW COMPLETE IS DDD?

It is time to answer the big question now. How complete is DDD? From the discussion above apparently this is very much a product specific question. A product's direct sales, status with monthly reporters and non-reporters, account contracting status, therapeutic area, market, specialty and its time in the market all can have an impact on how complete its data is.

DDD has comprehensive coverage and includes almost all of the data it attempts to collect. DDD does not include projected data. At the national level, IMS puts the completeness of the data above 90%. This can vary regionally and by therapeutic class. What should matter to you is the completeness of the data for your markets and that estimate should not give you any comfort when a key product in your market may have anywhere from 0-100% of its data included.

For competitor products, the most important question for you is whether their direct sales are included in DDD. Other missing data will be in proportion to your own products' missing data. For your own products, you can estimate the completeness of the DDD data through the following steps:

- Determine the status of your direct sales. If direct sales are not reported get direct sales from company records
- Estimate the sell-in for non-reporting warehouses, mail service, etc.
- Estimate sales for blocked accounts from contract data if available
- Get the amount for outlet reject data from IMS
- Get an estimate for late reporter and T/O warehouse missing sales from IMS
- For weekly DDD get an estimate for monthly warehouse sales from IMS

Principles of Adjusting Sales

Adjusting is the process of modifying the DDD data to alter the level of detail of certain transactions or the addition of new data that is entirely missing. The following principles must be observed when making adjustments.

The Replacement Effect

Certain adjustments have a replacement effect on the data. This applies to replacement of an account's sell-in with its sell-out. For amounts of sales going into DDD an almost equal amount must come out to avoid duplication. Sell-in is captured as a single transaction. Sell-out comes in many transactions, one per account served typically.

An account's sell-in and sell-out can vary for a given reporting period but over time they are approximately equal. You can prorate the sell-out you are adding to DDD to match the sell-in you are removing, in which case an exact equal replacement takes place. Alternatively, you may let the two vary up or down, and smooth themselves out over time. There is no significant net sales volume increase with these adjustments.

The second method represents demand more closely and avoids calculations yielding decimals. DDD does not use decimals in the unit data. Non-reporting warehouse and mail service pharmacy adjustments have a replacement effect.

The Additive Effect

Some adjustments have an additive effect on the data, as in the case missing account sales from DDD. Overall the net sales volume increases as a result of these adjustments. Adjustments of this type include those made for direct sales, late reporters, T/O warehouses, reject data and blocked accounts.

Adjusted Sales Affect Data Applications

As a rule of thumb all data applications using benchmarking with competitor data must have adjustments for all products or adjustments should not be used. For data with an additive effect, by altering your product's side of the equation you overstate your market share. For sub-national level data, adjustments with a replacement effect change the sales composition for accounts and territories resulting in uneven comparisons of sales performance between your own and your competitor's products.

Coding Adjustments

Adjustment data is available at different levels of detail. Applications require data at different levels of detail as well. The detail of the adjustment data must match that of the application. For database integrity, adjusted account data should be at the same level as similar account data already in DDD.

Coding of the adjustments should follow general DDD principles. Account data should be assigned DDD account numbers where applicable. Transaction dates should be translated to DDD weeks and months using the DDD calendar. Adjustment data should be formatted to match the DDD data format for easy integration.

You must add the adjustments to the appropriate sales category. A record ID should be introduced for each adjustment type to distinguish between original DDD and types of adjustments.

DEFINITIONS

This section deals with DDD market definitions and coding. These definitions are important in order to understand the DDD data.

Market Channel

There are four major channels in DDD: Wholesale, Retail, Hospital and Out-of-Country. DDD uses category codes to define the market channels. Every channel except the wholesale is represented by a single category in DDD. For the wholesale channel DDD uses two categories for reporting and non-reporting wholesalers. Below is list of the category codes.

- Category '1', also referred to as retail channel, captures sales to retail pharmacies and the distribution out of mail service pharmacies. Data for Category '1' is included in DDD.
- Category '2', also referred to as hospital channel, captures sales to hospitals and their outpatient clinic and pharmacy departments, staff model HMO's and federal facilities. Category '2' transactions are included in DDD.
- Category '1(2)' is not a separate category. Simply, accounts in this classification are assigned by default to category '1' with the option to move them to category '2'. When that happens, category '2' is referred to as the non-retail channel. From the data perspective, the main difference between Categories '1' and '2' is that Category '2' data can be seen in greater detail. Outlets of this type, referred to as 'movables', include clinics, non-reporting mail service pharmacies, other closed-wall pharmacies, long-term care facilities and other miscellaneous accounts.
- Category '3' captures sell-in to non-reporting warehouses. Their data is included in DDD because there is no sell-out available for these warehouses.
- Category '4' captures out-of-county transactions for non-USA territory accounts. Category '4' outlets belong in the POC tier and are included in

DDD. Category '4' transactions are mostly used in top line demand calculations and rarely in sub-national analysis.

- Category '9' captures sell-in to reporting warehouses. To avoid data duplication category '9' is not included in DDD because DDD includes already the sell-out for these warehouses.

Category	Code	Outlets in Market Tiers	Data in DDD	Lowest Detail Level
Retail	1	POC	Sell-in	ZIP
Hospital	2	POC	Sell-in	Outlet
Movables	1(2)	POC, Mfct.	Sell-in	ZIP or Outlet
Non-Reporting Wholesalers	3	Wholesaler	Sell-in	Outlet
Out of Country	4	POC	Sell-in	Outlet
Reporting Warehouses	9	Wholesaler	None	N/A

Figure 18. DDD Categories

Market Segment

The market segment in DDD is defined as 'class-of-trade'. All accounts in DDD are exclusively assigned to a market segment. Below are listed the ten classes-of-trade used in DDD:

- Chain Pharmacy
- Independent Pharmacy
- Foodstore Pharmacy
- Mass Merchandiser Pharmacy
- Mail service Pharmacy
- Hospital
- Healthcare Plan
- Clinic
- Nursing Home
- Miscellaneous

There is no perfect alignment between classes-of-trade and DDD categories. Chain, independent, foodstore and mass merchandiser pharmacies belong exclusively in the retail channel or category '1'. Hospitals belong exclusively in the hospital channel or category '2'. Clinics, mail service pharmacies, LTC facilities, healthcare plans and other miscellaneous accounts have outlets in either category.

TIP: You can define your own classes-of-trade by combining certain IMS classes-of-trade. Some companies prefer for example to see all retail pharmacies as one class-of-trade.

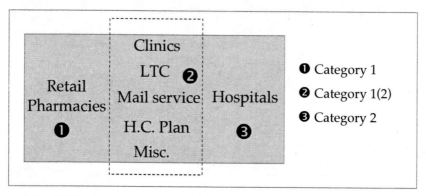

Figure 19. DDD classes-of-trade

Sub-Segment

Classes-of-trade are further broken down to sub-segments or sub-categories. Sub-categories are groups of outlets with similar characteristics. Each class-of-trade has one or more sub-categories exclusively assigned to it. Clinics, for example, are represented by sub-categories based on specialty, which include oncology, emergency centers, etc.

A two-character coding scheme is used for sub-categories starting with a letter and ending with a digit like C1, P2, etc. DDD assigns outlets to sub-categories based on their business type.

Sub-categories are very important. They reveal a lot about the outlets they represent and the reporting intricacies affecting their data. DDD uses more than 90 sub-categories.

TIP: You can use the sub-categories to create custom market segments or classes-of-trade. IMS provides lists of sub-category codes.

Account

DDD uses the outlet to define an account. The outlet is the lowest level in the market hierarchy definition. DDD outlets are assigned based on customer ship-to addresses and may represent a manufacturer, a wholesaler or any point-of-care location. An outlet is exclusively assigned to a sub-category.

In some cases, an outlet represents more than one customer. Such is the case of physician offices at the same street address which DDD groups by certain major specialties, or the case of retail pharmacies which DDD groups by ZIP code. This customer representation makes it impossible to break the sum of the sales down to its parts for these outlets.

For larger and more complex customer sites, DDD assigns multiple outlet numbers - one for each ship-to location. In this case, a single customer such as a hospital is represented in DDD by more than one outlet number. For example, the inpatient and outpatient pharmacies, any outpatient clinic or other department of a hospital may be assigned a separate outlet number in DDD.

An outlet in DDD is given a DDD number, which consists of its ZIP code and a three-digit sequence number uniquely identifying the outlet from other outlets within the ZIP. DDD reserves sequence number ranges for specific outlet types. For example, sequence numbers 001-149 are reserved for pharmacies.

OUTLET NUMBER

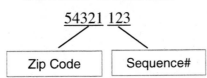

Figure 20. The DDD outlet number

The use of ZIP codes in the outlet number offers the advantage of easy geographic positioning and alignment of the outlet to a geographic territory. However, it has a serious drawback. The customer in DDD does not have a static identification number, in sharp contrast with the norm, but the number changes as the post office re-designs and re-numbers postal areas.

This type of account numbering requires extensive maintenance and cross-referencing to keep the continuum of historical sales data. The example below shows a hypothetical outlet number change as a result of a ZIP code change from 91234 to 91239. The sequence number may or may not change.

91234 200 ➞ 91239 202

Outlets that physically move from one location to another within the same ZIP code maintain their identity in DDD as the same outlet, with the same sales history but a different address.

Outlets that move to a new location outside the ZIP code are considered new outlets. The new outlet has a new DDD outlet number and address and sales history that begins with the first day of operation at its new location. The outlet at the old location gets inactivated and maintains all of the sales history up to the time of the move. Inactive outlets and their sales history are not removed from DDD in order to preserve the data integrity.

Perhaps the most challenging task for the manufacturer is maintaining the cross-references between the company customers and the DDD outlets. The cross-references must be updated on monthly basis as IMS publishes updates for new or changed outlets. The use of ZIP codes in the numbering of the DDD outlet further complicates the task.

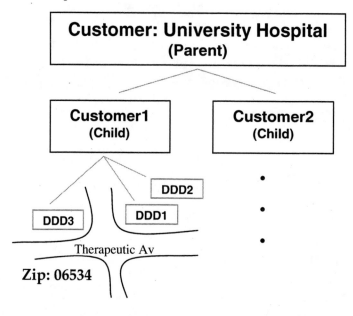

Figure 21. Parent, child customer and DDD outlets

The cross-referencing must be done at two levels. First, outlets of the same entity in the same immediate area are grouped to define a 'child' customer at that location. If the customer operates other locations, a similar process is followed to define a customer for that location as well. This location must be defined separately, because geographically it may belong to a different territory. Once all 'child' locations are individually defined, they can be linked at a higher level to a 'parent' customer. Using DDD, you can evaluate the performance of an outlet, a customer at a location and the total customer.

Figure 21 demonstrates the customer re-definition process. DDD outlets DDD1, DDD2, DDD3, define Customer1 in ZIP code 06534 and Customer2 is defined similarly in a different ZIP code. Customer1 and Customer2 are the 'children' accounts of the 'parent' account University Hospital.

TIP: Using outlets you can re-define sub-categories. This is useful in certain situations where you try to determine product usage by indication.

To summarize, in DDD the market channels, segments, sub-segments and accounts are defined hierarchically using IMS' category, class-of-trade, sub-category and outlet respectively. For practical purposes, the manufacturer can manipulate all of the above to create custom definitions of channels, segments and customers.

What Does Data Look Like in DDD?

One important fact about DDD is that it does not report data at the same level of detail it collects it. DDD collects a lot more data and in finer detail than what it provides to its clients. This is necessary to protect the interests of the data suppliers, certain market participants, the patient and the manufacturer. As such, DDD must alter the output to conceal some information. First and foremost, the ability to tie data back to a supplier is removed by eliminating references to the seller in the output records. By default, the seller in DDD becomes the manufacturer.

The vendor sets the lowest allowable level of detail for data categories. The manufacturer, on the other hand, has a few options in terms of product and customer detail and with respect to own vs. competitor sales data.

In general, the level of data detail required is dictated by the application. Finance and forecasting applications typically are the least demanding, requiring top-line data. Sales force applications on the other hand require a lot of customer and product detail. The rule of thumb is to start with lower level detail data and roll-it up to higher levels as required.

Retail Pharmacy Data

The pharmacy identity is masked in DDD and product sales for all retail accounts within a ZIP code are aggregated and assigned to the ZIP. This is necessary because pharmacies operate in a much more competitive environment than non-retail accounts, like clinics and hospitals, which enjoy some level of exclusivity. The ZIP is the closest you can come to the customer in the retail segment. The following figure demonstrates the transformation of the pharmacy data collected by DDD to the data reported.

Data Collected　　　　　　　　**Data Reported in DDD**

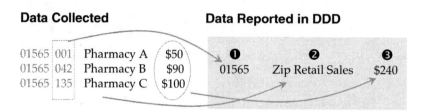

- ❶ DDD outlet numbers are masked & data is reported at the zip
- ❷ Account names are masked and data is reported generically as 'Zip Retail Sales'
- ❸ Retail account sales are aggregated and reported at the zip

Figure 22. Collected vs. reported retail data

Mail service Pharmacy Data

DDD collects and reports distribution data from reporting mail service pharmacies. The distribution is reported at the ZIP code of the prescribing physician. That way the territory creating the demand gets the credit for the sales, as opposed to the territory of the pharmacy filling the prescription.

Mail service data can be aggregated together with retail pharmacy data and reported at the ZIP as in the previous example. When reported separately, however, it is under a DDD number that consists of the ZIP code with a sequence number of '148'. The figure below demonstrates an example of mail service distribution data.

Data Collected　　　　　　　　**Data Reported in DDD**

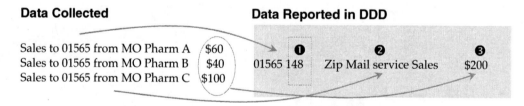

- ❶ The DDD number for mail service data consists of the zip code and the sequence number of '148'
- ❷ Mail service distribution is reported generically as 'Zip Mail service Sales'
- ❸ Mail service distribution to the zip is aggregated

Figure 23. Collected vs. reported mail service data

NOTE: *In a few cases mail service distribution is collected at the ZIP code of the patient. Due to new HIPAA guidelines, patient ZIP data must be rolled-up and reported at the 3-digit ZIP* *code. The DDD number for patient ZIP data for the above example would be "015<u>00</u> 148". The amount of mail service data from patient ZIP codes is rather insignificant.*

Hospital Data

The retail data rules above apply equally to manufacturer's own and competitors' products. Non-retail data rules are less restrictive, however, and the manufacturer's own product sales can be shown at the outlet level. The figure below demonstrates an example of collected vs. reported hospital data in DDD for the manufacturer's own products. There is virtually no difference between the collected and reported data.

Data Collected				Data Reported in DDD			
01565 200	Hospital A	ownProd	$300	01565 200	Hospital A	ownProd	$300
01565 230	Hospital B	ownProd	$600	01565 230	Hospital B	ownProd	$600
01565 235	Hospital C	ownProd	$350	01565 235	Hospital C	ownProd	$350

Figure 24. Collected vs. reported hospital data

DDD typically defines hospital inpatient and outpatient departments separately. The inpatient department is assigned a DDD number with class of trade of 'Hospital'. Outpatient clinics, dialysis centers and pharmacies may be assigned their own DDD numbers with class of trade of 'Clinic'. It is often the case that purchases made by the inpatient pharmacy are used in the hospital's outpatient departments. DDD cannot track this kind of spillover from the inpatient to outpatient departments.

It is worth noting here that for any hospital designated as a PHS (Public Health Service) covered facility DDD has its PHS sales for covered outpatient drugs carved out and reported separately from its non-PHS sales. Covered drugs are significantly discounted subject to procurement on the Federal supply schedule. For PHS facilities DDD assigns a separate DDD number with a subcategory of H9 to represent its PHS business. The total hospital sales, therefore, would be the sum of its PHS and non-PHS sales. This concept applies to certain other account categories besides hospitals.

PHS covered entities receive federal assistance for serving indigent populations. The PHS designation is granted by the Office of Pharmacy Affairs based on criteria outlined in section 602 of the Veterans Health Care Act. Organizations that may qualify for PHS status include Urban and Tribal Indian Health centers, Native Hawaiian Centers, Tuberculosis Clinics, Hemophilia Treatment Centers, Black Lung Clinics, Title X Family Planning Clinics, Sexually Transmitted Disease Clinics, HIV Early Intervention Projects, AIDS Drug

Assistance Programs, Disproportionate Share Hospitals and various Community, Migrant, Homeless, Public Housing and School-Based Health Centers. The requirements for covered entities prohibit duplicate discounts or rebates under another program such as Medicaid and the resale or diversion of drugs purchased under the program to non-qualifying patients.

Clinic Data

Data for hospital outpatient clinics, VA clinics and surgical centers is straight forward, captured and reported at the outlet much like hospitals discussed above. Physician data, however, deviates slightly from the non-retail rule. Because of the large number of physician offices, the task of tracking sales by physician office is enormous; as a result, DDD reports sales for all physician offices at a given address aggregated by specialty. There is a finite number of specialties for which data is reported separately and include dialysis, reproductive, oncology, nephrology, emergency care, orthopedic and X-ray/radiology/urology. All other specialties are reported together generically as 'outpatient clinic/doctor' sales. When the sales volume is insignificant, sales at the address are reported generically as 'ZIP physician sales'.

For a medical building, in other words, physician office sales are reported under a maximum of nine accounts regardless of the number of physician offices at the building. More likely, that number would be much smaller since rarely all of the above specialties can be found at the same location. The outlet name in most cases is 'Multiple Doctors' and in fewer cases a named physician or clinic. The DDD subcategories for the above nine groupings are D1, D2, D3, D5, D6, D7, D8, D9 and Z3.

Figure 25 demonstrates an example of collected vs. reported physician office data in DDD where transactions for seven different accounts at the same street address are aggregated and reported under three DDD outlets.

This method of reporting DDD physician office sales is very limiting for targeting because the activity of one physician office is indistinguishable from the next. Chargeback data provides some visibility here but only for contracted accounts. A more robust solution has been introduced by IMS with its DDD-MD product.

DDD-MD taps into the warehouse transaction data reported to DDD and matches the customer to an MII facility or to a physician from the Xponent universe instead of a multiple-doctor DDD outlet. MII is a customer profiling database. As such, it is a richer, more granular database than the DDD universe. In the case of physician offices, it could be profiling more than one office for a single DDD number. DDD-MD makes the connection between the multiple-doctor outlet and the matched accounts and allocates the actual sales accordingly.

DDD-MD retains the balance of sales that cannot be matched to either an MII facility or an Xponent physician at the DDD multiple-doctor.

Data Collected		Data Reported in DDD			
		❶	**❷**	**❸**	**❹**
Oncology Clinic A	$150				
Oncology Office B	$190	01565 165	Multiple Doctors	D6	$340
Urology Office C	$300				
Radiology Clinic D	$200	01565 180	Multiple Doctors	D9	$500
Pediatric Office E	$250				
Eye Specialists F	$150				
Cardiology Clinic G	$200	01565 185	Multiple Doctors	D1	$600

❶ Multiple physician offices at the same address may be assigned to the same DDD number

❷ A generic account name is assigned most typically to the DDD number

❸ A maximum of eight subcategory codes represent the physician specialties

❹ Sales at the location are aggregated by subcategory

Figure 25. Collected vs. reported clinic data

In the example below the multiple-doctor DDD transaction is broken down to its parts; the two DDD-MD records. In this example the data was not matched entirely to a DDD-MD account and as a result a third line is required to carry the balance of the multiple-doctor sales. In many cases DDD-MD reveals just a single account behind the DDD multiple-doctor number.

34256 150	**Multiple Doctors**	prodA	$10,000
❶	**❷**		**❸**
0000012345	ABC Oncology		$5,000
0012345	Dr. Doe		$3,500
34256 150	Multiple Doctors		$1,500

❶ DDD-MD uses either the MII ID or the IMS Prescriber Number from Xponent

❷ Account and physician information from MII or Xponent

❸ The balance of un-matched data is retained under the multi-doc DDD number

Figure 26. DDD multi-doc vs. DDD-MD

DDD-MD is relatively new with some room for enhancements, nevertheless, of great significance to many applications. At the present time its coverage is better in certain therapeutic areas than others. It is also more applicable to certain products than others, namely drugs dispensed or administered in physician offices. From the data processing standpoint, its production schedule lags that of DDD by a few days. Ideally, you want the two available at the same time in order to fully integrate them. The integration would involve replacing the DDD multiple-doctor records with their DDD-MD equivalents.

Long Term Care Data

DDD captures LTC sales at the nursing home level for nursing homes with in-house pharmacies and at the pharmacy level for pharmacies that supply this segment. Depending on what your sales objectives are this can be good and bad news. This segment is quite complex and the objectives vary.

Given the importance of the pharmacist, one objective might be to target the pharmacies. In this case DDD serves the objective well capturing the sell-in for in-house and free-standing LTC pharmacies. Subcategories N1, N2, N3, N4 and P7 round-up the sales. You may include in the list the VA nursing homes with subcategory G9. Subcategories Z7 and Z8 were intended for nursing home pharmacy sell-out, however, presently DDD reports only pharmacy sell-in without immediate plans to change that.

Things are getting more complicated with objectives involving the nursing homes. Data at the nursing home level exists for the minority of accounts with in-house pharmacies. For all other nursing homes the data is summarized at the supplying pharmacy. One approach here would be to apportion the pharmacy data to the nursing homes using nursing home-to-pharmacy affiliations and the relative size of the nursing homes weighed by occupancy rates, etc. Verispan's SMG captures these affiliations.

Prescriber level objectives can be met with Xponent, which captures prescriber script activity for the segment as we will see in the following chapter. The following example demonstrates LTC sales at the pharmacy and nursing home.

Data Collected			Data Reported in DDD			
01565 550	LTC pharmacy A	$300	01565 550	LTC pharmacy A	N2	$300
01565 505	Nursing Home B	$550	01565 505	Nursing Home B	N1	$550
01565 501	Nursing Home C	$600	01565 501	Nursing Home C	N1	$600

Figure 27. Collected vs. reported LTC data

Account profiling data is perhaps more important in this segment than any other. For nursing homes at the minimum you need the key personnel, occupancy and the parent entity as a great number of them are part of a chain.

For pharmacies the profiling information provides key personnel like the chief pharmacist and other pharmacists, the affiliations to the nursing homes and the parent entity. Again, as many of the pharmacies are part of a chain, the ability to roll-up the data to the corporate account level is very important for contracting purposes. Both MII and SMG provide nursing home profiling data.

Other Non-Retail Data

Below are examples of collected and reported data for different types of non-retail accounts including non-reporting mail service pharmacy and warehouse sell-in. Here also there is virtually no difference between the data the vendor collects and the data it reports.

Data Collected			Data Reported in DDD			
01565 410	N-R MO pharm A	$300	01565 410	N-R MO pharm A	S5	$300
01565 305	N-R Wholesaler B	$550	01565 305	N-R Wholesaler B	W2	$600
01565 250	Nuclear Pharm D	$750	01565 250	Nuclear Pharm D	A3	$750

Figure 28. Collected vs. reported non-retail data

Competitor Non-Retail Data

The rules for competitor non-retail data are more restrictive, limiting visibility somewhat. For individual competitor products DDD offers sales data at the territory level, where territory is defined as three or more outlets with sales. Alternatively, DDD offers competitor data at the outlet level only for combinations of three or more products from the same therapeutic area. The manufacturer must report their direct sales in order to receive competitor data.

Figure 29 demonstrates the data limitations for competing products in DDD. In the first example, sales for compProd1 from three non-retail accounts are aggregated to form a territory 1101 under which sales are reported. In real world applications the almost random aggregation of outlets to form territories for the purpose of reporting sales is not very practical or meaningful. This is used more frequently with actual sales territories to report total sales for competitor products down to their strength.

In the second example, three competitor products were selected and their sales to Hospital A were aggregated to get the outlet level sales. This is very practical in typical applications. More likely all competitor products would be aggregated to get the total competitive activity at the account. Even though you cannot isolate any one product's sales the combined competitor sales give you a target to work with. The problem with this option is that if you have fewer than three direct competitors, introducing another product in the mix may distort the true competitor activity.

Data Collected   **Data Reported in DDD**

01565 200 Hospital A   compProd 1 $100   ❶
01565 410 M.O. Ph. B   compProd 1 $200   Territory 1101   **compProd1** $600
01565 156 Clinic   C   compProd 1 $300

01565 230 Hospital A   compProd 1 $200   ❷
01565 230 Hospital A   compProd 2 $300   01565 230 **Hospital A** compProd 123 $900
01565 230 Hospital A   compProd 3 $400

❶ Competitor non-retail sales for individual products must be aggregated at the territory
❷ Competitor sales at the account are available for combinations of 3 or more competitor products

Figure 29. Collected vs. reported non-retail competitor data

The table below summarizes the level of detail rules for the retail and non-retail market.

	Retail	Non-Retail
Own Products	ZIP	Outlet
Competitor Products	ZIP	Outlet ❶ or Territory ❷

❶ For combinations of three or more products from the same USC class with reporting of direct sales

❷ Minimum of three outlets with sales in each territory

Figure 30. Lowest level of data detail matrix

TIP: For competitor sales at the outlet level, selecting the right three products is imperative. Including non-direct competitor products in the mix distorts the data. The sales volume of the products in the combination and their retail/non-retail sales composition are the key metrics to look for.

Product Detail

In chapter 3, we saw that the product is defined by its brand, form and strength. Product brands and generics can be grouped into therapeutic classes.

You can use any of these definitions and groupings in DDD to report sales when building reports. Further, you can group products from related therapeutic classes to define a custom market. In fact, DDD will allow you to group products in a totally arbitrary fashion mixing strengths, forms or brands.

Your business needs will determine which product data you will need and how the products should be grouped. The reporting of sales on these groupings is subject to the rules for customer detail discussed above. Namely, if you choose to report sales for a single competitor's product the lowest level of customer detail will be the territory. To go below the territory level you must group the product with two other competitor products from the same therapeutic class.

DDD uses product groups, 3-digit numbers, to represent anything from single product strengths, all strengths of a form, all or any number of strengths and forms of a brand or multiple brands.

Abbreviated Time Periods

DDD uses standard abbreviated periods in hard copy reports. Below is a list of them. If you use hard copy reports you must familiarize yourself with these abbreviations. For consistency with DDD you may want to adopt the DDD abbreviations in your reports.

CM	:	Current Month	**YTD**	:	Year-to-Date
QTR	:	Quarter	**TY**	:	This Year
MAT	:	Moving Annual Total (rolling 12-months)	**LY**	:	Last Year

DDD uses the combination of time period and year to define the length of time covered as shown in the example below.

YTDTY	=	Year-to-Date This-Year
MATLY	=	Moving-Annual-Total Last-Year

The DDD Calendar

DDD calculates monthly sales using a special calendar it introduced referred to as the 4-4-5 calendar. The 4-4-5 calendar differs from the regular calendar in that the month starts always on a Sunday and ends on a Saturday. Months are made up of four full weeks with every third month having five weeks, hence, the 4-4-5 naming. Certain days of the calendar month may fall in a different 4-4-5 month as in the example in figure 31.

S	M	T	W	T	F	S
3	4	5	6	7	8	9
10	11	12	13	14	15	16
17	18	19	20	21	22	23
24	25	26	27	28	29	30

S	M	T	W	T	F	S
1	2	3	4	5	6	7
8	9	10	11	12	13	14
15	16	17	18	19	20	21
22	23	24	25	26	27	28

S	M	T	W	T	F	S
29	30	31	1	2	3	4
5	6	7	8	9	10	11
12	13	14	15	16	17	18
19	20	21	22	23	24	25
26	27	28	29	30	1	2

Figure 31. DDD 4-4-5 calendar

The purpose of the 4-4-5 calendar month is to assure a fixed number of working days in months to aid year-over-year comparisons and trending. Based on how the weekends fall out at the end of the year, in some years the last quarter is reported as 4-5-5 quarter.

The implication of using the 4-4-5 calendar in DDD is that x-factory sales and chargebacks must be converted to the DDD calendar month for sales comparisons to be meaningful. Figure 31 provides an example of a DDD 4-4-5 calendar quarter.

BUILDING DDD

This section examines conceptually the vendor's main steps of data collection and processing. The process involves recruiting new data suppliers, assuring a steady stream of reported data, cleansing the data and performing the necessary quality assurance checks before the data is made available for use. It is important to understand this process because what is later identified as a data problem most of the times it has its roots here.

Data Supplier Recruitment

Ideally, every manufacturer and wholesaler should have their sales reported to DDD. Additionally, every mail service pharmacy, depot or other outlet in the POC tier that conducts business in a geographic area broad enough to cross-territory boundaries should have their sell-out in DDD. That is not always the case, however, and a number of non-reporters exist in every tier. It is the vendor's responsibility to continuously look for and recruit new data suppliers willing to sell their data. IMS gives higher priority to the larger suppliers because they can have a bigger impact on the manufacturer's data.

There are two prerequisites for reporting. The suppliers must be willing to report and must have the technical capabilities to meet certain requirements. There are always a number of warehouses unwilling to report and occasionally, a data reporter chooses to stop providing data. The technical capabilities of data supplier are also critical to meet the following criteria:

- Report data through electronic media or online transmission
- Report on a certain frequency
- Meet reporting deadlines
- Report using a consistent format
- Provide specific required data elements
- Meet quality standards

Not every candidate meets these criteria and those that do not, fail to get recruited. The recruitment can take several months to allow for thorough testing of the recruit's incoming data.

Manufacturers are often faced with compelling situations that necessitate the recruitment of new suppliers. These non-reporter situations typically impact the quota and compensation applications. Sales reps are generally unwilling to put effort on accounts that they do not get credit for due to lack of data. Although the manufacturer has other options, the course of action should be to refer the matter to the data vendor. Manufacturers have considerable leverage to persuade non-reporters to sign-up as data suppliers.

TIP: Manufacturers in specialty markets are more likely to encounter recruitment issues because specialty product distribution is concentrated through fewer suppliers. However, these suppliers may have low overall sales volume, making them not the best recruitment candidates for the vendor.

The recruitment process also applies to new outlets of already reporting suppliers. These outlets are not brought into the system automatically by virtue of the parent company being a reporter. They are also subject to the same quality standards as every other supplier. In this respect, reporters may have temporarily partial data until all new locations are integrated in the process.

In general, the area of concern with non-reporters is the mail service business with numerous non-reporting outlets affecting small areas but significantly. The wholesalers are well covered in DDD and are less frequently an issue. In terms of data integration, new supplier data in DDD is well handled. Typically, DDD brings in full 24-month history right away or partial history initially and full history right after. On the other hand, Xponent does not bring in the prescription history in almost every case. See more on this subject in Xponent.

As we mentioned earlier, the reported sell-out of a data supplier is more desirable over their sell-in. An adverse effect from a mail service pharmacy becoming a reporter is that going forward you cannot size the volume of its business. Given the rules for protecting the confidentiality of reporters, the manufacturer permanently looses access to the outlet's sell-in. This information, although not important to the sales reps, is vital to corporate account groups looking to contract with high volume accounts. They can segment the non-reporters by volume but not the reporters. The paradox in this case, from the corporate accounts standpoint, is that they get more information for those that are unwilling to share their data.

Reporting Frequency

Data suppliers are expected to report data to DDD on a weekly or monthly cycle. The preferred reporting frequency is weekly, however, it is not always possible and a few warehouses report their data monthly.

The reporting schedule is such that the data vendor has enough time to process the data and generate the reports for its clients. The vendor tracks the receipt of data and makes sure that missing data from suppliers is eventually recovered.

DDD reports data to its clients weekly or monthly. DDD delivers weekly data approximately 10 days after the close of the reporting week. Weekly DDD includes sales reported by weekly reporting warehouses only. DDD delivers monthly data approximately 3-4 weeks from the close of the reporting month and includes sales reported by both weekly and monthly reporting warehouses.

DATA CLEANSING

Reporting sales data to a vendor is simply supplying invoice data in electronic form. The data is extracted from the data supplier's computer system. Processing the data, for the vendor means dealing mostly with the disparity of the data reporters' business systems. Figure 31 demonstrates the process.

Looking back at the discussion of the invoice, two things on the invoice are not readily identifiable - the product and the customer. That is because each data supplier has its own unique numbering and naming of the product and customer. Other invoice elements such as quantity, date, unit price and total amount are straight forward in their interpretation.

Part of the process is to make a positive identification of the product and customer on every invoice. IMS maintains product and customer cross-reference tables to match records. The cross-reference tables connect data supplier identification numbers to internal DDD database numbers.

Records that fail the product or customer match are initially placed in a holding area, the reject bin. Then they are prioritized and matched manually based on dollar amount and length of time in the reject bin. Large amount transactions and transactions long in the reject bin have a higher impact and are given higher priority.

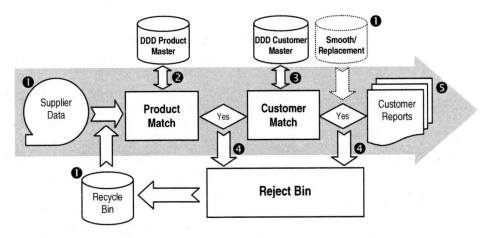

- ❶ DDD inputs - new supplier data, recycled & smooth/replacement
- ❷ The product referenced in the transaction must be matched to the DDD product master
- ❸ The customer referenced in the transaction must be matched to the DDD customer master
- ❹ Transactions without product or customer match to be matched manually
- ❺ Only fully matched records are seen in customer reports

Figure 32. DDD data processing

The reject bin potentially can hold transactions up to 2 years for outlets that rejected and 15 weeks (for weekly data) to 9 months (for monthly data) for products that rejected. Un-processed transactions after the respective periods are lost. Reject data is concentrated is the recent few weeks and the amount of it drops precipitously after that.

The rejection and recycling process is perpetual and it is the natural result of the matching process. As data in the reject bin gets matched and moved to the recycle bin it gets replenished again by the matching process of the next processing cycle. At any given time the reject bin holds an almost steady amount of rejected data. Similarly the recycle bin holds an almost steady amount of data to be re-processed every week.

The DDD data process has three main inputs:

- **Data suppliers –** This is new data reported by external data sources. It includes data for the current reporting period and possibly, previously unreported back data owed.

- **Recycle bin** – The recycle bin holds data for re-processing. This is data that failed a processing step in a previous cycle and went through a manual match.
- **Sales History File** – DDD taps into the sales history file to borrow 'smooth' or 'replacement' data for significant, 'must see' warehouses that are temporarily off reporting. Smooth and replacement data is not re-processed but just added.

Corrections are other minor inputs to DDD and fix erroneous data. They involve typically a small number of transactions and can add, remove or alter data. Data removals from DDD are common and they involve 'smooth' and 'replacement' data when the actual data is received.

Naturally, the higher the number of data suppliers, the bigger the task to keep the cross-referencing updated. Supplier consolidation works favorably in that respect. Newly launched products are more prone to product-no-match rejections as a number of wholesalers are introducing new product numbers.

Similarly accounts switching wholesalers have new customer numbers assigned to them by the new supplier, with a good chance of their data rejecting. Mergers can have a larger scale impact as customer records are migrated and converted from one system to another. DDD takes steps to deal with all of these situations.

Transactions that get successfully matched continue on to have their dollars calculated based on the WAC price or other price as mentioned in the invoice discussion.

Implications

The diagram in 32 reveals some important facts about the processed data:

- Some but not all of the data not submitted by the suppliers is going to be missing from a manufacturer's reports. Missing data is recovered and processed at a later time.
- DDD includes some historical data in the place of actual missing sales.
- Data that fails the product or customer tests is not included in the manufacturer's reports. This data is manually matched and reported at a later time.
- The manufacturer's reports include new data for the current week and month but also new data for previous weeks and months not reported earlier, which causes sales history to change.

DDD ACCURACY

Data accuracy is the subject of debate often between analysts and sales reps, especially when it comes to applications of quota and compensation. To understand the DDD accuracy you must look at it from different perspectives. Accuracy is about errors, the frequency by which they occur and how long they persist until they are eventually corrected. Accuracy is less of a threat to your application when you understand the causes of errors and their magnitude. With that understanding, you can at times come up with solutions to minimize its impact.

Accuracy is more relevant when talking about lower levels of data detail. At higher levels, as the point of reference changes and the volume of sales increases the impact is minimized. For national level sales, for example, it does not matter if sales are credited to the wrong outlet as long as they are accounted for. At the outlet level, however, accuracy is critical because the account potential and performance can be miscalculated.

Data errors can be introduced by the data suppliers, the data vendor and the manufacturer. They exist in the data or can be artificially created by erroneous report definitions. Most of the times errors can be attributed to the product or customer dimension of the transaction.

Product Mismatches

The product match is one major step of the DDD data processing. Because of the large volume of data processed by DDD it is inevitable that a number of mismatches will take place. A product mismatch can involve the wrong strength, form or pack of a product and potentially the wrong brand altogether. This kind of error affects two products at the same time with one product's sales typically overstated and the other's understated.

Different strengths have proportionally different prices; therefore, the magnitude of the error for strength mismatches is a factor of the price differential of the two strengths to the plus or minus side.

Different form but same strength products typically have the same price but some form devices come with a premium. Crediting sales to the wrong form can result in an error the magnitude of which is proportional to the premium.

Pack level mismatches have the potential for the biggest impact. In this case, a pack may be interpreted as a pack unit or vise versa. The magnitude of the problem is proportional to the number of units in a pack.

On the wholesaler side, product errors have a financial impact both on the wholesaler and its clients and cannot persist for long. There, a product error is the equivalent to selling the wrong product at the wrong price. On the data vendor side there is no financial impact and the problem may persist longer, especially if the magnitude of the error is small.

Errors can occur because the product information was set up incorrectly in the product master table. Newly launched products can be particularly vulnerable to product errors, as are products sold for the first time by a warehouse. Error fixes result in data corrections retroactively altering the sales history of the products involved.

Outlet Mismatches

There are a few causes for outlet mismatches. Some of those originate in the DDD data processing where outlet matching may result in the identification of the wrong customer and sales attributed to the wrong outlet. From the sales perspective, this does not impact the overall sales volume. At the territory level, however, if the matched outlet falls outside the territory of the correct outlet, it understates sales for a territory while it overstates sales for another.

Recycling of customer numbers by wholesalers does not occur often but it is a problem when it does. It happens when over time a wholesaler re-uses an old customer number.

A third situation involves a perceived outlet-matching problem. DDD literally defines the shipment drop-off location as the outlet. This may be one of many receiving locations at a campus. The manufacturer's expectation may be to see sales at an adjacent location where the product was actually used.

Outlets moving to a new location in a new ZIP are considered new outlets. The new outlet does not carry the sales history, which stays with the old outlet. This can also be a perceived error with the data. Name changes and splitting outlets are other situations of perceived data problems.

Unlike product mismatches, which are scrutinized mostly by the company owning the product, outlet mismatches impact all manufacturers. Potentially, a number of them may be trying to correct the same outlet problem. When a manufacturer discovers and reports the problem to DDD, the fix benefits everyone and sales for all products are routed to the right outlets.

The persistence of these types of errors depends on their magnitude. The magnitude of an outlet mismatch is equal to the sales volume of the transactions involving the outlet. The larger an outlet's missing sales amount is the sooner it will be identified and dealt with.

Smooth and Replacement Data

Smooth and replacement data are historical sales used to prevent trend brakes and large gaps in DDD when reporting warehouses fail to report their data on time. The fact remains that they are just proxies for the actual sales. In reality, they maybe lower or higher than the actual sales. Smooth and replacement data have the potential to:

- attribute too much credit to outlets
- attribute too little credit to outlets
- not attribute any credit to outlets with sales
- attribute credit to outlets without sales

Smooth and replacement data are normally used only temporarily for a particular wholesaler and there is some amount of it almost always in DDD. They become an accuracy problem only when they stay too long in the data as a result of the wholesaler not being able to produce the back data promptly.

Once you come to recognize the problem there is no further action until the warehouse submits the actual data. Infrequently, some warehouse situations become permanent, in which case, the replacement data stay in the database indefinitely; however, DDD eventually stops supplementing for these warehouses.

"Replacement' data are historical sales used for suppliers reporting weekly. For significant or 'must see' warehouses, DDD starts replacing un-reported sales with historical data from the same week of the previous month immediately with the first week of missing sales. For all other warehouses, DDD replaces sales for all missing data weeks but the most recent one, so that, these warehouses are missing at most one week of data. However, the last data week of the month, these warehouses have their missing data replaced for all weeks in order for the monthly data to be as complete as possible.

Data weeks are matched because of possible varying buying patterns throughout the month. DDD continues to compensate for missing sales during the following weeks until the warehouse resumes reporting. Eventually, the data supplier provides the actual data, at which time the replacement data is removed from DDD.

For monthly reporting warehouses DDD replaces un-reported sales with 'smooth' data starting with the first month of missing sales. Smooth data is the warehouse's average sales for the last three months.

The method of smoothing and replacing DDD may over or under compensate for missing sales both at the account level and in total. Otherwise, it is a good proxy for the missing sales.

Data Reports

A common source of data accuracy problems is the vendor's reports. Reports are defined by setting various parameters. The wrong report setup can duplicate, exclude sales or include sales at the wrong level.

There are occasionally examples of reporting warehouses having both sell-in and sell-out data. This is not a problem for territory application but at the national level it duplicates data.

In other instances, the report may be excluding sales for certain warehouses or have special conditions for specific outlets and sub-categories that redirect data. These exclusions and overrides surely can impact national or territory totals.

Having strengths at the wrong level will result in inaccurate outlet level data. This problem may be masked by the fact that some data for other strengths of the brand are at the outlet level.

The manufacturer has some visibility into the report setup but not all aspects of detail. Report problems occur more often than they should. This can be a training issue for the vendor. One way to treat this problem is to keep reports simple.

Similarly, the manufacturer's own data processing can generate data errors through faulty report definitions and programming logic as wells as improper or misinterpreted business rules.

Mail Service and Re-packer Units

DDD includes dispensed prescription data from reporting mail service pharmacies. A prescription varies in size and it can be a fraction of the pack unit. For example, the pharmacist may fill a prescription of 20 tablets of a drug out of a bottle of 30 tabs. DDD does not report fractional units and in pack-unit reports it rounds up fractional units. Consequently, mail service units can be overstated in DDD.

Re-packers have also the potential of overstating DDD units. Re-packers customize the quantities of the products they re-sell. They may, for instance, buy the product in quantities of 100s and resell it in quantities of 30s. The vendor attempts to capture re-packer units at the actual size whenever possible. Additionally, some re-packers try to take advantage of overfill in injectable vials by pre-filling syringes. The excess quantity results in extra units.

DDD does not convert mail service units to dollars; instead it uses actual reported dollars, thus, avoiding the problem of overstating dollar sales. There is no action required to correct mail service and re-packer units unless a particular supplier has a profound effect on your data. In that case, you may choose to have the particular reporter excluded from your DDD reports.

TIP: You should avoid converting units to dollars. Instead you should use dollar data provided by IMS in order to avoid inflating product sales. This is particularly important for specialty products and products with significant mail service sales.

Data Suppliers

Data suppliers can affect the quality of the data by introducing errors or by not supplying data for a period of time. When a warehouse goes 'temporarily-off' the reporting system the vendor is forced to use replacement or smooth data in DDD impacting the account, territory and the overall accuracy. Ultimately the warehouse's ability to continue reporting, the timing of the recovery and ability to produce past data is critical to DDD. Computer system upgrades are common causes of this problem. Mergers and acquisitions, which typically result in computer system consolidation, can be equally destructive.

DEALING WITH DATA ACCURACY

The process of dealing with data accuracy involves problem identification, problem resolution and implementation. For best results, both the vendor and the manufacturer's office and field-staff should engage in the process.

The first step is to identify the problem. Quality assurance processes of the vendor or the manufacturer can identify problems systematically. A very effective method for manufacturers is the use of chargebacks to validate sales. This uncovers specific problems for contracted accounts or general warehouse problems. Automated trend-break and zero-sales checks at the account and territory level are easily implementable by the manufacturer.

Sales rep inquiries are perhaps the best source of identifying problems, especially when they are well documented. The manufacturer must have a process to deal with sales rep inquiries. This process should validate the rep's claim, provide supporting documentation to the vendor and manage the responses with the proper communication to the field.

Once problems are identified and referred to the vendor, the vendor can now verify them and plan their resolution. The timing of the implementation varies from one to several data cycles depending on its impact. If the resolution affects many customers significantly, DDD prolongs the implementation to allow its customers to make any necessary adjustments. The corrections are likely to be seen first in the weekly DDD data. The monthly data cycle is one whole month; therefore, some problem resolutions take several months to complete.

For the manufacturer, what is more important is the problem identification and verification. For critical processes, such as the close of the compensation plans at the end of the term, when there is practically no time to wait for error fixes, the manufacturer can make his own territory sales adjustments.

WHY DOES DDD SALES HISTORY CHANGE?

History corrections are changes made to DDD for data weeks and months past the current reporting period. History correction can affect any of the 24 months of active DDD data but typically impact recent weeks and months the most. As the data 'ages' it becomes more stable with lower likelihood of being altered.

Unlike the typical accounting process, closing the month and freezing the DDD sales history is not possible. DDD tries to consolidate data from numerous sources without control of their timing. That is why it allows the flexibility to add, remove and correct data beyond the current period. Below are some of the causes of the history changes.

Temporarily-Off (T/O) Warehouse Back Data

Back data is data not reported previously by certain warehouses due to their 'temporarily-off' reporting situation. Back data affects mostly the very recent data weeks considering that many warehouses go 'temporarily-off' reporting for just one week. Occasionally, a warehouse may resume reporting but not provide the back data until a later time. In that case, back data affects weeks further in the past.

The total impact of back data for T/O warehouses with smooth or replacement data is minimal; however, at the account level there may be significant adjustments. For warehouses without smooth or replacement data, back data typically has a positive effect boosting overall sales; except perhaps for accounts with more returns than purchases in the specific reported time period. The magnitude of the changes depends on the size of the warehouse.

Smooth/Replacement Data

Smooth or replacement data for an account stay in DDD until their actual data is received. At that time, the smooth and replacement data is removed for the same time period as the actual data received.

Smooth and replacement data have a negative effect, reducing sales, only to be neutralized by the actual data going in. The end result is a small positive or negative impact on national sales.

The impact is greater potentially at the account and territory levels and it depends on how well the smooth and replacement data 'predicted' actual sales. For accounts with fairly stable buying patterns there is probably little impact, while for other account it would depend on any unusually large transactions.

New Data Suppliers

Occasionally, a new data supplier joins DDD. DDD requires that new warehouses provide two years of sales history. That is done to assure the continuity of the sales trend. The new data replaces the sell-in for the new supplier without a significant overall sales volume change; however, the account and territory sales composition can change significantly in the geographic area served by the new reporter.

Small specialty warehouses can affect relatively few products but have a large impact. New data can reveal new significant accounts within a territory affecting targeting. Compensation is impacted the most because sales are added to the current-performance side of the equation. Adjustments to the quota are absolutely necessary in this case.

Release of 'Interrupted' Data

Infrequently, blocked outlets release their 'interrupted' data to DDD. The release of the back data has an additive effect because this is entirely new data unaccounted for in DDD, increasing overall sales volume from the account level to national. The considerations for new supplier back data discussed above apply here as well. Omnicare is one example of blocked accounts to have released interrupted data to DDD.

Account Sales Corrections

Account level corrections are made to rectify situations where sales were attributed to the wrong account. The net change could be zero with one account's sales reduced by a certain amount and another's increased by a similar amount. If the accounts are in different territories, the sales volume of both territories is affected; otherwise, there is no territory volume impact.

Product Sales Corrections

Product sales corrections are made when sales are attributed to the wrong product strength, form or pack, or to an entirely different product. Product sales corrections can have a replacement and an additive effect on the data at the same time and impact account, territory and national totals. Sales for a given account are shifted from one product to another. If the correct product is a larger or more expensive pack, the adjustment adds to the overall sales volume; otherwise, it reduces it accordingly. If the problem originates in a warehouse, the sales history for all customers served by the warehouse is impacted.

Recycles

Recycled data is new data that was previously rejected due to a product or customer no-match. Recycles have an additive effect and impact account, territory and national totals. Recycles may include returns, which would decrease sales. Recycled data originates in many warehouses; therefore, their impact is broad across regions. They affect recent weeks more than previous weeks with high concentration in the last three months.

Outlet Reclassifications

Outlet reclassification is the change of an outlet's sub-category code, which may result in the alignment of the outlet to a new class-of-trade or category code. These changes happen when an outlet is erroneously classified or its business has changed enough to warrant placement in a new sub-category.

Sub-category changes do not affect the overall volume of sales, but can shift sales from one segment or channel to another and possibly change the level of data detail when moving from one category to another. The outlet sales history does not change but sub-category, class-of-trade and category sales may as the outlet is displaced to a new sub-category and class-of-trade or category.

Price Updates

Price updates deal with incorrect product WAC prices or unreported price changes. The corrections reach back to the effective date of the price change. Sales data for the period is restated with sales increasing or decreasing, according to price increases or decreases. The magnitude of the change is proportional to the percent price change. The impact of price changes is relatively low for all data applications, and broad, affecting every sales transaction for the products whose price changed.

ZIP Code Changes

DDD outlet numbers are based on ZIP codes and as a result a change in the ZIP code of an outlet causes the outlet number to change. There is no net change in the overall sales volume but sales shift from one outlet number to another.

For outlet moves from one territory to another, historical sales stay intact with the old outlet number while the new outlet appears not to have any sales history. This problem can be treated in reports by cross-referencing the two outlet numbers and if applicable, your internal customer numbers.

For re-numbered or redrawn ZIP codes by the post office, outlets are given new DDD numbers with full transfer of the sales history from the old to the new. ZIP changes can be problematic when ZIP codes on the boundaries of adjacent territories are redrawn to combine areas from both territories. In cases like that, at the minimum, one territory would loose the retail accounts in the portion of the ZIP moving to the other territory. You can keep non-retail accounts with the old territory by overriding the new default territory; however, if you are using a straight ZIP-to-territory alignment, treating exceptions may not be very practical.

TIP: New ZIP codes must be aligned promptly to avoid automatic alignment of outlet and ZIP sales to the default 'Unassigned' territory, consequently, understating sales for certain territories.

DEALING WITH SALES HISTORY CORRECTIONS

Dealing effectively with the history changes requires answers to these questions:

- Who gets affected?
- How much?
- How long of a time period?
- What action is required?

Who Gets Affected?

The answer to this question is that at any given time everyone almost is affected by one or more data problems. What you want to focus on here is the accounts and territories affected significantly.

Sales history changes for 'Temporarily-Off' warehouses, new data suppliers, smooth and replacement data and product sales corrections have their roots at a warehouse. Knowing which warehouses are currently affecting data is a good first step.

Their geographic locations can suggest which territories they may impact. Your chargeback data can tell you the contracted accounts they serve. These are not actions you take every week or month, but potential actions when a problem persists for a long time.

Problems from these sources are concentrated in certain areas and clusters of accounts. Concentration of data problems as opposed to random occurrences has more significant impact on applications.

Account sales corrections and recycles affect outlets at random across all territories with less impact to any one territory. The focus here should be to identify the high volume outlets impacted. Looking for trend and sales breaks in high volume outlets and variances between DDD sales and chargebacks for contracted account are good proactive actions.

Outlet re-classifications and ZIP changes are more technical in nature and are easy to deal with at the outlet or territory they occur.

Price updates have a very broad affect on every outlet and a cumulative effect at the territory and national level.

How Much?

If an outlet's history changes, the key question is how much. Action should be focused on high volume changes for a few reasons. Accounts whose sales increase dramatically will need to be called more frequently, major ZIP code changes may trigger realignment within a district, and enough sale volume adjustment can shift the forecasting curve, for example.

History changes happen over time and have a cumulative effect. While you may notice subtle changes periodically, at the end of the quarter there may be enough accumulated changes to require a review of your applications.

How Long of a Time Period?

Sales history corrections can affect data for a single reporting period, a few reporting periods, or the full two year of active DDD sales history. Recycles, outlet, product and price corrections and back data for T/O warehouses affect history for one or more data periods. Corrections from new suppliers, release of 'hostage' data, outlet re-classifications and ZIP changes can affect all 24 months of active data.

It is important to know if full or partial history corrections are applied by the vendor. Some changes are implemented in stages, one timeframe at the time. For new suppliers, for example, data for the current year may be integrated immediately while the previous year's sales are integrated later.

What Action Is Required?

You determine the action by putting history changes in perspective with the application. The two complicating factors here are the frequency by which these changes occur and their criticality at the time they occur.

Some history changes occur on a constant basis, as in the case of back data from T/O warehouses, smooth and replacement data and recycles. These changes would require tremendous effort to follow at the account level on a weekly basis with little benefit. They are best dealt at summary level, monitoring total activity for each category, the warehouses involved, their reporting history, and the weeks of unreported data.

On the other hand, sales history changes from new data suppliers, release of 'hostage' data, account sales corrections, product sales corrections, outlet re-classifications, price updates and ZIP changes occur with varying lower frequencies. These changes can be evaluated as they occur to determine if immediate action is required; otherwise, applications should be reviewed periodically and adjustments should be made accordingly.

The criticality and immediacy of history corrections should be determined by the applications they affect. Alignment applications are very sensitive to ZIP code changes, for example, and territory targeting lists should be updated immediately when new data reveals new significant accounts. Forecasting is updated by some companies as data becomes available, although, unless the volume from history changes is significant, it has no effect on the sales trend. Quota and compensation programs on the other hand are evaluated quarterly and are not prone to weekly fluctuations in the data.

DDD REPORTS

A sales transaction is fully described by the customer, product, date of sale and the product amount. The fifth dimension, the seller, is assumed to be the manufacturer. DDD maintains a number of attributes for each of these dimensions as shown below:

Customer: Name, address, state, ZIP, category, sub-category, class-of-trade, MSA
Product: Brand, form, strength, pack
Time: Week, month
Amount: Pack, strength & volume units, dollars, market share, sales index

You can use attributes in combinations to create different views of the data. By aggregating sales of customers in the same state you can create a view of the state sales. By adding the sub-category you create a state view broken down by sub-category. You can introduce new attributes to extend DDD and create more complex views.

Extending DDD

The key to extending DDD is the link between standard DDD attributes and the extended attributes. The territory, district and region are extended geographic attributes of the ZIP code.

Extending DDD through industry standard data elements like the ZIP code is very easy. The difficulty lies with proprietary attributes such as the DDD number. You could try to link DDD data to an external database of hospital profiles, but without the ID cross-references that would be a very difficult task. When working with external databases you need to make sure that they are compatible with DDD to avoid extensive manual matching of key attributes. The external databases should provide the links to DDD.

These databases are very important because they allow you to create views for customers in the influencer tier. Influencers have no part in the sales transactions and DDD does not attribute directly sales to them. Sales for influencers are derived from their association to POC tier outlets. GPOs are defined as a collection of the hospitals they serve, PPMs as a collection of the member physician offices, etc.

Evaluating the performance of these customers will depend on your ability to link them to DDD. IMS offers its own solution in this area, the DDD Integrated Views (DDDIV). DDDIV provides customer profile information integrated with DDD sales. Other databases such as SMG provide that extendibility as well. Claritas, CACI and others provide extended attribute data for demographic analysis, and the post office provides geographic databases for alignment applications. Your ability to create views of the data will only be limited by the access and connectivity to new data attributes.

Report Types

DDD provides formatted, ready to use paper and electronic reports and raw data files for manipulation by its clients. Fixed reports provide a single view of the data, are inflexible for further manipulation, inefficient, containing few data elements and lengthy.

Raw data reports come in electronic form and provide maximum flexibility for manufacturers because they can be extended by using additional attributes to provide multiple views of the data.

Fixed Reports

IMS has a suite of standard fixed format reports but it also offers customized solutions. When choosing a report you must select options for the following dimensions:

Product or Market – You have the option to track your own product sales (basic report) or sales for the whole therapeutic area (Therapeutic Class Report or TCR).

In TCR reports, the previously discussed level-of-detail limitations for competitive products apply. TCR reports are the source of market share data.

Level of Detail - You may choose from outlet, ZIP, territory, district, region, sub-category, class-of-trade or even national level reports, considering the limitation for competitive products.

Time Periods - You may choose from IMS' standard time periods CM, QTR, YTD and MAT for the current and previous years or custom periods.

Data Types - Options include DDD dollars, pack, volume or strength units, market share or sales indexes.

Raw Data

Raw data files provide more options for manufacturers with capabilities to process data in-house. They come in several standard IMS file formats to suit the manufacturer's needs. Using raw data files, manufacturers can report sales in various ways, align data for different sales forces, and introduce new data attributes to extend DDD.

File Formats

The most important consideration for selecting a file format is the platform on which you will be processing the data. Packed data is friendlier to some platforms than others, for example.

The applications and productivity tools you use will be your next consideration. You should select file formats that are easier to read with these tools. Delimited data are typically faster to define than fixed length data.

Formats vary in number of time periods and SRA (Sales Reporting Area) fields. Time periods range from one, for the current period, to 24 or 106 data periods for monthly and weekly data respectively. Using file formats with a single timeframe may meet your current requirements but ultimately a format with the most time periods will meet all requirements.

There are typically between two and four SRAs in a file. Having more SRAs in a file allows you to pack more levels of data in a deliverable for complex reports.

Staying consistent with one file format is perhaps your best strategy to maximize productivity. You can design a single routine to read any of your deliverables cutting down your development and maintenance costs.

Levels of Data

Raw data files allow you to add products in a deliverable more than once, at more than one level, aligned more than one way. Although it is best to include products at the lowest allowable level and roll-up data to higher levels, it is more convenient to have data already rolled-up in your deliverables. You may include strength, form and brand level data for a product in a file at the same time. You can have data for a product at the outlet level and at the same time have the same data at the territory.

Raw data files are not reporting tools but rather delivery platforms where a single instance of them delivers data to address one or more needs.

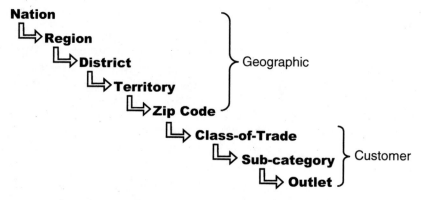

Figure 33. Customer and geographic levels

Data records have one key attribute identifying the level of data detail. Data attributes applicable only to certain data levels do not have reserved fields in data formats, but are instead assigned to SRA fields. SRA fields are variable fields that you populate with the data attributes as needed. For ZIP, outlet, sub-category and territory levels of data, you need to assign the ZIP code, outlet number, sub-category code and territory number to SRA fields, for example, or the data will not be meaningful.

SRA fields are not populated with values for every record. For territory level data you cannot have lower level of detail attributes like the ZIP code or the outlet number SRA fields populated, for example. As a result, SRA fields are populated with values only for records of certain level of detail.

The Anatomy of the DDD Record

The typical DDD record consists of four sets of fields that correspond to four dimensions found on the invoice: customer, invoice date, product and amount. Because DDD removes references of the actual supplier, all DDD sales are traced back to the manufacturer in DDD.

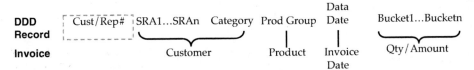

Figure 34. DDD record dimensions

- The customer and report numbers identify the DDD client (typically a manufacturer or supplier) and the specific report. These are constant values populated consistently in all records in the file.

- The SRA fields hold values for customer attributes such as the outlet number, sub-category codes, class-of-trade abbreviations, ZIP code, state, territory number, other geographic codes, etc., depending on the data aggregation used in the file. Along with the category, they define the customer or group of customers when data is at a level higher than the outlet.

- The category is used to distinguish retail, non-retail, wholesale and out-of-country transactions.

- The product group represents one or more products. While the invoice references products individually, in DDD you may aggregate sales for several products when lower detail adds data volume but not data value.

- The data date represents the most recent reporting period with data in the file. It is typically a week of month and it is consistently populated in all records in the file. A value of '0105' in a monthly data file indicates that the most recent month with data is January of 2005.

- The data buckets hold up to two years of sales history. By contrast, the invoice is a snapshot of a single sales transaction in a moment of time. The leftmost bucket represents the most recent data period. Weekly files have up to 106 data buckets with monthly up to 24.

The following figure demonstrates a typical DDD record layout.

Figure 35. Anatomy of the DDD record

BUILDING SALES HISTORY FILES

DDD keeps current and supplies up to two years of data at a time. Data beyond the two-year period drops off and gets archived. It is a good practice to accumulate historical, non-current sales data. DDD changes from data period to data period, therefore, a historical sales file should include only data periods on their last update. That is, when they become the oldest data period in a deliverable. For weekly data, it is the 106th data week, and for monthly data, it is the 24th data month on the current data file. These two data periods will drop off with the next update and a new week or month will be added. The rest of the data periods will likely adjust.

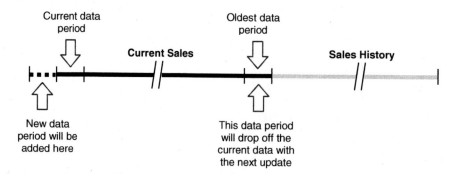

Figure 36. Constructing sales history files

Similarly, you must also maintain a historical outlet master file to preserve the links between sales and outlets. The DDD outlet master lists all active and inactive outlets that have sales in the current two-year period. Inactive outlets with no sales in the last two years drop off the outlet master. The outlet change log lists changes in the outlet master from month-to-month and can be used to build a cumulative, historical outlet master file.

PROCESSING DDD DATA

DDD provides a very simplistic view of the data and the base foundation on which you can build more complex applications. That view consists of the sales data file, the category code-translation table and the product cross-reference file, all provided by the vendor. The manufacturer's product master is optional.

The outlet master and sub-category definitions are also optional and required for outlet level data only. The data may be pre-aligned by the vendor using an alignment file provided by the manufacturer, or post-aligned by the manufacturer.

The DDD number is unique to accounts and ZIP codes and should be used as the primary key for this level of data as well as for the integration of external data with DDD. The diagram below shows the basic table relationships:

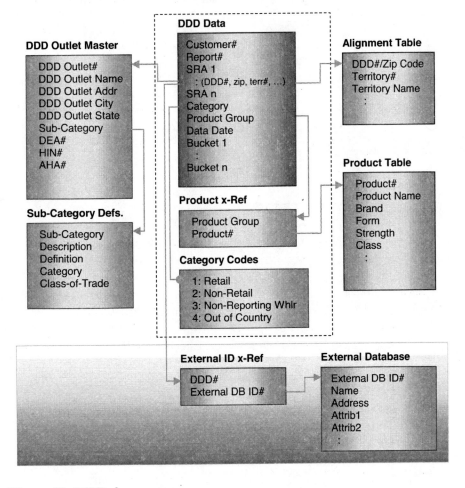

Figure 37. DDD data structures

DDD works fairly well as is for most applications, especially for companies with limited resources. Sometimes, companies will take certain steps towards filling some gaps in DDD as discussed under the DDD completeness. The following section provides a framework for implementing those steps integrating DDD with supplemental data. The schematic below demonstrates the steps required:

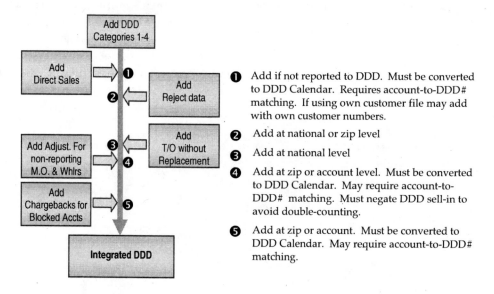

Figure 38. Data integration steps

The rules for integrating these types of data were discussed earlier. Below is a summary of them.

1. New data added should be coded by type to give users the ability to include or exclude them from certain applications. One way to do this is to use the category code field and introduce a new category code for each new type of data. DDD reserves categories 1-4 and 9 to code every transaction in the sales data. You could use category 5 for instance to code reject data.

2. Data must be put in a format compatible to DDD sales. The record layout of the added data must match the DDD sales data record layout. Having extra fields or unpopulated fields in either will prevent seamless integration. When adding new data, make sure not to add incompatible types of units. DDD comes typically in pack units while internal company sales are often in packs. When adding dollars, also make sure

that the price types used in the calculations are compatible. DDD typically uses WAC pricing unless requested otherwise.

3. Transaction dates should be converted to DDD calendar periods. The DDD week starts on a Sunday and ends on a Saturday while DDD months start with a full DDD week and end with a full DDD week, with 4 or 5 weeks in a month. IMS provides DDD calendars.

4. Match the level of detail of data as much as possible. If the DDD data, which is the core data, is at the brand level there is no reason to add new data at a level below brand. On the other hand, if the DDD is at a lower level than the added data, you can still add the data at a higher level and limit its use to the applications that can deal with this level of detail.

5. Applications need to filter only the data that is applicable to them. Some of the added data is applicable for top-line sales calculations and most of the new data is not useful for market share calculations. You can review some of the rules in the 'DDD Completeness - Enhancing DDD' section.

WARNING: Some of the methods discussed above require considerable company resources to implement. In this book we are exploring potential options but not recommending their implementation indiscriminately. More simplistic approaches yield fairly good results and will undoubtedly be more applicable to certain companies.

Once the adjustments have been integrated with DDD, the customer and alignment overlays should be applied. The customer overlays group the DDD outlets into manufacturer-defined customers as discussed earlier. This is an optional process that requires significant maintenance.

DDD data is aligned to territories geographically or on exception basis or a combination of both. Geographic alignments assign ZIP codes to territories. ZIP and outlet DDD data records are then aligned to territories based on the ZIP code. You can override the default alignment of a certain account by explicitly assigning its DDD outlet number to another territory. This method allows you to assign all of the accounts in a ZIP code to a territory but a select few. This is the method of defining special alignments such as for hospital-focused sales forces, etc.

TIP: You can use a straight outlet-to-territory alignment; however, without a default ZIP-to-territory alignment, new accounts would fall into a generic 'unassigned' territory. Accounts in newly created ZIP codes fall in the 'unassigned' territory until the ZIP code is mapped to a territory.

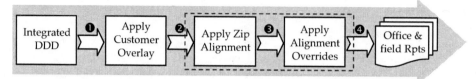

❶ This process groups DDD outlets to customers as defined by the manufacturer

❷ Geographic alignment of territories must precede exceptions

❸ Exceptions can be made for ZIP codes and DDD outlets

❹ Reports must filter appropriate categories

Figure 39. Customer and alignment overlays

MANAGING DDD DATA

To ensure the continuous, stable flow of DDD data, a number of activities must take place on a regular basis. The activities are the joint responsibility of the manufacturer's staff together with the data vendor staff and focus on data quality, data deliverables, schedules, alignment files, direct sales files, price changes, new product tracking and recruitment of new suppliers. The following section discusses the importance of these activities to the data integrity and flow.

Data Quality

Data quality requires the vendor to implement and report on a number of controls. In turn, the manufacturer must review the reports and determine what action if any must be taken. To be successful with data quality, the data vendor and the manufacturer must have a good level of cooperation and act together to promptly resolve problems. Below is a list of data quality steps and reports available to the manufacturer.

Mechanized Validation

The Mech Val, as it is referred to by the vendor, is a process that checks the reported sell-in of a warehouse against the sell-out of the warehouse. The idea behind this test is that, adjusting for inventories, sales should equal purchases.

Mech Val is expressed as a percent of sales-out over sales-in, and has an expected value of approximately 100 percent for a 12-month period with an acceptable range of ±20%. When the results are outside that range the warehouse may be experiencing reporting problems. Monthly values can vary outside the range without necessarily a data issue. Zero percent validation for any given month, however, is an issue.

Mech Val is a high level test and does not offer clues about other warehouse reporting issues related to accounts or products. It is performed selectively on a company's top products only. Mech Val does not work well with new products because the inventory level is high compared to sales and the validation is typically low and outside the acceptable range. In this case its utility is limited to identifying warehouses without sales.

Because of the rather large acceptable range of values, Mech Val is slow identifying problems. Moving from 80% validation to over 120% can take some time, for example. The most obvious problem it can identify is zero sales-in or sales-out. Mech Val validates above 100% when wholesaler inventories decrease and below 100% when wholesaler inventories increase.

Only top-line Mech Val reports are available to manufacturers because of warehouse confidentiality. The manufacturer can and should review Mech Val reports at the vendor's site quarterly, especially the early months of product launches when the risk of unreported sales is high. There are additional tests to safeguard the data quality.

DDD Data Management Reports

DDD publishes a number of reports on monthly basis that monitor the integrity of the data. Changes related to outlets, products, ZIP codes and warehouses and their reporting status are recorded and reports are provided to manufacturers. The manufacturer must review the reports and determine what internal action, if any, is necessary, always in coordination with the vendor. Most of the changes do not have an immediate impact or the impact is not significant enough to require immediate action from the part of the manufacturer. The section below lists these reports and their importance to the manufacturer.

Warehouse Reporting History Reports - This report provides alphabetical and state lists of warehouses with their reporting status. A third listing outlines the months in the last two-year period for which the warehouse supplied data or months with smooth or replacement data due to a 'Temporarily-Off' situation. These listings are an excellent reference to address field inquiries on the reporting status of warehouses.

Data Source Change Report - This is a series of mini reports with each capturing warehouse reporting changes. The warehouse data situation listed here may have implications on the data quality and must be reviewed carefully on monthly basis. Below is a list of the key reports with the potential implications and actions that may be taken:

- *Newly reporting warehouses* are warehouses recruited to report data to DDD. These are wholesalers and mail service pharmacies not reporting to DDD previously, or new warehouse locations of reporting wholesalers or chains. New reporters can be brought in with up to two years of sales history. The added sales history from new reporters affects quota. You should monitor new additions throughout the quarter to determine if quota recalculations are necessary. The sell-in of a warehouse from past data months can help you quantify its impact to the quota. For insignificant sales history volumes you can defer recalculation for the following quarter or even the close of the year. It is important to keep in mind that the sell-in for the warehouse will not show any longer in DDD, which might appear as loss of sales. In reality, the warehouse sell-in is replaced with the sell-out at the ZIP or account level. As a result sales for accounts, ZIP codes, categories, subcategories, and territories change. You must make sure that the sell-in to the warehouse is now zero. The sell-in of a reporting warehouse in reports duplicates sales.

- *Restarted warehouses* are warehouses that were previously taken off the system with a lapse in their reporting to DDD. It is important that the warehouse provides its unreported sales for previous months. You must consider the affect of the historical sales to applications.

- *Monthly/weekly warehouses with smooth/replacement data and 'Temporarily-Off' system* are warehouses with temporary reporting problems. The report indicates the recoverability of their data. Most of the times the data is recoverable. Check this report to identify warehouses with smooth and replacement data. Smooth data cover the entire month. For replacement data the report indicates the specific weeks for which the warehouse has replacement data.

- *Back Data Processed* lists weekly and monthly warehouses for which previously unreported data was received and processed. Smooth or replacement data for these warehouses for the same data periods is removed. Perhaps the best way to deal with T/O warehouses with smooth and replacement data and processed back data is to keep a cumulative list over time showing the data periods with problems and an update for data fixes. That way you have a current list of warehouses with outstanding problems year-to-date. It is important to remember that smooth and replacement data helps correct the overall sales volume problem for missing data. At the account level the variance between replacement and actual data can be significant. Knowing how many warehouses and reporting periods of smooth and replacement data you have helps you understand the magnitude of the problem. Additionally, it allows you to correlate areas with high number of rep data inquiries with the locations of the warehouses and their T/O time periods.

- *Newly off system warehouses* are effectively warehouses taken off reporting with their sales no longer in DDD. You cannot readily assess their impact but you can ask the vendor for an assessment.

- *Closed Warehouses* are warehouses whose business is absorbed most often by another warehouse location. This can be the result of a buyout, merger, or a new facility. The transition can be problematic. You may want to request the vendor to monitor your product sales from the new location to make sure there is no loss of sales volume. A quarterly review of the Mech Val reports should include closed warehouses to confirm higher sell-out from the warehouses picking up the business of the closed ones.

- *Warehouse conversions* lists typical changes in the reporting frequency of warehouses from monthly to weekly and vise versa, which rarely occur, as well as the count of weekly and monthly warehouses. The preferred reporting frequency is weekly. On the positive side, data for warehouses converting from monthly frequency to weekly have their data now available in the weekly DDD. On the down side, warehouses converting to monthly reporting frequency continue to have their data in monthly DDD but no longer in the weekly. In this case you experience some loss of sales. The ratio of weekly to monthly warehouses is approximately 3 to 1; however, monthly warehouses while significant in number they account for only 5% of the overall sales. That is because included in this group are many manufacturers reporting insignificant amounts of direct sales.

- *Warehouse Description Changes* are rather insignificant except for warehouse moves. During the move, warehouses tend to take care of the more important business with the potential of reporting interruptions. Check the Mech Val report to confirm sell-out from the new location.

Significant Outlet Changes Report – The report highlights ZIP code and outlet changes. Outlet and ZIP changes are very visible to the sales reps and should be dealt with effectively to avoid reporting problems. The report consists of a series of mini reports in the two categories discussed below:

- *ZIP Code Changes* – These changes are important because they affect the DDD outlet coding, account sales history and create new DDD outlets. ZIP changes result in outlet renumbering, outlet moves result in new and inactive outlets, and outlet splits create new outlets. Account changes have a direct impact on the sales territories especially if you are reporting sales on the DDD outlet number. If you are cross-referencing DDD outlet numbers to your own customer numbering, you can make these changes transparent to the sales reps. The three things you need to look for here are the cross-referencing of old to new outlets, the alignment of new ZIP codes and outlets and any account moves across territories. Changes listed in these reports are not all inclusive. Refer to the DDD Outlet Change Log for a comprehensive list of all of the changes.

- *Category Changes* – The report lists outlets changing category as the result of a sub-category re-classification. Changes from category 1 to category 2 enhance the visibility into the sales detail going from ZIP to outlet. For movables already in category 2 this is simply a sub-category change. Changes from category 2 to category 1 compromise the level of detail with sales going from the account level to being aggregated along with other retail sales at the ZIP. Other category changes listed are for warehouses changing reporting status with territory data implications especially when they go from reporting to non-reporting. Segment and channel reports are affected because of data shifts between sub-categories or categories.

Warehouse Recruitment Status Report - The report summarizes the activities of IMS to recruit new data suppliers. It lists warehouses actively pursued for reporting as well as warehouses for which activity has ceased. For active recruitment warehouses, the report indicates if they have submitted test data. Warehouses with test data are a step closer to reporting; however, the process may take several more months to complete depending on the quality of the submitted data. Warehouses with poor data quality are dropped. This report is a good reference for addressing warehouse reporting issues raised by the field. It tells you if the warehouse is in the process of being recruited, the status of test data indicates how close it might be to reporting, lists the warehouses deleted from the recruitment list, warehouses refusing to negotiate and low potential warehouses. Depending on the warehouse's current status you may consider pursuing other alternatives.

DDD Interrupted Data Report - The report provides a historical perspective on the data situation of blocked accounts. It lists chronologically the major events, status changes and efforts to remedy their situation.

TIP: If you are using the list of blocked accounts provided by DDD, make sure to update them frequently. There are discrepancies between the accounts provided by DDD and those provided by the groups themselves. If you contract with any of these groups, you should consider using the list of accounts specified in the contract instead.

New Product Notice Report - The report consists of three sections for branded generic and OTC products. The term 'new product' covers new packs, repacks and new forms and strengths of existing products as well as new product brands. The reports can serve two purposes; data integrity and competitive intelligence.

On the data integrity front, the reports are an excellent source to monitor the market for new products and to keep your market definitions updated. Ideally, DDD should be updating the market definitions used in reports automatically for new forms and strengths, but that does not happen always. Without all of the form and strength data captured in the reports, the competitor data is going to be understated and your market share inflated. The New Product Notice report can get lengthy, but you can narrow your search to markets of your interest using the therapeutic class field.

In the competitive intelligence area, the reports allow you to read into your competitor's strategies. Price discounts and premiums, introduction of easy to use administration devices, less frequently dosed forms, etc., suggest a few things about their strategies. For competitive intelligence the search for new products should probably extend beyond the direct competitors to related therapeutic classes.

Product History Adjustments Report - The report highlights sales adjustments to correct product coding errors. It provides the warehouse where the error originated along with the timeframe for which data was adjusted. Corrections involve typically the misinterpretation of product packages or attribution of sales to the wrong product, as well as some other exceptions. In the case of misinterpreted product packages, when a large pack or a more expensive pack unit is coded as a smaller pack or less expensive pack unit sales are understated. Sales are overstated in the opposite case. When two different products are involved, inevitably, there is a shift of sales from one product to the other.

In either case, product history adjustments can impact a territory's sales positively or negatively. You should evaluate the magnitude and the direction of the adjustments. Small volume adjustments and adjustments that boost territory sales probably require no action and they are part of the natural transformation of DDD. Large volume adjustments and adjustments that lower territory sales on the other hand may need some handling. You can use the warehouse location to identify territories with potential impact.

Another situation for which product sales are adjusted is when data is entirely wrong and as a result removed from DDD. In other cases the data is removed, recalculated and reinstated. The variances they produce before and after the adjustments is again the key determinant for action.

Product Grouping Status Report - The product grouping status report is important because it allows the manufacturer to verify the products included in the data deliverables. A product group is a code assigned to a collection of strengths, forms and brands of products in any combination.

When a product group is included in a report, the report provides aggregate sales for all the products listed under the product group. Although you can define product groups in random, product groups make sense in the following situations:

- A specific strength of a product for specific strength sales
- All strengths within a form of a brand for total form sales
- All forms and strengths of a brand for total brand sales
- Combination of three or more brands for outlet level competitive data
- All equal strengths from different forms of a brand for total strength sales
- An entire therapeutic class for total class sales
- Any other combination the sales of which have some meaningful business application

A product group is defined within a file code together with other product groups. You define the products to be included in a data report by assigning one or more file codes to the report. Multiple file codes must be used when the report includes data of different levels of detail. A file code is assigned entirely to a level while different file codes are assigned to different levels.

The *Client Report Profile & Change Summary* report provided by the vendor shows which file codes are assigned to what reports. Reviewing the file codes assigned to reports gives the manufacturer a limited way of checking the report composition. What the file code cannot tell you is if there are any missing strengths from the product definitions. Unless you have a better way to check on all available forms and strengths of a product you might be at risk of missing some data. Every time you add or change file codes make sure to review them before reports are run.

The report also reflects price changes and their effective dates for all product strengths listed. Whenever possible, validate the competitor's prices against an independent source. DDD has instituted new checks with third party sources to validate prices.

Your own product sales data is the most important data to you, and for its accuracy, you must make sure that the vendor has the right product information. The *Prime Product Master List* is a list of a manufacturer's own products. You must review the report to make sure product descriptions, NDC numbers, form and strength descriptions and current prices are all accurate to ensure data integrity.

Report Definitions

Your reports are the delivery vehicles for the data, but as much as the collected data may be right the wrong report definition can seriously distort it. Additionally, your monthly data refreshes, which most of your applications are based on, are limited to twelve runs in a year. The recovery from errors depends, first, on the time it takes to discover them and, second, on the vendor's production schedule. Naturally, the question here is how many failed runs can you afford in a year? And the answer to that should be none.

Unfortunately, the manufacturer does not have full visibility into the report definitions. Your service representative is your key person to make things right. A lot of interaction, questions and the review of report changes by a senior service person can reduce the risk of erroneous reports considerably.

The risk from report problems is exponentially higher as a function of the report's complexity, but there are trade-offs with simple and complex reports. See the 'Building Data Deliverables' section for more on that subject.

The vendor provides DDD report profiles for review by the manufacturer. The profiles give a thorough description of the report setup; however, this is only a description of the intent and not necessarily the way things were executed. Moreover, this is a retrospective review and by then the error would have occurred already in a previous report run. Prospectively, you may want to focus your discussions with the vendor service team for all new changes on level of data detail, file code application to categories, SRA assignments, warehouse inclusions and exclusions and outlet and sub-category overrides, so that they are executed flawlessly.

Control Totals

The DDD control totals are summary reports of data files. At most, they provide national level sales by category and time period for each product group in the report. The purpose of the control totals is to validate that data generated by the vendor and data processed by the manufacturer match and to eliminate the possibility of errors introduced in between. It is important to understand that control totals are accurate only with respect to their companion data files. Control totals can not identify report problems. If the report is defined incorrectly and produces erroneous results the control totals will be equally wrong.

Control total files are now available for full automation and they should be integrated into the manufacturer's data processing. The process is simple. You summarize the sales in the data file by product group, category and data period and you compare that to a corresponding summary record in the control file. The numbers are expected to match exactly and any deviation indicates an error.

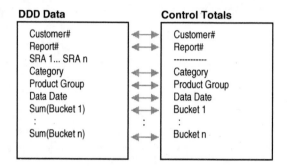

Figure 40. DDD comparison to control totals

Whenever you add a new product to your reports or if you have doubts about the accuracy of the sales for a particular product in a report, you should compare its DDD sales to another source to make sure there is no fundamental problem with the setup of the product in DDD. You need to perform this test for a given product only once.

One such source is the National Sales Perspectives™ (NSP), another product of IMS that has its roots in the same data as DDD. Because NSP does not use the same complicated report definitions as DDD, query results should be free of report errors. NSP, however, uses off-invoice pricing which can be quite different from WAC, especially for heavily discounted products. In most situations NSP will provide a good baseline for a product's sales. If NSP produces considerably different results you may need to search yet for another source, perhaps the financial disclosures of the product's manufacturer.

Ultimately, control totals provide some degree of confidence in the data; however, it is the sale analyst who is most familiar with the sales trends of your products and the competitor's products. The sales analyst should validate these trends with every new data cycle.

Direct Sales

For DDD to be complete it must capture the manufacturer's direct sales. Keeping your direct sales from DDD has certain implications on your ability to subscribe to DDD data. Chances are that your direct sales are very low anyway, which does not make for a good argument not to report them. Your sales are incorporated in DDD in full confidence, making it impossible for anyone to isolate sales for your direct accounts. Lastly, your competitor's sales are important to you and your access to it depends on the sharing of your own direct sales.

DDD has well established guidelines for submitting direct sales data outlined in the 'DDD Direct Sales Policy'. The manufacturer should implement those guidelines to assure the timely and uninterrupted flow of data to DDD. Below are some key points to keep in mind:

- Report sales on the ship-to address. This is the basis of DDD and must be strictly followed.

- Make sure that you report product returns correctly. Returns should be debited to the accounts they originated from. Some chains and warehouses use third party vendors to collect and process returns that may not be reported appropriately to the originating accounts or not reported at all. In that case you may have some level of overstatement in DDD.

- Free goods should not be reported as sales because the product is not for re-sale. Companies ship free product for indigent use, clinical trials or as samples. Typically, transactions of these types have a zero sales dollar amount but a quantity other than zero. Customer rebates given in the form of product are exceptions to this rule and should be counted as sales because the product is resalable. Work with the vendor to properly identify and process these records.

- Drop-shipments should be reported appropriately in DDD. Drop-shipments are initiated by distributors but executed on their behalf by the manufacturer. Drop-shipments happen due to out-of-inventory situations with warehouses. To expedite filling the order for a client, the product is shipped directly by the manufacturer but invoiced by the warehouse. The manufacturer and the vendor must agree on the method of reporting drop-shipments.

Incorrect reporting of direct sales has data integrity implications that will likely surface as inaccurate or incomplete data. The manufacturer and the vendor should work together to create a sound process.

Data Deliverables

Data reports are the actual deliverables of your contract with your vendor. Your report design has certain implications on cost, risk of error, internal effort and report timing. You must develop a strategy when it comes to deliverables and stick with it, realizing that when you deviate from it there will be some impact. There are certain trade offs for selecting a strategy over another, analyzed in the following discussion.

Strategies for Building Reports

Cost is the first consideration. Deliverables come with incremental costs. These costs are the least productive use of your data budget. Consolidating the deliverables will save you money. This money is better spent in more unbudgeted data than in report charges. You can now buy more data with the same amount of money.

Your vendor is also not making good use of their resources having to invest in more people to handle all of the additional deliverables. Internally, the more deliverables you have the more effort they will require to handle them.

Consolidation comes at the risk of increased error rates. From the vendor's standpoint, report maintenance is more challenging. Consolidated reports are more complex and rigid. Their design is difficult to understand and changes are difficult to implement. Service reps need to be savvy in report design and very familiar with your strategy to properly manage these deliverables.

Alternatively, you can design simple reports, easy to maintain, for a higher cost, but with substantially reduced error risk. Work with your vendor on solutions that make sense for you. The figure below demonstrates the cost, risk and complexity relationships with data deliverables:

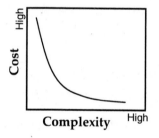 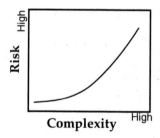

Figure 41. Complexity vs. risk & cost

The degree of consolidation you will achieve will primarily depend on four variables. The number of markets you track, the data types, the number of alignments and the levels of data. Each of these variables uses one or more report 'levels'. Report have a finite number of levels that once used you can no longer add new data except at an existing level.

The more markets you enter the more sales forces you must deploy. In fact, for the same market you may be using several sales forces that include sales reps, clinical specialists and national and corporate account managers with each sales force having its own alignment. It is possible to have more than one alignment in a report. Dollar and unit sales add new dimensions as the types of units do. National, territory and outlet levels of data require different report levels.

You can start the process by taking an inventory of all of the dimensions of the four variables. You can work with the vendor to discuss alternative report designs. The idea here is not to come up with a single deliverable, although it is possible for small companies, but with a number of optimized deliverables.

Building Data Deliverables

This section discusses the process of building a new data deliverable. Some of the choices you make up front will be difficult to change later on, therefore, take time to consider them carefully.

- **Data Format** – Select one of the applicable file formats based on the platform you are using. Use formats consistently. See previous discussion on data formats.

- **Data Type** – Select from dollars, units and unit types based on your needs. Some companies derive their dollars from a unit conversion. This is not a value-added process and should be avoided.

- **Frequency** – Select from weekly, monthly, quarterly, semi-annually or other. Frequency refers to the production schedule and not to data summarization. Quarterly frequency reports can still have data columns for weeks and months.

- **Media** – IMS offers a variety of data media options. Considering the alternatives and the benefits they offer the clear winner is electronic data transfer via VPN. There is a cost associated with this option; however, the trade off is speed. Every other option comes with a time overhead for production and shipping.

- **SRA Assignments** – The SRA assignments depend on the levels of data added. Select file formats with maximum number of SRA fields for future expandability of your deliverables. Avoid changing the SRA assignments when making report changes. Processing previous runs of files with changed SRA assignments can be challenging.

- **Inclusions & Exclusions** – You have the option to customize your DDD reports to include certain categories only, exclude warehouses that cause data anomalies and exclude certain sub-categories or move them to a different category.

TIP: It is recommended that you use any inclusions and exclusions consistently through out all your reports. This is often the reason why sales for the same product in two different reports do not match. One way to deal with this is to create a report template and use it consistently with every new report to make sure that its parameters match existing reports.

- **Product Groups** – Work with the vendor to define product groups and organize them into file codes. See previous discussion on product groups and file codes. File codes re-use product group numbers. You should not use file codes with duplicate product group numbers in the same report because they overwrite each other. Although not required by DDD, if possible, you should use product group numbers exclusively for specific products. Use the product group consistently across weekly and monthly DDD and prescription data files. This may be difficult to implement especially when you have a number of deliverables.

- **Alignments** – You should keep as much control as possible of data alignments having the vendor align only the data you cannot align in-house. That would be mostly competitive data at the brand level or below and some special situations such as retail sub-category level and class-of-trade data. If you are using multiple sales forces for the same market you may need to align data more that one way. You need the control to align data in order to apply last minute alignment changes before data is sent to the field. The company's own product sales and competitor ZIP and outlet level sales for combinations of products should be aligned in house.

TIP: Apply the same alignment to own and competitor sales data for market share calculations. Variances in the alignment can produce inaccurate results. You can get around the limitation of aligning in-house the competitive data if you are using straight ZIP alignments by creating TCR sales reports at the ZIP level.

- **Levels of Data** – You can have the vendor produce and deliver different data cuts for every level of detail for you. This is convenient because you can effortlessly access the data from the source files. However, it creates multiple versions of the same data in the source reports and a lot of duplication. It is recommended that you only take the lowest level data possible and build higher-levels from it. Keep in mind that strength level data rolls-up to form and brand, and ZIP and outlet level data rolls-up to territory, region, nation and other geographies. You can use the matrix below to determine what you need to get for what you need to build.

Data Type: DDD$

	Retail				Non-Retail			
Product	Zip	Terr	Distr	...	Outlet	Zip	Terr	...
Product Brand A	✓	R	R	R	✓	R	R	R
Form A	.	.	.	.	.	.	.	.
Strength A	.	.	.	.	.	.	.	.
Product Brand B	✓	R	R	R	C	R	R	R
Product Brand C	-	✓	R	R	-	-	✓	R
Product Brand D	-	-	-	✓	-	-	-	✓
:	:	:	:	:	:	:	:	:

(Left axis label: **Monthly**)

R: Rolled-up from lower level

C: Combined with other competitor products

✓: Available

- : Not Available

Figure 42. Matrix of data levels

Report Timing

The vendor's data cycle begins from the moment the data is due from the suppliers until its clients' reports are all delivered. The manufacturer's data cycle starts when data is due from the vendor until all of the internal clients and field-staff have received their reports. Obviously time is critical and you should try to manage it tightly. Part of it is in the vendor's control. The vendor must first produce your reports before you can begin your internal processing. Generally IMS guarantees delivery of the DDD information 28 days after the close of the month. However, if earlier receipt is required, arrangements can be made for an additional fee. Using the general delivery method of 28 days after the period (DAP) or the close of the month, March data would be delivered on April 28th.

Internally, you would think you have more control of time, but often you do not. Simple, efficient, automated systems and good, fast communication capabilities produce best results. Instead a number of counter-productive activities plague the processes.

The first common mistake is trying to fit complex technologies to solutions. Simplicity is the key here. The last part of the analysis is often performed with common productivity tools. The closer to the productivity tools your systems are the better results you will achieve.

The second common mistake made is data 'cloning'; moving and duplicating data endlessly around computer platforms and applications wasting a lot of effort. If you want data fast you will need to take the simplest, shortest, clearest path to your clients.

DDD APPLICATIONS

The most obvious application of DDD data is the performance evaluation of an account. Simply stated in dollar amount or in number of units purchased the information confirms that a given entity is a customer. That by itself, however, does not answer other relevant questions. Such as how important that customer is in relation to other customers, if this customer is more or less important to your competitors, changes in the customer's performance overtime, etc.

DDD can be used in a number of standard, structured applications that address many business needs. These applications are relatively simple, yet important to evaluate the company's performance at various levels. DDD, however, is not the only applicable dataset for every application. Therefore, you should first determine the most appropriate data for your application. There you have to decide between the weekly and monthly versions of DDD and its related product the National Sales Perspectives (NSP). Chargebacks and direct sales, although not complete solutions, they come to complement DDD and provide answers at times as well.

The following discussion offers a quick comparison of weekly and monthly DDD and contrasts DDD with NSP, chargebacks and direct sales to aid you in the selection of the right data for your application. Then it goes on to provide a general overview of the common applications of DDD data.

DDD vs. Chargebacks

Chargebacks can be a very important data source for manufacturers that can make good use of it. They are an excellent source for validating questionable DDD sales. They are also a great alternative source for accounts with blocked data in DDD. Chargebacks are not a replacement for DDD, except perhaps for products 100% under contract. In that case, a manufacturer could rely entirely on its chargeback data for its own products but would still rely on DDD for access to competitor data.

The complexity with using DDD in combination with chargebacks is the matching of the contracted accounts to DDD numbers. Chargeback data is more granular than DDD. This is particularly true with clinics where a multiple-doctor outlet may represent sales from more than one contracted accounts. In situations like this the comparison is almost impossible without perhaps the use of DDD-

MD. DDD-MD can assist in identifying the facilities behind the DDD multiple-doctor outlet.

The principal limitation with chargebacks is that the data is available only for contracted accounts. Because of that its completeness can vary drastically by product. More expensive and less broadly distributed drugs are likely to have more of their sales under contract. The applicability and usability of the chargeback data will depend a lot on its completeness.

DDD vs. X-Factory Sales

X-factory sales are any sales out of a manufacturer's facility to wholesalers and sites of care. X-factory sales are not a great indicator of demand because a significant part of these sales become, at least temporarily, wholesaler inventories. DDD on the other hand which includes manufacturer direct sales and wholesaler distribution measures more accurately product demand.

In general, for a given time period, x-factory sales and DDD should be close; however, differences exist for several reasons. First, DDD does not capture 100% of a product's sales. Assuming an average 5% of missing sales in DDD, without any adjustments, x-factory sales would be higher by at least that percent. Unless adjusted, in a financial model the missing DDD sales become inventories that keep growing over time.

Another reason is the periodic wholesaler inventory loading and inventory management around the end of the year and ahead of price increases. The effect of that are temporary inventory spikes that take a few weeks to translate into DDD sales. During this time, comparison of x-factory sales to DDD is likely to tip the scale heavily towards x-factory sales. In subsequent weeks wholesalers will reduce their purchases until the inventories are depleted and DDD is likely to be higher than x-factory.

Inventory buildup contributes to the variance of DDD and x-factory. In order to maintain a given number of days of supply for a product with growing sales, wholesalers must increase their inventories. For example, one week's inventory for a product with $100 million dollar in sales is roughly $2 million. If the product grows to $200 million one week's inventory is $4 million.

X-factory sales, although not a great indicator of demand, together with DDD can help monitor inventory trends. X-factory sales are very accurate, however, because of the DDD imperfections inventories cannot be calculated precisely.

Weekly or Monthly DDD?

Both weekly and monthly DDD are substantially based on the same collected data. The monthly DDD includes data from all reporting warehouses. The weekly DDD includes data only from warehouses on a weekly reporting schedule. The number of monthly-reporting warehouses is significant and includes many pharmaceutical manufacturers reporting their direct sales. Although large in number, the monthly-reporting warehouse sales volume is very low; therefore, the difference between weekly and monthly DDD due to the monthly-reporting warehouses should be rather small. Your vendor can help you quantify that difference.

Monthly DDD smoothes missing data for all warehouses and all data periods. Weekly DDD does not smooth data fully, except for the last week of the 4-4-5 month for which it smoothes data for all warehouses in preparation for the monthly data generation. In terms of completeness, therefore, the monthly data is more inclusive.

We mentioned earlier that completeness affects accuracy. An account supplied by monthly and weekly warehouses would have its sales understated in weekly DDD, whereas, an account supplied only by monthly warehouses would appear in weekly DDD with zero sales. Only accounts supplied by weekly reporting warehouses have their data captured equally in weekly and monthly DDD. The monthly DDD bucket being an aggregate of 4-5 weekly buckets tends to mask data problems. In monthly DDD a week of missing sales appears as a mere understatement of sales where three or four weeks of good data smooth out the bad week. By contrast, the same situation in weekly data can be exaggerated. Accounts with sales for the week and no replacement data could appear having zero sales, and accounts with no sales but with replacement data could appear as having a significant amount of sales.

Weekly DDD data provides smooth, intuitive trending almost at all levels of detail except perhaps the account level. Depending on its size, an account's weekly buying patterns may be erratic with no sales for some weeks and large sales for others. Weekly trends are affected by speculative buying, holidays, data errors, etc. Volatile account level data may show spikes that if taken in the wrong context may trigger the wrong action, especially when targeting extensively with weekly data. A subsequent data update usually validates the accuracy of the numbers or reflects any corrections applied.

By contrast, monthly patterns for accounts are more stable. The aggregation of weekly data to monthly averages out high and low data points for a smoother trend. The complicating factor with trending monthly data, however, is the 4-4-5 calendar and its highs and lows. This holds true at every level of detail. With monthly DDD you may have to use some kind of rolling average in order to read the true trend.

Where weekly DDD truly has the edge over monthly is the update frequency. Before you can get a new monthly update you have three or four weekly snapshots of market performance that can serve as early warning to newly developing trends. All of that with the understanding that the most recent data buckets can have drastic adjustments on the next update. Also, it is likely that the weekly data will reflect first the aging of account data.

All these should be considerations for the use of DDD in applications. Generally, monthly DDD is more suitable for compensation, segmentation, alignment and deployment applications. Time sensitive applications such as targeting and demand, inventory and revenue forecasting are typically based on weekly DDD. It is prudent to use weekly data at a minimum for general product, market, channel and segment trending, in which case, subscription at the subcategory or class-of-trade level is sufficient.

DDD or National Sales Perspectives?

The NSP belongs in the same sales data family of products with DDD. NSP was designed as a market research tool giving market researchers access to sales data for all drugs, markets and therapeutic classes. As such it reports sales at higher levels of detail with the lowest level being the market segment and geographically the nine census regions. The trade-off to NSP's lack of detail is its affordability compared to DDD. DDD is typically subscribed at lower levels of detail and for markets with in-line products only.

NSP draws from the same data collected from manufacturers and distributors with a few major differences. NSP is not based on WAC pricing like DDD but actual, off-invoice pricing. This is as close to net sales as a syndicated data product can get, but it does not account for additional discounts offered typically as invoice terms and back-end rebates. NSP includes sales for drugs such as OTC, herbal products, vitamins, medical devices, etc., that are not found in DDD. NSP is slightly projected for the amount of data not captured by the data collection process. By contrast, DDD is un-projected, comprehensive data with only a small percent of missing data on average.

NSP projects both direct and indirect missing sales where possible. The projections vary for the DDD and non-DDD products and by segment. On the direct sales side, sales reported by manufacturers are not adjusted in any way. Unreported direct sales for non-federal hospitals are projected based on size and type from a panel of approximately 350 hospitals reporting both direct and indirect purchases. Unreported direct sales for the clinic, HMO, LTC, HHC and miscellaneous segments are modeled based on the ratio of direct-to-indirect sales for the segment. The ratio is then applied to estimate the missing direct sales for these outlets. Unreported direct sales for retail pharmacies and federal facilities are not projected.

Indirect sales for DDD products are projected for non-reporting warehouses and chain pharmacies by region based on their estimated size. Warehouse sales for non-DDD product are projected from a panel of warehouses reporting their sales. Chain and food-store pharmacies are projected from panels of pharmacies providing their data.

As a result of the projections DDD and NSP sales vary somewhat. The unit data should vary only by the number of projected units in NSP with NSP slightly higher than DDD. The dollar data varies both by the amount of projected sales and the difference between the product's WAC price and it's the weighted average of the invoice prices. Without that price difference NSP would always be higher than DDD because of the projection. Assuming that manufacturers offered no discounts, and wholesalers charged AWP, with AWP at 20-25% above WAC, NSP could be higher than DDD by that much plus the projected sales. However, deep discounting of products can push the average off-invoice price much below list price, enough to offset NSP's projection advantage. There are indeed examples of products with NSP sales significantly below DDD.

NSP is updated monthly and is made available a little over 30 days from the close of the month. It offers the DDD data measures as well as additional calculated measures that include market share, growth trends and elements of growth. The elements of growth measure attempts to attribute the growth to price increases, volume increases, new product introductions, line extensions and price changes.

Given their differences, DDD and NSP are not interchangeable in applications and they should be consistently used without substituting one for the other. To preserve that consistency from the account to the national level your choice should be DDD, as only DDD provides all of these levels of detail. If you are not adjusting your DDD for missing sales, you could leverage the completeness of the NSP unit data in national level applications; however, with a lot of caution and the appropriate notations. You should avoid distributing two different sets of numbers, especially the dollar figures that can potentially be very different.

For markets without DDD data NSP will be your only choice as the DDD cost may not justifiable until there is truly a need for sub-national data. That is likely to happen as you get close to a product launch. Here also, consider which dollar measure is more appropriate for your application and consider deriving list price dollars from the units and the product's WAC price.

Despite their differences, a product's DDD and NSP sales should trend closely and any deviations should be analyzed as there are some legitimate reasons for that.

NOTE: *NSP is used by Wall Street Analysts to monitor sales trends and the performance of pharmaceutical products and companies. Monitoring what the analysts see through NSP allows the investor relations groups to prepare for their interactions with the analysts.*

Sales Trend Analysis

Sales trend analysis compares sales for sequential time periods or current time periods to the same periods of the previous year. The goal is to identify subtle or profound differences in the sales over time.

Short term trends are identified by comparing sales for current data periods with periods immediately preceding them; current week, month or quarter to previous week, month and quarter, for example. Short term comparisons are important to identify changes in the long term sales trend. The long term sales trend may be showing an increase in sales, however, the most recent months of sales may be declining gradually. Depending on the product, these comparisons may be prone to seasonality. You can use rolling averages to deal with the seasonality. Also, sequentially, DDD months have 4 or 5 weeks making them un-comparable without some adjustment for the extra week.

Long term trends are identified by comparing sales for current data periods to the same data periods from previous years. Year-over-year comparisons eliminate the seasonality issues. The shorter the timeframe compared, the more prone it is to error because it may include one-time, unusual transactions. The DDD calendar makes sure that time periods in the current year include equal number of days as the same period the year before, therefore, making the comparisons more meaningful. Some years have an extra week in the last quarter that can affect year-over-year comparisons. Make sure to adjust for the extra week.

The formula below calculates the year-over-year percent change in sales for a time period, in this case the current quarter:

$$(QTRTY - QTRLY) / QTRLT * 100$$

Market Share Calculations

The market share is a benchmark of performance for a given time period against your competitors. The first and most important step in the process is to define the market you are competing in. That may include one or more products, except for single-product markets and orphan status drugs that have 100% market share.

It is important to define the market properly to get a good sense of the true market share. Excluding products from the market makes your market share look higher than it really is, while defining the market broadly you may be targeting unnecessarily. The market is set most appropriately by your marketing department or you can use an industry accepted definition such as the therapeutic class of the product. Be sure to specify the market definition when quoting market share for a product.

With market share, the current percent value is as important as the trend. A high percent share is good news but not when it comes with an eroding trend. You may calculate market share one data period at a time, week or month, and observe the trend between periods sequentially over time. The formula for calculating market share for a product is:

Product-A$ ÷ Market$ * 100

TIP: *When tracking market share over time make sure to use the same market definition consistently adding to the market new forms and strengths of the products or new brands of products as they come in the market. If you must change the market definition, make sure to recalculate all of the market share data points.*

Market share is applicable at any level from the account, to territory to national. The calculations are valid when the data for all products is comparable. DDD is suitable because it uses the same methodology for data collection in the market. One exception might be un-reported direct sales by some manufacturers.

One-sided data adjustments distort the results and should not be used. The data completeness is not an issue for top-line market share calculations because statistically the market share in the missing data should equal that of DDD. Additionally, as a percent of total, the missing data is too small to have an affect on the market share. At the territory and account level, however, missing data has the potential of distorting true market share by a few points, depending on the circumstances.

Products with multiple indications definitely affect market share because part of their sales belong to a different market. If the indication is based on form and strength you can exclude those forms and strengths from your calculations. Generally your ability to precisely divide sales by indication is limited especially with competitor products because of the data detail limitations. See section 'Sales by Indication' for more detail.

Last, but not least, comes the issue of unit vs. dollar market share. Dollar-based market share is easy to understand but has certain limitations. First, price increases tend to favor products with aggressive pricing. While everyone changes prices, not all changes happen at the same time and by the percent increase or decrease. A higher price increase boosts market share, assuming there is no unit erosion from higher prices. Second, dollar market share is influenced by the overall level of pricing. For example, because of the large difference in price, a more frequently prescribed generic may appear to have a much lower dollar market share. One argument in favor of dollar market share is that it is revenue that counts regardless of units sold.

Unit market share eliminates the pricing influences but it has its challenges as well. Units must be equivalent to calculate market share. First, you must determine the unit equivalencies between the products often taking into consideration daily dosages and days of therapy. Refer to Chapter 3 for a full discussion on the topic.

There is value in both the unit and dollar market shares. From the financial standpoint dollar market share is more meaningful. From the sales trend standpoint unit market share is more insightful.

Sales by Indication

Drugs are indicated for the treatment of one or more diseases. Sometimes the same form and strength can be used for all indicated diseases and other times one disease may require a specific form and drug potency. However, even when strengths are indicated for specific diseases, physicians deviate from the label, using the strengths interchangeably for all indicated diseases.

The question begging for an answer here is 'what indication was the drug used for?' There are a few steps you can take using DDD and other sources to answer this question. The assumption here is that the product was primarily used as indicated with a few exceptions.

The approach will be to allocate initially all sales for forms and strengths to their corresponding indications. Then shift some sales between indications for certain forms and strengths based on certain criteria. The methodology assumes that DDD category 1 is made up of retail pharmacies and sell-out of mail service pharmacies with DDD category 2 capturing all non-retail sales.

It should be noted that the task is rather easy for heavily retail drugs. To gauge the usage by indication in the retail segment you must analyze its composition of prescriptions by physician specialty using Xponent or NPA. Typically, prescription activity is dominated by one or more key specialties with a number of other specialties contributing to a lesser degree. Some specialties may be easier to attribute to specific indications than others and with some educated guesses and a degree of error tolerance you can fairly accurately come up with the ratio of prescriptions between indications for each form and strength of the product. You can apply that ratio to DDD category 1 to allocate sales by indication.

Non-retail sales should be dealt on a sub-category basis. Physician offices and clinics are grouped in DDD into sub-categories by specialty for major specialties. They make up for many products a substantial portion of the non-retail sales. When the specialty sub-categories lend themselves to this kind of segmentation, you will be able to allocate a substantial amount of the sales volume to indications. Depending on the desired degree of precision, you may have to go below the sub-category level and assign outlets to indication. This process may require substantial effort. DDD-MD should provide some insight into the multiple-doctor accounts.

Hospitals are the other major component of the non-retail market. Hospital profile information can provide clues about drug use by indication. The indication itself may reveal clues. One indication may require hospitalization while another may not. Other secondary market research data, the number of diagnoses and the procedures performed and claims data can also be used for this purpose. Whenever that determination cannot be made, the default indication for the form or strength should be used.

Primary research, while expensive, can be used to establish an average split of sales for certain segments. And then, there is the sales rep. The sales reps can provide valuable information about the drug usage within their accounts based on their knowledge and interactions with the physicians.

DDD in Quota & Compensation

Quota setting and compensation calculation is one of the main sales applications of DDD data. It works best, however, for the non-retail part of the business. DDD does not resolve the 'traveling script' issue; consequently, scripts written in one territory and filled in another are not credited to the territory that generated the demand. Traveling scripts for adjacent territories cancel each other out to a great degree; however, to remove the uncertainty it is best to use script data in quota and compensation applications for the retail channel.

Quota and compensation applications have financial implications for people and they require a great degree of data completeness and accuracy. There are unlimited variations of compensation plans but they all use sales data one of few ways to which completeness and accuracy can be more or less critical. The following section looks at different ways DDD is used in these plans and the pros and cons of these plans with respect to data.

Commission Plans

These plans are based on actual units or dollars sold and compensate sales reps a specific dollar amount per unit sold or a percent of sales. For a sales rep to receive fair compensation, every unit or dollar sold must be accounted for. Commission plans require adjustments from all available sources. That would include reject data, sales from non-reporters, blocked accounts, etc. Simply put these plans require perfect data.

Additionally, for sales reps to have an equal opportunity to earn, their territories must have equal potential. That does not happen often because territories are balanced based on a number of criteria only one of which is sales potential. Sometimes sales potential is compromised for geographically large territories in order to reduce the size of the territory and make it more manageable. Commission plans favor small territories in large metropolitan areas usually. These plans are often used for newly launched products.

Year-Over-Year Growth Plans

These are among the most common compensation plans. These plans consist of three components. The previous year's sales, an expected growth rate and a sliding scale reward system. A territory's plan may look like the example in figure 43.

Year-over-year growth plans obviously are not applicable to newly launched products. In fact, they are even challenging for products on their second year on the market because they require you to predict fairly accurately the sales growth for the next year. If your sales forecast is pessimistic, every sales rep becomes a superstar, and for optimistic forecasts everyone can miss the target by a mile. The plan should be based on realistic expectations. These plans work best for mature products with stable growth curves.

Perhaps the biggest advantage of year-over-year plans is that they are very 'forgiving' with both the completeness and accuracy of the data. When it comes to data completeness what matters for these plans is the sales growth rate in the territory. The growth rate can be derived from partial data given that there are no extraordinary circumstances in the missing data. In other words, the growth rate for the accounts with data is equivalent to the growth rate for the accounts with missing or blocked data.

Last Year's Sales:	$1,000,000		
Target Growth:	10%	$1,100,000	
Payout on Achievement:	95%	$1,045,000	$5,000
	100%	$1,100,000	$10,000
	105%	$1,155,000	$20,000
	110%+	$1,210,000	$35,000
Actual Achievement:	101%	$1,111,000	$10,000

Figure 43. Example of year-over-year growth plan

Even when one or more accounts with missing data are growing at a rate faster than the territory average, it is not certain that adjusting for their data would have an impact on the plan overall. The accounts must have both a much higher than average growth rate and their total sales to weigh significantly in the overall sales of the territory in order to move achievement up by even one percentage point.

In the next example we are revising the territory plan from the example above adjusting for one or more missing accounts totaling 10% of the territory sales and having a growth rate of 50%. The previous year's sales are adjusted to $1.1M and the target growth to $1.21M. Although adding their sales to the plan moved territory achievement up by three percentage points that was not enough to move the territory to the next payout level. The payout scale is very critical in this kind of plans. The smaller the ranges the more sensitive the plan is to data imperfections.

Last Year's Sales:	$1,100,000		
Target Growth:	10%	$1,210,000	
Payout on Achievement:	95%	$1,149,500	$5,000
	100%	$1,210,000	$10,000
	105%	$1,270,500	$20,000
	110%+	$1,331,000	$35,000
Actual Achievement:	104%	$1,261,000	$10,000

Figure 44. Example of year-over-year growth with adjustments

DDD accuracy may or may not be a concern with year-over-year growth plans. When the data is credited to the wrong account within the territory it gets included in the calculations. If, on the other hand, both the sales history and current sales of an account are credited to a different territory, it becomes more of a missing data issue discussed above.

The real problem is with mismatched data where the history is in one territory and the current sales are missing or credited to another territory. In that case, the territory with the history has its quota inflated without current sales to offset it. The other territory gets a boost on its current sales performance without sales history in the quota. These situations are few and once identified they get rectified in subsequent quarters with account sales corrections and recalculation of performance. Product mismatches alter both the quota and current sales proportionally minimizing their impact to the plan.

Aging of the data is an important consideration for these plans; therefore, you may want to allow at least one data period past the close of the incentive period before calculating the final payout. Alternatively, you can make adjustments for rejects, outstanding sales inquiries or even consider a one or more percentage point achievement-bonus to compensate for data imperfections depending on the plan and the payout scale.

In summary, year-over-year growth plans should require few, if any, missing sales adjustments and for high growth accounts only. The focus should be on accounts with quota without current sales and data aging. Territories close to a threshold for the next level of performance are more at risk. Sales adjustments should be made only after alternative options, discussed later in this chapter, have been considered.

Market Share Plans

Market share plans offer sales reps incentives for achieving a certain level of market share against their competitors, increase market share from the previous year's level, or against a baseline such as the national average. They are very suitable for products in their early years in the market when they have the most upside potential, or their later years in the market when defending from various market threats.

Unlike year-over-year growth plans where growth could come strictly from overall market expansion and price increases, market share increases come at the expense of the competitors and require sales growth higher than the rate the market is expanding. A better efficacy and pharmacoeconomic profile contribute to the achievement of this goal.

The most important consideration with market share plans is to keep the two sides of the equation, own product sales and competitor sales, comparable and aligned consistently.

The concepts related to data completeness discussed for year-over-year growth plans apply here as well. The assumption is that in aggregate the market share for missing data equals that of the DDD data. The market share for the missing sales would have to be drastically different and the volume significant to move a territory's overall market share by a point or more on either direction. Large accounts using exclusively a product over another can tip the balance in a territory. When there is evidence of it adjustments could be made.

Mismatched sales within the territory are included in the calculations and have no affect. Accounts with sales history that have their current sales missing or the current sales are attributed to another territory, do not have a material impact when they remove or add sales to territories in proportions similar to the territory's market share. For example, removing the sales of one or more accounts with aggregate market share of 60/40 from a territory with an overall market share of 60/40 leaves the territory with un-altered market share.

Data aging is not as critical for market share plans because they impact own and competitor sales proportionally; therefore, a grace period for data aging, reject data adjustments and rep inquiry adjustments should not be necessary.

In the real world there will be deviations from these assumptions. The payout ranges are important here as well and affect the sensitivity of the plan. The closer the territory performance is to the upper limit of the range the higher the risk of miscalculation.

Dealing with Compensation Plans

The goal with compensation plans should not be to rectify every data problem to make the plan right. The fact is that not every data situation has a material effect on a plan. The goal should be instead to understand the nature of the data problem, wherever possible quantify it to determine if corrective action is necessary, and most importantly understand the potential alternative solutions. This section discusses the various issues to be considered when dealing with compensation and quota plans.

Setting Quota

Ideally, quota should be set at the beginning of the year to give sales reps an annual goal to aim for. Setting quota with the most recent data available you are likely to set the quota too low because recent-month data has not aged and is likely to adjust quite a bit higher in the following few data periods. The quota could be set early and adjusted later.

History Changes

A few months into the current year, the previous year's sales will have aged enough to 'fix' the quota, however, history changes from new reporting warehouses can happen at any time during the year. Therefore, quota recalculations ideally should take place with every payout calculations.

Typically, companies pay out compensation on quarterly basis. Payout should be recalculated for previous periods to avoid underpayment. For calendar year plans, fourth quarter payout could take place with December's data and full year closeout with recalculation one or two data-months later and after the data has aged.

Adjusting for Missing and Incorrect Data

Rejects and data investigations are incremental sales for the current year having overwhelmingly a positive bias in favor of the sales rep. They should be

174

applied only when closing out a plan, not earlier. Other types of adjustments affect both sides of the equation and they may not necessarily result in higher payouts. Reject data can be obtained from the data vendor at the ZIP code and aligned by territory. Reject data includes warehouse-to-warehouse transfers and unusually large transactions should be excluded. With adjustments you may compensate for certain accounts more than once, however, these sales adjustments are rather small and the impact low.

Pending data investigation transactions should be reviewed and whenever there is reasonable evidence, the sales rep should be given the benefit of the doubt. These transactions should be included in year-over-year growth and commission plans and only when closing out a plan.

For blocked accounts, chargeback data should be used wherever possible. If you do not contract with these accounts it is unlikely you will be able to obtain their data. When adjusting for blocked accounts you must adjust both the previous and current years.

Non-reporter data will impact year-over-year growth plans only if the growth rate and volume are very high. There are hundreds of these accounts, primarily mail service pharmacies. Non-reporting wholesaler and large mail service accounts could be aligned to the district or regional house accounts with credit re-allocated to all territories. You can leave small mail service pharmacies in the default territory. Setting a threshold will help you determine large from small accounts.

When moving a mail service account from a territory to a house account beware of situations where retail pharmacy sales are shifting to mail service. In other words, mail service is gaining at the expense of the retail pharmacies. These mail service pharmacies typically have much larger percent growth than the territory as a whole. When you remove them from the territory, essentially you are removing too much of the territory's current performance and not enough quota.

Another method for dealing with mail service data is to make adjustments. To adjust for non-reporting mail service pharmacies you need to know the territories affected and the proportions of sales going to these territories. For year-over-year growth plans, adding to a territory roughly the right proportion of sales at roughly the right growth rate can be sufficient. You can make the assumption that a mail service pharmacy's sales are growing at the same rate in all territories. To allow for enough volume, you can use a higher than equal proportion of sales for each territory. For example, if you had five affected territories you could allocate one-third the volume to all of them. At this rate you are over-adjusting or under-adjusting only slightly each individual territory. The fact that you are calculating a percentage as opposed to an absolute number provides some cushion from gross miscalculations. Precise proportions are necessary for commission plans. Adjustments with purchased data should be few and rare.

For territories close to the next payout level, you may want to move them to the next level, giving the representative the benefit of the doubt. Rounding up all achievement calculations provides a small buffer also. Occasionally you may over compensate a territory; however, not having to incur data purchase and processing charges that can be quite a bit higher offset that cost.

Purchasing data from non-reporters is a direct incentive to them not to cooperate with data vendors and should be avoided. More importantly, the practice encourages other reporters to abandon reporting for more lucrative direct data contracts with manufacturers, putting the integrity of DDD data and other industry data at risk.

Forecasting

Forecasting is another key application with company wide implications that uses many times DDD as a key input. Forecasting is not intended to predict 'the number', because that is practically impossible but rather a range within which actual sales are expected to fall. Based on the range of predicted values the company plans, prioritizes and budgets its short and long term activities. If the best case scenario unfolds the company executes all of the activities as planned. Otherwise, activities are scaled back in order of priority and according to the actual performance.

There are many forecasting techniques, mainly categorized as quantitative and qualitative but more likely to be used in combination. It is the quantitative techniques that use DDD data. Other quantitative data inputs used in forecasting include prescription, epidemiology and promotional spend data. Qualitative input comes in the form of primary research and surveys, upcoming events, opinions, Delphi sessions and other inputs from company experts, consumers, industry experts, the sales force, etc.

For mature products, their historical DDD sales are used to forecast their future performance using time series, exponential smoothing or other regression techniques. The forecast is then adjusted to account for certain future events that can affect the sales growth. These events include promotional programs, releases of pharmacoeconomic studies, new product launches, etc. The potential outcomes of each event are quantified and probabilities of occurrence are assigned to them. Using simulation techniques, a range of potential outcomes is calculated from the base forecast. The upper bound of the range represents the optimistic forecast scenario while the lower bound the pessimistic, with the best case scenario the middle of the range.

For pre-launch forecasts and even new products in the market there is no sufficient DDD data on which to build the model. For these products you can study the launch profiles of analog products to predict your product's adoption rate and market share. The forecast is fine tuned with data for important factors such as the market size, the product's clinical profile, the order of entry in the market, pricing, promotional spend on share-of-voice and DTC programs, etc.

Long term forecasts are typically based on patient models. Patient models use epidemiology data to estimate the market size in terms of incidence and prevalence of disease, and number of diagnosed and treated patients. Prescription and claims data together with persistency and compliance data are also used in the estimation of the number of treated patients. Once the market size is estimated, certain assumptions about the product's market share are made. Using averages for days-of-therapy and dosage you can calculate unit sales. Future revenue streams can also be calculated using inflation adjusted prices.

Forecasting uses national level DDD data and in terms of data accuracy and completeness it is the least demanding and easiest to accommodate application. Accuracy does not affect forecasting most of the times because at the national level the scale of most errors is insignificant.

Completeness, on the other hand, is important but can be easily handled with national level adjustments. The national sales should be adjusted with reject data and sales estimates for T/O warehouses without replacement data provided by the vendor. For non-reporting warehouses and mail service pharmacies their sell-in is equally usable as their sell-out for national level sales. For contracted products chargebacks can make up for missing data from blocked accounts.

These adjustments will account for most but perhaps not all missing sales in DDD. An analysis of the persistent variances between the adjusted DDD and x-factory sales will help you calculate a final adjustment factor for the remaining unaccounted sales.

Chapter 6
Xponent
Data

XPONENT® DATA

Xponent is a product of IMS HEALTH and captures physician prescribing activity for scripts filled in retail, mail service and LTC pharmacies. In essence, this is sales activity out of the retail segment of the Point-of-Care tier to patients. However, unlike other sales data, the focus of prescription datasets is not to tie sales activity to the customer, in this case the patient, but the decision maker, the prescriber. The manufacturer desires to identify and target these key decision makers with the intent of influencing them to prescribe more of their products resulting in increase of sales.

There is something new about Xponent since the last edition of this book. IMS proceeded recently with its Next-Generation Prescription Services (NGPS)™ initiative to re-engineer the entire prescription family of products. That includes the Xponent, Xponent PlanTrak, EarlyView™ and National Prescription Audit (NPA)™ brands. The first wave of upgrades was completed with release 1.0 in January of 2005 and the rest due with release 2.0 in January of 2006.

Key improvements include the introduction of a patented product-level common projection methodology for these services out of the same sample, a sample stabilization process through the use of imputed data, use of alternative sources of data to enhance the sample, the introduction of weekly compensation grade data, projection methodology for restricted plans and the projection of LTC data.

What is the Source of Xponent Data?

The source of the prescription data is strictly the retail, mail service and LTC pharmacies. The prescriptions are written mostly in solo and group practices, clinics, long-term-care facilities, and to a small degree in hospitals but filled in the retail sector.

Independent pharmacies report data to IMS through the software vendors managing their computer systems and many of the larger chains report directly to IMS. Data from chains and independents are based on cash prescriptions and adjudicated prescriptions (Medicaid and third-party) entered into the pharmacy software systems. Long-Term Care prescriptions are supplied by the pharmacies serving the segment. Figure 45 demonstrates the data flow.

Xponent cannot capture dispensing and drug utilization inside inpatient hospital settings, clinics, physician offices, health plan facilities and other closed-wall pharmacies. True demand data is not available for these segments similar to the retail and LTC channels. Only the outflow of scripts from the facilities to retail, mail service and LTC pharmacies can be captured in Xponent.

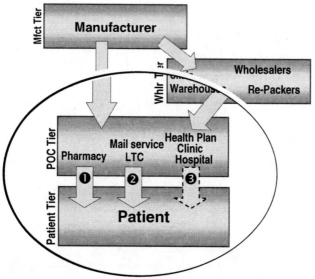

❶ Xponent captures scripts from a large number of retail pharmacies
❷ Xponent captures data from reporting Mail Service & LTC pharmacies
❸ Xponent does not capture dispensing in hospitals, clinics and HMOs

Figure 45. Channels in Xponent

Xponent projects the retail pharmacy scripts from a very large sample of collected data. Xponent captures a significant amount of the mail service scripts which offers un-projected. With NGPS, Xponent now offers a non-recommended option for projected mail service data. In the Long-Term Care area, with the addition of Omnicare, Xponent increased its sample significantly to make it projectable. The table below summarizes the data captured in Xponent.

Outlet Type	Rxs in Xponent®
Retail Pharmacy	Projected
Reporting M.O.	Un-Projected
Non-Reporting M.O.	Option for projected
Reporting LTC	Un-Projected
Non- Reporting LTC	Projected
Hospitals	Hospital outflow only
Clinics	Outflow to retail pharmacies only
Health Plan Facilities	-

Figure 46. Segments and Prescription data matrix

The Prescription

A prescription is initiated by the physician providing his patient a prescription slip to obtain his medication. Unlike the invoice, the prescription is not the final document of a sales transaction. In fact, the final sale may involve a product other than the one written by the physician because of the pharmacist's ability to intervene and alter a prescription in certain cases. The prescription is just an order for medication that may or may not be executed. Patients occasionally do not fill their prescriptions or the physician may write a prescription to be filled only when certain symptoms persist, for example. Figure 47 demonstrates a sample prescription slip.

Main Street Medical Group, Inc.
200 Main St, Suite 100
Maintown, CA 92002
(213)/999-9999

John Doe, M.D. DEA#AB1234567
Mary Doe, M.D. DEA#BC7654321

Rx

Name _____ Date _____
Address _____ Expires _____

< prescribed product(s), quantity, dosage >

☐ Refill ____ times

☐ DO NOT SUBSTITUTE _____, M.D.

Figure 47. Sample prescription slip

Only processed prescriptions generate sales, therefore, the distinction between a written and a filled prescription is material. A filled prescription is logged into a pharmacy computer system, recorded and reported to IMS. A written but not filled prescription gets discarded by the patient. Xponent captures only filled new and refill prescriptions. Below is a description of the prescription slip data elements:

Prescriber name – The whole idea of script data is to tie sales to the key decision maker, the prescriber. This is the single most important information on the prescription slip. In group practices, the name of the practice may appear on the slip and often the slip lists all of the physicians in the practice. This can cause some ambiguity when the prescriber cannot be determined conclusively. The pharmacist tends to clarify these ambiguous situations by calling the practice particularly in the case of scheduled or narcotic drugs; however, there is a chance of allocating the prescription to the wrong prescriber. In other cases, NPs, PAs, interns and residents may use the supervising physician's prescription pad or a hospital pad when writing prescriptions for patients. The physician DEA number may also be available.

Patient name, address – The patient name and address are used by the pharmacist to identify the patient in the pharmacy's database and verify his benefit eligibility. HIPAA guidelines prohibit the use of the patient identity for marketing purposes by any party. Patient information is important to the manufacturer for tracking the progression and patterns of diseases and treatments. To meet HIPAA requirements, anonymous patient information is shared with the use of identification numbers that cannot be decoded to derive the patient's true identity. Patient metrics such as age and gender had previously been available only through patient datasets. Now vendors are starting to introduce integrated prescription and patient datasets.

The Prescription Date – The date the prescription was written and the date it was filled can be different if the patient is not prompt in filling his prescription. The fill date is the important date and the actual date recorded on the final transaction.

Prescribed Product – The brand, form and strength of the written product is listed. The pharmacist has the liberty and often the obligation or incentive to substitute the written drug with a generic. Sometimes the pharmacist has also the incentive to attempt and get authorization from the physician to substitute the drug with a therapeutic equivalent. It is again the dispensed drug that matters more than the prescribed and the one that gets recorded in the data.

Quantity – The total amount of the prescribed product and it is subject to change if the written drug is substituted.

Dosage – The quantity dosed and frequency. Both are subject to change if the written drug is substituted.

Refill Indicator – Instructs the pharmacist that the prescription can be refilled.

Number of Refills - If the prescription is to be refilled, it indicates the number of refills allowed.

Substitute Indicator – Instructs the pharmacist to fill the prescription as written when the 'Do Not Substitute' box is checked. That prevents the pharmacist from substituting the 'written' drug with a generic.

The prescription slip includes the essential information for the pharmacist to dispense the prescription but not all of the critical information for the pharmacist to run their business or to construct Xponent. Consequently, the pharmacy and the vendor provide some supplemental information. The pharmacist adds for instance the payer or plan paying for the script, the patient age and sex, the product NDC number and the acquisition and retail cost of the prescription. The vendor matches the prescriber to a master database to extract the prescriber's address and specialty and standardizes the data in reportable form before making it available to its clients.

What is the Importance of Xponent Data?

In the DDD discussion we saw that the pharmacy sell-in was captured and aggregated at the ZIP code. DDD also captures reporting mail service data at the prescriber ZIP and LTC pharmacy sell-in. So, what benefits does Xponent deliver? You can narrow its benefits down to four major ones:

- **Provides pharmacy sell-out** – We stressed previously the importance of sell-out over sell-in. Pharmacy sell-out is true demand while sell-in includes inventories. Additionally, the pharmacy sell-out provides a wealth of information with numerous prescriber transactions compared to the single sell-in transaction. Prescription data has a tremendous advantage over DDD in the retail segment.

- **Captures the prescriber** – Sales data involves the seller and the buyer of the product. Prescription datasets capture the influencer; the prescriber in this case. Recognizing who is the key decision maker takes your data to a higher level. At best, DDD captures mail service prescription activity from reporting mail service pharmacies but reports it at the ZIP level only. DDD does not identify the prescriber.

- **Provides competitive data** – In DDD there are added complexities with competitor data even when you are able to overcome issues with your own product's data. Prescription datasets deliver own and competitor product data at the same level of detail without limitations.

- **Solves the problem of the 'traveling script'** - The term refers to situations where the script is written in one territory and filled in another. This occurs very frequently with patients traveling a distance to see their doctor and filling the prescriptions in the neighborhood pharmacy. Filling prescriptions on the road while traveling is another example. Xponent traces the prescription back to the prescriber and ultimately the territory that generated the demand. According to IMS, 99.3% of prescriptions are matched to the territory of origin.

XPONENT vs. DDD

If Xponent offers such important advantages over DDD can you substitute DDD with Xponent? The answer to this lies primarily with the percent of product sales going through the non-retail channel of distribution.

This question is applicable to individual products rather than product portfolios. For products with substantial usage inside the clinics, hospitals and HMOs, where Xponent does not give you any visibility, you absolutely need DDD. For retail drugs sold almost entirely through the retail channel it is possible to only purchase Xponent. However, because total sales are always a desired piece of information, it is probably prudent to use at least national level DDD for its broad coverage of all the market channels.

Many times and when there is some level of sales in both the retail and the non-retail channels, using DDD for the non-retail channel and Xponent for the retail makes most sense. This option gives many people the comfort of the un-projected, almost complete sales of DDD, the account detail in the non-retail and the prescriber detail in the retail channel.

For a specific drug, calculate the split of its retail and non-retail business from DDD and analyze your applications to determine which data product or component of product you will need. Forecasting applications rely on DDD data for its completeness. Targeting requires Xponent for prescribers and DDD for non-retail accounts. Compensation may use components from both or exclusively any one of the two.

You can have the best of both worlds by constructing one data set that includes DDD with the retail category '1' replaced by your script data. For this to work, you must make sure to match the sub-categories that make-up category '1' in DDD precisely to the sub-categories included in Xponent. Also, the unit of measure in both components must be comparable. For comparability purposes, keep in mind that each uses some unique measures. The pack unit, a common DDD measure, is not available in script data and the Rx is not available in DDD. Both track volume units as well as dollars with certain limitations. Conversions into some measures are possible.

Additionally, they may report sales on a different calendar basis. DDD uses the 4-4-5 calendar. Xponent previously offered data only on calendar month basis. With NGPS Xponent can deliver data either on 4-4-5 or calendar months. To start, DDD monthly sales are not directly comparable to monthly prescriptions because the first represents sell-in while the second sell-out. The 4-4-5 calendar further complicates comparisons on a monthly basis with DDD sales 'spiked' every third month.

Figure 48 demonstrates some of the key differences between DDD and Xponent. In this example the product has a substantial amount of retail business. The non-retail line is unique to DDD and its position relative to the DDD retail line varies based on the retail and non-retail sales mix. The two comparable lines are the retail DDD and Xponent.

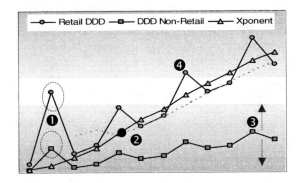

❶   Initial channel loading spikes
❷   Xponent catches-up with the DDD moving average line
❸   The line's relative position to the retail line varies depending on the type of drug
❹   The distinct peak of the third month of the quarter of the DDD 4-4-5

Figure 48. Xponent vs. DDD

The most notable feature of a DDD trend line is the initial product loading during launch. It usually happens in a period of one or two weeks. The second notable feature is the distinct pattern of peaks and valleys on the DDD line due to the 4-4-5 calendar, while the Xponent trend may be smooth depending on the reporting option.

During launch and with supply outpacing demand DDD leads Xponent. Eventually demand catches up and at some point the Xponent line and the smoothed moving average DDD line run close in parallel. The two should keep pace with each other until eventually Xponent leads in the product decline as demand slows down towards the end of the product's lifecycle.

In summary, the physician level data is the ultimate level of detail whenever possible. That is where prescription datasets offer superb solutions over DDD.

On the other hand, DDD is indispensable for its completeness and coverage of the non-retail activity.

Measuring Rxs

The basic Xponent measure is the script (Rx). One Rx is equivalent to one prescription fill or refill of a drug. A prescription counts as a new script (NRx) the first time the patient presents the prescription slip to the pharmacist. The pharmacist assigns it a prescription number and all refills are credited towards that number. A refill through another pharmacy qualifies as a new script at that pharmacy. When the prescription slip is presented to the same pharmacy more than once it qualifies as a refill. In order to get a refill, the refill indicator and the number of refills on the original prescription slip must be marked appropriately. A prescription slip is good for a total of n+1 fills where n is the number of refills indicated. The sum of new and refill prescriptions equals the total scripts (TRx).

TRx = NRx + Refills

With two measures in Xponent, the user's dilemma will be which of the two measures to use. Both are very important, but ultimately it is the TRx count that matters most because it captures the whole prescribing activity. However, it is the NRx that must be followed more closely, as a slowing trend in new scripts is troublesome and may be indicating lack of new patients on therapy. You will use TRx in almost all applications and monitor the NRx trend. Here are two important facts about prescriptions:

- Prescriptions vary in size by patient but are counted in Xponent as equal. For example, patient-A may receive a prescription for 30 tablets of a given product while patient-B receives a quantity of 20 tablets of the same product. Both are counted as one Rx each. The Rx as a unit of measure captures the action of filling a prescription. It is the equivalent of one actual visit to a retail pharmacy or a virtual visit to a mail service pharmacy. To measure volume dispensed or number of tablets, you must use the quantity data type instead. The difference in the prescription sizes is more pronounced between retail and mail service prescriptions, with mail service prescriptions larger typically by a factor of 2 to 3. Mail service pharmacies fill prescriptions for patients with larger quantities but less frequently.
- A new script does not always imply a new patient. A patient may visit the physician and receive a new prescription for the same condition more than once. In this case, you have one patient with an NRx count greater than one. A patient with a recurrence of a condition at a later time could qualify as a new patient, in which case you could have a count of two patients with an

equal NRx count. The NRx count is closer to the number of patients for symptomatic diseases that are treated with a single prescription. For chronic diseases, the NRx count could be substantially higher than the number of patients. In that respect, Xponent is not the best source for patient counts.

The Look of Script Data in Xponent

Xponent includes data at the prescriber, hospital and ZIP code levels. Usually the prescriber is identified by his ME number, name and address. Hospitals are identified by their DEA number, name and address. ZIP code records are referenced simply by the five-digit ZIP. The example below demonstrates various options for different levels of reporting.

❶ Prescr. ID	❷ Prescr. Name	❸ Product	❹ Rx Type	❺ Quantity
0000120432	Dr. Joe Doe	BrandA	Retail	20 TRxs
0000120432	Dr. Joe Doe	BrandA	Mail	10 TRxs
A78912345	Hospital A	FormB	Retail	50 NRxs
(12345)	(Prescriber Zip)	StrengthC	Both	10 ml

❶   The prescriber ID may be the physician's ME number, hospital DEA#, zip code, or other

❷   Xponent includes scripts matched to a physician or hospital, otherwise, reported at the zip

❸   Data is reported at the strength, form and brand levels or combinations of the above

❹   Retail and mail service scripts can be reported separately

❺   Activity is quantified in terms of new and total Rxs, volume units and dollars

Figure 49. Prescription data detail

XPONENT PROJECTION

The general theme with prescription data is projections. Technology limitations at some pharmacies, industry dynamics and economics make it impossible to collect the prescription data from every store. Statistics, on the other hand, eliminate the need to have every bit of the data collected from its source. Projections are used very commonly for estimating totals from samples. The government, more than anyone, uses projections because of the prohibitive length of time, effort and cost to collect census data. When the government quotes a figure on almost anything, chances are that the figure was projected.

Projections require only a sample of the data. For certain projections the data sample can be very small, often less than 1% of the total. The required sample size for different degrees of accuracy is estimated using statistical formulas depending on the error tolerance. The sample used in projections must be representative of the whole data. You must have enough occurrences of the characteristics that matter in your sample. Samples with too few or too many occurrences of certain characteristics are biased and the projections potentially flawed.

With NGPS, Xponent offers projected retail pharmacy scripts and un-projected mail service scripts as it did earlier. However, it now includes an option for projected mail service data. Because the prescription patterns and the projection principles - discussed in the next section - do not hold true with mail service pharmacies, IMS does not recommend the use of this option. Finally, in LTC IMS acquired enough new data to make the data projectable and now offers projected LTC scripts. The following section describes the projection methodology of Xponent.

Retail Pharmacy Projection

Xponent data is used in compensation applications and to achieve the high degree of accuracy required, Xponent uses a very large data sample in its projections. According to IMS, the Xponent sample represents approximately 67% of the pharmacies which account for approximately 75% of all retail prescriptions. Samples of this size are atypical for most projections. To eliminate biases, Xponent includes in its sample data from all types and sizes of retail pharmacies. This way Xponent achieves the level of accuracy at the physician level that makes the data applicable for targeting, compensation and other applications.

Xponent projects scripts individually for each prescriber at each un-sampled pharmacy before it aggregates all of the scripts from all stores for the prescriber to derive their total activity. The projection assumptions are rather simple. The prescribers whose scripts were filled in the store to be projected are the same as the prescribers of the surrounding pharmacies in the sample. The script volume of these prescribers is proportional to their volume in the sampled stores. Therefore, the surrounding sample stores have a great influence on a store to be projected. These influences are driven by two main factors:

■ Store Size – Larger stores have higher influence than smaller stores and their prescribing patterns for these stores are more heavily weighted in the projections.

■ Store Distance – The prescribing patterns in the un-sampled stores are similar to those seen in the nearby sampled stores. It is implied that the high volume prescribers for nearby sampled stores are high volume prescribers for un-sampled stores. The closer two pharmacies are, the closer their patterns. The patterns between two stores break gradually the further the two stores are apart.

Figure 50 demonstrates the two principles. Store-B has a high volume influence on Store-A's projection because of its size, but its influence is moderated because of its distance from Store-A. On the other hand, the smaller Store-C has low volume influence on Store-A's projection but its influence is boosted because of its close distance to Store-A.

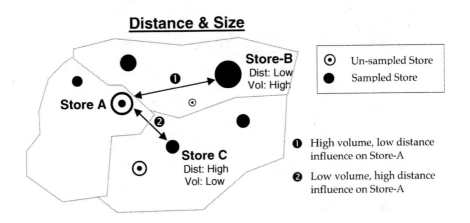

Figure 50. Xponent projection

Xponent determines the number of scripts to project for an un-sampled store by the store's size using DDD as a key input. DDD tracks the sell-in of almost every retail pharmacy. The Hayes directory of pharmacies is also used in certain situations. Before NGPS, Xponent came in two flavors, each one defining store size differently. The standard version of Xponent defined the store size based on the aggregate sales for all prescription drugs sold to the pharmacy combined. While that works for many therapeutic classes of drugs it is far from accurate for specialty drugs such as oncology, HIV, etc. Large stores do sell more antibiotics in proportion to their size but not chemo agents, for example. Specialty drugs are carried by fewer pharmacies and in many cases smaller stores by the above definition. These small stores may far outperform large ones in sales for specialty drugs and unless the projection accounts for it, projections for such drugs can be distorted and biased by the prescription patterns of the large stores.

IMS addressed the problem with specialty pharmacies by introducing Xponent SR (Specialty Retail). Xponent SR solved the store-sizing problem by considering the pharmacy sell-in for the individual product being projected rather than the aggregate sell-in of all products. This method elevates the importance of small stores with high sales for the projected product and demotes the importance of stores with high overall sales but low sales for the projected product.

NOTE: For projecting new products in the market while their DDD sales history for the first six months of the launch is unstable, Xponent uses the sales history of the market to size the stores.

Xponent SR did not identify new prescribers because it used the same sample as standard Xponent. Prescribers appear in Xponent only if they have at least one script in the sample. What Xponent SR did better was resizing the store and setting the projection factors for specific products based on the DDD sell-in, as a result, affecting the relative ranks and deciles of many prescribers. The overall script count also changed as a result. The large stores caused the over-projection of specialty products in the standard Xponent when you compared the results to DDD. Xponent SR also may over-project DDD but by a smaller margin.

NGPS adopted the superior SR methodology as its core projection method across its entire prescription family, along with some other features from the other projection methodologies. A more important one, used previously in NPA, is the national projections across census regions. In NGPS the census regions were increased significantly for better accuracy. Xponent uses these projections to adjust and reconcile its prescriber level projections with national level projections.

Another important enhancement is the introduction of a kind of smoothing for stores in the sample without data for a particular reporting period. To avoid prescriber activity trend breaks NGPS now uses historical data for the store in place of its missing scripts. In addition, to enhance the sample, particularly for areas known to have lower than normal coverage, NGPS for the first time turned to alternative sources of data beyond its usual channels. Those include Medicaid data from IMS' own DNA product as well as managed care Third Party payors.

Even though NGPS maintained the brand name of Xponent, the product resembles more Xponent SR rather than the older, standard Xponent.

XPONENT DATA COMPLETENESS

Xponent data has quite unique aspects and the way we look at its completeness will vary somewhat from DDD discussed earlier. First, Xponent is not a census database but projected. Xponent is a static database not subject to history changes like DDD the completeness of which is affected by history adjustments. Also, Xponent has three distinct components, retail, mail service and LTC, each of them to be considered individually. We will define the data completeness here again by:

- The amount of data captured and reported
- The data being reported at the right level of detail
- The number of prescribers identified

Retail Pharmacy Data Completeness

By virtue of projection, in terms of total scripts, the retail pharmacy data is 100% complete. Xponent projects the retail pharmacy scripts from a large sample using DDD sales as a guide to estimate the upper bounds of the projection. Moreover, smaller geographies like territories are projected with a high degree of accuracy to their universe as well. Territory data completeness can be affected by the alignment of prescribers to territories, however.

Xponent's approach assures its completeness but includes a certain amount of data not at the optimal level of detail and a small amount of data not representative of true demand. Naturally, the desired level of data detail is the prescriber. The ZIP where the prescription originated is a distant second choice, however, usable in many applications including compensation. Xponent matches and reports approximately 97% of the transactions back to the prescriber. The remaining 3% of the transactions are matched and reported mostly at the ZIP code of the prescribing physician and the territory where the script originated, with the smaller part matched to the store ZIP code and possibly a territory other than the one the script was written.

In terms of identifying every prescriber of a product, the precondition for Xponent is that at least one of the prescriber's scripts is filled in one of the pharmacies in the sample. Although it is difficult to quantify how many prescribers are not identified in Xponent, there is enough evidence that this happens. The conditions under which all of the scripts of a prescriber are filled in pharmacies not in the sample are quite unique and occur infrequently. The scripts for these prescribers are accounted for in the total script count but allocated to other prescribers.

NOTE: Xponent includes data for prescribers indicated 'deceased' or 'retired'. Although there is no value in that data from the targeting standpoint, these records are included to maintain the completeness and trending of Xponent intact.

FACT: The projection does not require any specific retail pharmacy to be in the sample. If a pharmacy is not in the sample, its scripts are projected.

Mail Service Data Completeness

Xponent captures overall more than 80% of the mail service prescriptions according to IMS. For certain therapeutic areas and for specialty drugs the percentage of coverage could be significantly lower. You can determine the percent coverage for a given product or market by comparing the DDD sales for sub-categories S5 (non-reporting) and Z2, Z6 (reporting).

The default Xponent option calls for un-projected mail service data which simply does not account for the non-reporting mail service pharmacy scripts in any way. The new option in NGPS for projected mail service accounts for 100% of the scripts because the sell-in to non-reporting mail service pharmacies is known through DDD. However, you can be certain of misallocations of scripts at the prescriber level and that is why IMS does not recommend this option.

A very substantial amount of the mail service data in Xponent is reported by Medco. Medco previously offered manufacturers the option to contract for their prescriber level data. In 2004 they revoked that option and its scripts are now included in Xponent only at the specialty level within the prescriber's ZIP.

You can determine the amount of Medco data as a percent of total mail service – see later discussion on how to identify Medco records. Aside from Medco, a small amount of scripts is matched to the prescriber's ZIP or the patient's 3-digit ZIP with fair chances of being reported at the territory where the scripts originated.

For mail service pharmacies, IMS' strategy remains to continue recruiting aggressively new stores to capture as much of the data as possible. Meanwhile, the manufacturer will need to develop a strategy to deal with the missing data in this segment.

TIP: Currently new mail service pharmacies are added in Xponent without their prescription history. This can cause certain problems with compensation plans when it happens in the middle of a performance period. IMS has announced plans to address this issue in its upcoming major product upgrade.

Long Term Care Data Completeness

A major improvement in NGPS is the projection of Long-Term Care script data. Xponent increased its sample from about 40% previously to approximately 50-60% currently with the addition of Omnicare. The projection makes the LTC data virtually 100% complete. Non-reporting LTC stores are sized based on their sell-in data available in DDD.

Omnicare, a key player in the LTC arena, blocked its data previously making it almost impossible for companies to get an accurate read of the market without a direct data agreement. There are still limitations with this data, however. A manufacturer's product must be under a rebate contract with Omnicare to get prescriber-level access. Otherwise, non-Omnicare data is provided at the prescriber level and the Omnicare at the territory level. Each product's eligibility is determined individually and not as a manufacturer product portfolio.

Although the territory level of detail works for compensation, it is far from optimal for targeting purposes. The arrangement is such that Omnicare still maintains the leverage with manufacturers while making data management and integration through Xponent a little easier for the manufacturer.

Dealing with Unreported Mail Service Data

A typical scenario with mail service pharmacies is "plan-A requires mail service prescriptions to be filled through the non-reporting mail service pharmacy-X and territories 101, 102 and 103 are not getting credit for their sales". We mentioned in an earlier chapter that mail service pharmacies have the ability to manage costs and managed care has recognized that. Therefore, this problem is going to get worse not better and, while the problem gets worse, you are still left with the same options. At stake here is the approximately 17% of mail service data not captured in Xponent.

How do you deal effectively with this problem? Always the first step is to assess the overall situation as well as the situation of individual mail service pharmacies. Your key to this is DDD. The DDD sell-in can help you establish the total sales volume of the 'S5' sub-category that makes up the non-reporting mail service pharmacies, as well as the sales volume of each individual account. The pre-requisite here is that you must move these accounts from their default retail category in DDD to non-retail for visibility at the outlet level. This is a product specific exercise because products are impacted at different degrees by mail service.

By now you have determined which products are vulnerable to mail service and which mail service pharmacies have a significant impact on your business. There are more than 300 non-reporting mail service pharmacies and it is practically impossible to deal with all of them individually. You will not need to deal with most of them because of their low sales volume. You can set a sales volume threshold for pharmacies to deal with. You could assign low-volume pharmacies below the threshold to their default territories and medium-volume ones to house or district accounts in DDD.

Ideally the next step would be to identify the territories that each of the high volume pharmacies affect - an important distinction from the territories they serve. The pharmacies may serve a large number of territories with marginal business in many of them. This information can be provided by the sales reps as they come to the realization that their territories are affected. If you can, assign weights of severity of the problem to each territory. All territories within the area of influence are contributing to the accounts' sales.

At this point set some realistic objectives of what you want to accomplish. In the spectrum of options, from doing nothing to perfection, the only option not viable here is perfection. Setting out to adjust the data at the prescriber level may be a stretch because it is probably not necessary, unless you were trying to fine tune targeting. A more realistic approach might be to aim for ZIP or territory level adjustments. The prescriber level option narrows your alternatives down to one. The territory level option allows the most room to maneuver.

Another key objective is accuracy. The question is what level of accuracy do you expect from your adjustment method and is 100% the only option? Back in the DDD applications compensation discussion it was demonstrated that there is not always an impact for adjustments you make. Chances are that you can achieve your objectives with a less than 100% precise method. Again flexibility is the key to developing more alternatives. Ultimately setting an objective for substantial correction will take you further than a perfect solution one.

Finally, start developing some alternative approaches. Your first one always should be to make an effort to convince the pharmacy to report their data to your data vendor. Remember that this option gives you competitive data as well. Your last alternative should always be to purchase data directly from non-reporters. This is a high-risk option and was discussed in an earlier chapter. One of your options should always be to do nothing.

One complicating factor with these outlets is their sales history. Any adjustments would have to be applied both to current and past performance. You must make sure, however, that quota and current sales are aligned and changes in the market such as shift of sales from the retail pharmacies to mail service have not left territories with disproportional amounts of quota compared to current sales. This can be particularly true when you make mail service adjustments in DDD.

Always be mindful of the cost of adjusting sales for a mail service pharmacy. Most of the times there is a cost associated with the adjustment data and always a cost of processing that data in-house. One option might be to pay an amount equal or higher to the data and processing fees to the affected reps to compensate for the missing sales.

This works when the data costs are significant enough. For generous plans these funds may not be sufficient and a higher amount may need to be paid out. You can perform some simulations assuming that the affected territories move up one or more levels in the payout scale to determine what a reasonable payout amount should be.

The payout scale increments are critical. Plans with small intervals of 1% or 2% attainment points are more difficult to handle and more prone to estimate errors. For higher intervals you can estimate the probability of the territory making the next level with an adjustment based on how close it is to the next payout level. See the 'Quota & Compensation' section in DDD for more on the topic.

Other options require some formula of apportioning a pharmacy's prescriptions to the territories. These options are useful when you want to solve substantially the problem and must have some tolerance for error. See what effect equal apportioning has on compensation. Look for any information that would allow you to assign weights to each territory for prorated allocations. To allow for the imperfections in the formulas, increase the allocated amount to a territory by some percentage so that the allocated amount exceeds the pharmacy's total sales.

Some mail service pharmacies are too big, serving a very wide area and may be best treated by buying data. For those pharmacies consider using the previous year's allocation and buying data every other year. This will substantially solve the problem but not perfectly because the current allocation may change somewhat; however, it disturbs the pharmacy's dependence on data revenue and forces them to cooperate with the data vendors.

You have now assessed your mail service situation, set your objectives, considered your alternatives and decided on an adjustment method. It is now time to implement the adjustments, but where do you apply your adjustments? Mail service belongs in the retail channel of business and naturally the adjustments could be applied to Xponent. But you have already moved the non-reporting mail service accounts to the non-retail channel in DDD; therefore, you have an equal opportunity to apply the adjustments in DDD. In either case, make sure not to double count the pharmacy sell-in in DDD.

The method you use for adjustments does have to be perfect. It simply should be fairly accurate. One formula will not fit all, so have your analysts determine how each pharmacy should be handled and fine tune the formulas to eliminate as much of the error as possible.

Dealing with LTC Data

LTC is much like a niche market served by a niche group of physicians and a niche group of pharmacies. The physician's profile in this market is often different from his prescribing profile seen in retail Xponent and prescription filling is tightly controlled by chain and independent consultant pharmacies. Then, there is a rather small number of nursing homes with in-house pharmacies. The typical sales activities in this segment include targeting of prescribers in and out of nursing homes, consultant pharmacists at LTC pharmacies and nursing home staff.

DDD sell-in provides the measures of sales performance for LTC pharmacies that you can tie to the affiliated consultant pharmacists and other essential pharmacy staff. Xponent LTC covers the same pharmacies but ties their dispensing to the prescribers. The DDD subcategories N1, N2, N4 and P7 make up these pharmacies.

The addition of Omnicare to DDD and Xponent simplified a rather complicated data situation with this segment. Products under contract with Omnicare now qualify for complete account and prescriber-level DDD and Xponent data access. This is an ideal solution from both the targeting and compensation standpoint. For non-contracted products the outlet and prescriber visibility is limited to the non-Omnicare pharmacies only. However, Omnicare data for these products is available at the territory level or higher. This is still a significant improvement considering the usability of the data in compensation applications.

Customer profiling databases like MII and SMG are an absolute necessity for data applications in this segment. Some of the more important elements they provide are the affiliations of medical directors and other essential staff to nursing homes and the affiliations of consultant pharmacists to nursing home providers. The SMG database also captures the relationships of LTC pharmacies to the nursing homes they serve.

Dealing with Specialty Pharmacies

The bulk of the specialty pharmacies are found in IMS' mail service classification with DDD subcategories of S0 and S5. The issues with mail service specialty pharmacies are similar to those of traditional mail service pharmacies. The difference is in the volume of business they handle. There is typically high concentration of specialty drug sales through these pharmacies and a non-reporting store becomes a bigger data problem in order of magnitude.

TIP: *Bigger non-reporting mail service specialty stores are in IMS' recruitment list while smaller ones are given low priority. As such, if a small specialty mail service store is causing territory credit allocation issues refer it to IMS for recruiting.*

Specialty pharmacies classified as nuclear and home health pharmacies are the most challenging because DDD and Xponent do not currently recruit them for reporting. Even though the radius of the area of operation of these types of pharmacies is rather limited compared to mail service pharmacies, they may serve customers across several territories. The data issues with these pharmacies can be dealt with similarly to the non-reporting mail service stores.

Retail specialty pharmacies that are not in the sample are projected in Xponent. The projection methodology introduced with Xponent SR, which is now the core engine of the NGPS projection methodology, was designed to deal with the retail specialty pharmacies. The key to it is weighing the influence of the pharmacy in the projection based on its sales for the specific drug being projected rather than its aggregate sales. The methodology projects accurately the volume of the pharmacies; however, sample biases can affect the allocation of scripts to the right prescribers.

The situation with retail specialty pharmacies gets more complex as these pharmacies evolve through the stages of offering specialty drugs and services to a local market, to delivering drugs within a rather small radius, to a mixed business model of retail and regional mail service. As these stores expand their area of operation they render the Xponent projection methodology ineffective, at least partially. At this point the pharmacy should be either recruited or at least reclassified as mail service. There is currently a pressing need to identify the retail specialty pharmacies.

TIP: *If your company promotes specialty drugs you may want to use your field to gather intelligence on the operations of retail specialty pharmacies that pose a challenge for territories to analyze their influence and re-examine their business models. You can then pass the information to IMS to negotiate a potential solution.*

Specialty pharmacies can also be an issue when they form close relationships with clinics and hospitals. These relationships are typically limited to high cost injectables and infusion drugs. By directing all of their scripts through the specialty pharmacy, the physicians in these facilities do not appear to have any activity in Xponent when the specialty pharmacy is not in the panel of sampled pharmacies. In that case the prescriber is not projected in Xponent and their prescriptions are allocated to other physicians instead.

Inevitably, some of the scripts are sometimes credited to prescribers in surrounding territories. Even though Xponent projects the total prescriptions for the pharmacy completely, the spillover of prescriptions hurts the territory's performance while it benefits neighboring territories as figure 51 shows.

TIP: *Because of the intricacies of specialty pharmacies, when compensating reps on targeted accounts alone you are running the risk of not capturing all of their activity. Non-targeted account and ZIP-level activity may be very relevant to the plan.*

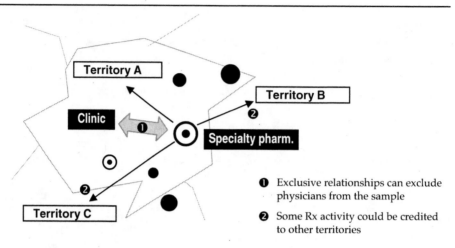

Figure 51. Specialty pharmacy

XPONENT DATA ACCURACY

We mentioned in the DDD discussion that data accuracy is about errors, the frequency by which they occur and how long they persist. We will stay consistent with that definition in Xponent as well. Our objective here will also be to understand the nature of the errors and the types of action that can be taken to correct them.

The fact that Xponent employs projections implies some level of error in the data. Similarly to DDD, processing data from disparate data sources requires standardization and, therefore, matching of product and customer information to the master databases. This process is a source of errors for Xponent as well. The following section discusses data accuracy in relation to these processes.

Prescriber Level Data Accuracy

Prescriber level projections can be affected by biases in the sample. Sample data is collected in a way that minimizes biases; nevertheless, residual bias will cause small inaccuracies in the projection. Prescribers overweighed in the sample will be over-projected. Over-projecting for a physician inevitably means under-projecting for others.

Xponent does not capture every prescriber in its sample. To have their scripts projected prescribers must have prescriptions in the sample. Prescribing physicians not captured in the Xponent sample are not projected and their prescriptions are allocated to other physicians inflating their script counts.

Prescriber matching can result in script allocations to the wrong physicians. This typically stems from imprecise data entry by the pharmacist in the adjudication software system. When the vendor attempts to match the physician entered by the pharmacist, the wrong physician could be identified and consequently credited with the prescription activity.

At times, a physician's sample data results in multiple matches to physicians with the same last names and similar but different first names. The physician's activity in this case is split and allocated to multiple prescribers. Often the unrelated specialty of one of the physicians will be the clue for the validity of the match. Other times the sales reps will provide feedback about non-prescribing physicians with scripts in the data.

Prescriber habits are often the reason for inaccuracies. Allocation errors can potentially occur when physicians do not use their own prescription pads or do not clearly mark their names on pads with multiple physician names listed. Pharmacists will attempt to correct most of these situations. NPs and PAs may use the supervising physician's pad for writing prescriptions passing the credit to them. 'Jr.' and 'Sr.' title omissions have been proven to be causes of matching errors as well.

All of these situations cause higher activity for some prescribers at the expense of others. Remember that this is activity shifted from one prescriber to another without a change to the overall prescription count. There are two key questions here. First, are the inaccuracies so pronounced to distort the prescriber's true potential and therefore affect targeting? And second, is there a spillover of prescribing activity between territories to affect compensation?

It is practically impossible to know the answers to these questions. The most you will be able to do is correct a few of the situations occasionally. Although Xponent safeguards against biases from store sizing in specialty markets, prescriber over-projections cannot be entirely avoided. Physician mismatches can be dealt to some extent by IMS with cross-referencing of DEA numbers. The fact of the matter is that as long as pharmacies provide imprecise identification for prescribers there will always be mismatches.

Situations of prescribers not in the sample cannot be corrected without the vendor recruiting new pharmacies. Any adjustments for these physicians would have an additive affect, inflating the overall script volume because their activity is already projected and allocated to other physicians. Unlike DDD, historical adjustments in Xponent are made in rare situations and data errors have typically a permanent affect on the data.

Territory Level Data Accuracy

Territory activity is the aggregate activity for all prescribers and ZIP codes aligned to the territory. As a result, at the territory level prescriber over and under-projections cancel each other out to a great extend to reflect more accurately territory activity. Here, the prescriber's alignment is more crucial than the prescriber projections. A prescriber must be aligned to the territory where the demand was generated. This may not happen in the following instances:

- The prescriber generated demand in a territory but their demographics place them outside the boundaries of the territory. This requires correction of their address and realignment to the right territory.

- The prescriber generates demand from more than one office in more than one territory but their demographics place them in a single territory. This can be fixed by apportioning part of their activity to the other office locations.

- Scripts matched to a patient's 3-digit ZIP or a pharmacy 5-digit ZIP can potentially originate in a territory other than the one credited with the activity. Lack of sufficient information does not allow for any action to correct these situations. Less than 1% of the data falls in this category.

The change of address of a prescriber permanently moves them from one territory to another. Xponent moves the history along so that there is no activity trend-break and provides a benchmark for the prescriber's future activity. Because the pharmacy sell-in stays with the store in the old territory, this creates a disparity between sell-in to a territory's retail outlets and the territory's prescribing activity.

TIP: Often the expectation is that a territory's pharmacy sell-in should match the prescribing activity in the territory. This is not a valid comparison. Pharmacies have fixed locations with respect to territories. Physicians on the other hand can be aligned freely based on one of their many addresses.

Xponent accuracy improves progressively at higher levels of geography. Xponent reports Rx, quantity and with some limitations dollars as the product of quantity. Generally speaking the Rx type is more reliable than the quantity simply because it is a mere count of observations and not subject to variability like the quantity data type. Pharmacies are expected to report quantities in volume units. However, that does not always happen, at least partially, and consequently quantities may be misstated. Injectable drugs are more susceptible to this problem than other drugs. Benchmarking Xponent quantities with DDD retail frequently identifies discrepancies between the two. These comparisons should be performed after converting the Xponent and DDD quantities to a compatible type.

Prescriber Demographics

A prescriber is a medical professional from a number of disciplines or specialties: MDs, DOs, interns, residents, NPs, PAs, optometrists, dentists, podiatrists, veterinarians or pharmacists. Anyone of them can potentially be a prescriber whose scripts will be captured in the sample and projected. For all of the prescribers the vendor must maintain some basic demographic data. Prescriptions and demographics are combined to form the Xponent dataset.

IMS compiles its physician demographic universe file from industry associates and other sources. There are at least eight resource files used to build the universe file. Some of the files used come from the American Osteopathic Association (AOA), the American Medical Association (AMA) and the Drug Enforcement Agency (DEA). For prescriptions reported at the hospital, the DDD outlet universe is used to provide the demographic information. When a physician's information is available through multiple sources, Xponent uses a priority hierarchy to determine which source to use.

Xponent is using a methodology to match a prescriber in the sample to a prescriber in the master physician file. For better reliability, the first attempt to match is made on the DEA number followed by the name and ZIP code combination. If no match is found, Xponent starts to 'loosen' up the matching criteria attempting to match on unique name or non-unique name. Ultimately, when a prescriber cannot be identified the record is matched preferably to the prescriber ZIP, otherwise, to the store 5-digit ZIP for retail prescriptions or the patient 3-digit ZIP for mail service. Prescriber matches to a ZIP code result in the ZIP level data in Xponent.

NOTE: Medco scripts are the exception to this rule. Medco scripts are reported in Xponent by default at the prescriber specialty level within ZIP code due to limitations imposed by Medco.

The data sources used for the physician demographics are not the most reliable sources for a physician's address of practice. These are mostly membership associations with many addresses listed being the physician's place of residence. As a result, the address information provided in Xponent in some instances is not usable. Additionally, Xponent does not split the prescribing activity by office location for physicians with multiple practices. Xponent provides a single record with the prescriber's default address and the aggregate number of scripts for all locations.

IMS offers options for dealing both with the address and the apportioning issues in Xponent. IMS has implemented a new procedure whereby the primary office address of a new prescriber is verified by calling the prescriber's office. The vendor's intention is to provide the best address for targeting, but also offers their clients the option to override the reported primary address on the universe with an address from the client's call file. Additionally, IMS clients can apportion the prescriptions across up to 20 office addresses.

Vendors, including IMS, offer premium databases with multiple addresses for prescribers. Some databases go beyond membership associations to incorporate claims data. This is the key information vendors needed to place a practitioner to a practicing location because the claim will likely reflect the address where the physician provided care. Additionally, the frequency by which an address appears in claims is used to rank a prescriber's practice locations and determine the 'best address'.

IMS' Healthcare Professional Services (HCPS) is one such database. HCPS uses external consumer, claims, subscription and other databases to compile its prescriber universe. Addresses are standardized and certified using the USPS (United States post Office) address database, primary research and manual lookups to identify and eliminate duplication. HCPS provides the prescriber's primary called-on address as well as secondary addresses. More importantly, it analyzes a prescriber's script activity to assign relative weights for each practice location that you can use in apportioning.

Tip: The practitioner's mobility makes them a difficult target to follow unlike any other provider. The successful implementation of Xponent in targeting and fair compensation hinges on accurate practice locations and alignment. Good prescriber demographic data is a worthwhile investment.

Call Files

Although Xponent by itself does not solve the best address and apportioning problems, it functionally supports them with the use of call files. Call files include address and territory override information and multiple practice locations for apportioning. The manufacturer specifies in the call file the address and territory they prefer for a particular prescriber. Xponent then substitutes the prescriber's default address and territory number with the address and territory provided in the call file.

The manufacturer can provide more than one address and territory for each prescriber for purposes of apportioning prescribing activity between several territories. Xponent replicates a physician's data enough times, one for each address in the call file. The manufacturer can choose between dividing the physician's prescriptions equally between the various office locations and allocating the full activity to all locations.

TIP: *Apportioning activity equally between physician office locations prevents the sales rep from seeing the physician's full potential. Apportioning at higher than 100%, on the other hand, duplicates the physician's activity and may over-compensate the reps depending on the plan. Sales support must decide which apportioning method works best keeping open the option of using both depending on the application.*

Databases such as HCPS offer now an evidence-based alternative to equal and full apportioning. The analysis of a prescriber's activity relative to their practice locations creates true split-factors that can be used to credit territories. IMS has not integrated HCPS into Xponent but offers it as a separate database.

Generating the call file, if one is used, is the responsibility of the manufacturer. Call files are optional if you are using a straight ZIP-to-territory alignment without overrides or apportioning. Applying the call file to Xponent can be done either by the vendor or in-house by the manufacturer. From the sales force application standpoint, the advantage of in-house processing is the added flexibility to implement immediately territory and alignment changes. Call files require a significant amount of lead-time to take effect in Xponent when applied by IMS.

XPONENT REPORTS

Xponent offers a number of hard copy report formats. Xponent hard copy reports can be very lengthy; however, you can control the size of the report by limiting the physicians shown on the report. Talk to your vendor about report options. Whenever possible you should generate reports in-house. The following section discusses Xponent raw data.

Raw Data

The raw data files afford you the flexibility to produce custom reports to meet your business needs. Perhaps the greatest benefit is the ability to integrate various data source such as DDD, Xponent, call activity, etc., to produce consolidated views of account and territory performance. Another major benefit is the ability to implement and change business rules on the fly. Prescription data is generally more complex in its implementation. See later section on Xponent implementation strategy.

File Formats

See discussion on file formats in DDD. In summary, select a format that best fits your platform and use it consistently across your deliverables. Extend the consistency to SRA assignments if possible and the order of new and total Rxs. Select a file format with maximum number of SRA fields and data buckets.

Note: *With NGPS IMS now offers additional format options for weekly and monthly data including options for 4-4-5 calendar month and split-week.*

Level of Data Detail

The lowest level of detail in Xponent is the prescriber or the ZIP code for records not matched to the physician. There is practically no difference in the level of detail for a company's own products and competitor products like in DDD. You are better off with a single copy of the data in your source files at the lowest level of detail and handling the roll ups in-house. For your market definition, all key products should be at the strength level. Generics and secondary products can be at the brand or class level. Consider splitting out mail service, retail and LTC in your data files even though you may show aggregated scripts in the reports.

The Anatomy of the Xponent Record

The typical Xponent record has four sets of fields; report identification, customer or geographic attributes, script data with qualifiers and product. Xponent includes any of all of the following types of records:

- Records matched to prescribers
- Records matched to hospitals
- Encumbered Medco mail service records masked at the specialty/ZIP
- Retail or mail service records matched at the prescriber's ZIP
- Retail records matched to the store ZIP
- Retail or mail service records matched at the patient 3-digit ZIP

Note: *Xponent captures and reports 'hospital outflow' scripts. These are scripts written on a hospital pad but without the physician identifying information they are credited and reported under the hospital name. This is different from drug utilization within a hospital.*

You should familiarize yourself with the characteristics of these record types to be able to identify them and apply your business rules. The key to identifying some these record types is the IMS Prescriber Number which is not a standard field in the file formats but can be added in an SRA field. The first two digits to the IMS Prescriber Number typically reveal the record type. Below is a list of those codes:

Hospital record	:	95 or 96 + 5-digit sequence# (not ZIP)
Physician-ZIP record	:	97 + 5-digit ZIP
Store-ZIP record	:	98 + 5-digit ZIP
Patient-ZIP record	:	99 + 3-digit ZIP
Medco ZIP record	:	NULL or 91 + 5-digit ZIP
Prescriber record	:	Other

* A 3-digit ZIP is a zero right-padded 5-digit ZIP code, i.e. '23100'

The figure below demonstrates a typical Xponent record:

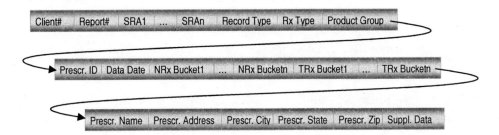

Figure 52. Anatomy of the Xponent record

- The Client and Report Number fields are provided for report identification.

- The SRA fields are assigned typically to customer attributes such as ID, specialty, geographic assignments like the ZIP code, territory, etc. The SRA assignments may vary between files depending on the file contents.
- The Record Type identifies the source of the data captured in the record. A value of '1' indicates prescriptions filled in retail pharmacies, '2' mail service and '3' LTC pharmacies. A physician with prescriptions for a product in all three categories would have three records in Xponent, one for each category. When data for all pharmacy types is aggregated in a single record the record type has a value of '1'.

NOTE: *The retail pharmacy sales should not be confused with the retail channel of distribution. Retail pharmacy sales are only part of the of the retail channel. When querying Xponent use record type 1 for retail pharmacy scripts and record types 1 and 2 for retail channel scripts.*

- The Rx Type field indicates the type of script data included in the record (N: NRx data, T: TRx data, B: Both NRx and TRx data).

- The Product Group identifies the product or collection of products for which data is captured on the record.

The Prescriber ID field includes any of nine types of IDs from different sources depending on the agency that supplied the physician demographics. In most records that ID is the physician's ME number because the AMA provides by far more physician demographics due to its broad membership. When IMS lacks information from one of the typical sources for a prescriber in the database, it assigns them a temporary Prescriber ID. The ID consists of the letter 'I", source code of '99' likely, and its IMS Prescriber Number. A temporary number may look like "I991234567". The temporary number is replaced by an actual one as soon as one of the sources reports the prescriber's information to IMS. The Prescriber ID field values are not unique. Some agencies use similar numbering schemes for member IDs. You must use this ID in conjunction with the Source ID to make the field values unique.

TIP: The ME number is eleven digits long. The last digit is the checksum of the first ten digits and IMS omits it. When matching ME numbers from Xponent with ME numbers from a different source, make sure to base the match on the first 10 digits only.

- The Data Date indicates the most recent data period with data in the file. It is typically a week of month and it is consistently populated in all records in the file. A value of '0105' in a monthly data file indicates that the most recent month with data is January of 2005.

- The typical Xponent file format has two sets of data buckets for new and total Rxs, with the new leading and total trailing. The leftmost bucket of each set represents the most recent data period.

- The Prescriber Name field holds the name of the physician or hospital for physician and hospital records. The physician's first, last and middle initial are concatenated to form a single value string. For other record types, the field may hold constant values depending on the record type. Zip code level data will likely have 'National Assignment' designation in the name field.

- The Prescriber Address field holds the physician or hospital address.

- The Prescriber State field holds the physician or hospital state.

- The Prescriber ZIP field holds the physician or hospital ZIP. The ZIP code may not be populated consistently in Xponent. The ZIP code for records matched at the ZIP is embedded in the IMS Prescriber Number. For Medco records reported at the specialty/ZIP levels it is either embedded in the IMS Prescriber Number or is in a separate SRA field.

TIP: The ZIP is a very important field because the default alignment most likely is based on it. You must correct the inconsistency by selecting and populating a field with the ZIP code for all record types. This should be done early in the processing of data.

- The Supplemental Data field is provided for the manufacturer to pass values to Xponent and have them displayed in reports or returned back through this field in raw data files. If your processes are self-sufficient you will have no use for this field.

There are other non-standard key fields that can be assigned to SRA fields and include the IMS Prescriber Number, Specialty, Source Code and Territory number.

- The IMS Prescriber Number is unique to a physician, hospital or ZIP type. ZIP records are assigned an IMS Prescriber Number for physician, patient and store ZIP code matches.

TIP: If the IMS Prescriber Number is null for Medco records, you can construct it by adding the constant '91' and the 5-digit ZIP. With the IMS Prescriber Number consistently populated you have a unique key for the customer.

- The Specialty Code field holds the prescriber's primary specialty. The code is an abbreviation of the AMA specialty name in most cases. Specialties for NPs and PAs are generally not available.

- The Source Code identifies the agency that provided the prescriber demographics. This code is often concatenated with the abbreviated Specialty Code and assigned to the same SRA field. The Source Code values are shown in figure 53. Source code '99' was introduced for legitimate prescribers for whom the actual source codes have not been determined yet.

- The Territory number for pre-aligned data can be included in an SRA field.

PROCESSING XPONENT DATA

The basic Xponent data structure consists of the prescription file, the product group table and a number of code translation tables for the source codes, specialty codes, record type, Rx type, and IMS Prescriber Number prefixes. The manufacturer alignment and product tables are optional.

The typical Xponent file has all of the customer information embedded in the prescription data file. As a result the customer demographic attributes are repeated for the same physician. Xponent utilizes a relational model for data delivery in which data is normalized.

Figure 53 below demonstrates a typical Xponent data structure:

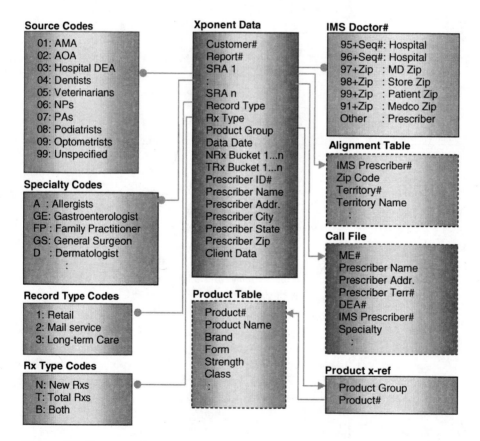

Figure 53. Xponent data structure

The IMS Prescriber Number is an excellent primary key for the data structure. By contrast, the Prescriber Number is only available for physician and hospital records and it is not unique across data sources. It can have for instance the same value for two physicians the demographics of which are provided by two different sources.

The prescriber number is also subject to change making it further unsuitable for data processing applications. There is a hierarchy of precedence when a physician's demographics are reported by multiple sources. A physician's prescriber number may change if a source higher in the hierarchy reports physician demographics previously available through a source with a lower hierarchy.

Because the IMS Prescriber Number is not a standard industry ID, when linking Xponent with external sources you may need to use the ME number or DEA number instead. Conceivably you could use a third party physician-to-hospital affiliation file to link hospital and physician activity to calculate the total hospital account value. The ME number could be used to link the affiliation file to Xponent and the DEA number to DDD.

The diagram below demonstrates the major steps for in-house Xponent data processing:

❶ Geographic alignment of territories must precede exceptions.

❷ This is the first step of the optional call file processing. It overrides addresses and creates records for multiple office locations.

❸ The second step of the call file processing apportions physician prescription activity.

❹ Aggregations at levels above territory in reports must filter out duplicate physician data when using apportioning at higher than 100%.

Figure 54. Alignment, overlays and apportioning

You can align Xponent data geographically using ZIP-to-territory assignments. Prescriber, hospital and ZIP records are aligned to territories based on the ZIP code in the address provided. You can override the default territory by explicitly assigning the physician to a territory. This can be accomplished by maintaining an exception file and assigning IMS Prescriber Numbers to territory numbers. These exceptions must be processed after the geographic alignment has been applied first.

You can maintain a straight physician-to-territory alignment; however, this is a very cumbersome process. Besides, the geographic alignment layer provides a safety net for new prescribers, automatically assigning them to territories based on their ZIP code. Those physicians would otherwise fall into a default unassigned territory.

A physician can be aligned to more than one territory with the use of a call file applied either by the vendor or the manufacturer. The additional addresses provided could be aligned to different territories. The script volume for these physicians may need to be adjusted here based on the apportioning method.

MANAGING XPONENT DATA

Similarly to DDD, the manufacturer must engage in a number of activities to ensure the integrity and flow of Xponent data. The activities center on data quality and designing and maintaining data deliverables. Additionally, the manufacturer should make sure that there is an Xponent implementation strategy that fits the business needs.

Other activities such as new product tracking, price updates and alignments are shared activities with DDD data management. For this reason, the manufacturer's DDD and Xponent data quality measures should be integrated.

Xponent Implementation Strategy

Xponent is more complex in its implementation than DDD due to the high volume of the data, the fact that Xponent is projected, data types, apportioning and physician alignments to name a few. Implementation decisions are certain to have some impact and are better made with data applications in mind and the collaboration of the business groups. The following section discusses the key implementation issues.

NGPS Impact – The enhancements introduced in NGPS leave certain aspects of Xponent intact. Yet, others are so profound that provide the opportunity to reconsider your whole implementation. If you opt for a low impact transition to NGPS, you can practically change nothing and continue with your current implementation virtually unchanged. You can fit the new data in the existing deliverables with potentially the only visible difference some trend changes in the data.

The ultimate solution, however, takes advantage of one key enhancement in NGPS, the common projection of Xponent, Xponent PlanTrak and EarlyView. Because the projections are calculated weekly, you can now switch your reporting to a weekly schedule entirely. In practical terms this means that now there is a weekly version of Xponent and Xponent PlanTrak. Additionally, EarlyView, now compensation grade, is a derivative of weekly Xponent or a mere set of branded reports.

Using a single weekly prescriber and plan level data file you can generate EarlyView-like reports in-house. Using the same data file you can generate Xponent and Xponent PlanTrak reports on a weekly schedule. You can also rollup weeks into months to produce your monthly trend reports. Rollups are possible either on the 4-4-5 or calendar-month basis with the use of additional fields in the data files to capture split weeks.

The consolidation of deliverables reduces significantly the data volume, data archiving and the incoming data feeds from the vendor.

Xponent Application – Although many companies have a great degree of confidence in projected data for applications such as deployment, alignment, targeting, segmentation and retail market share, others treat it with skepticism about its use in quota and compensation applications. Successful implementation of Xponent in quota and compensation means successfully addressing sales reps' concerns about the reliability of the data and answering questions about data completeness and accuracy.

The sales support group should be adequately trained and thoroughly understand the strengths and weaknesses of the data. More importantly you should have procedures correcting and compensating at least the major data anomalies, primarily around specialty and mail service pharmacies. Use the vendor's support to educate sufficiently the office staff. Before rolling out a plan, run and analyze some simulated territory reports and try to anticipate potential questions.

Data Types – Selecting the data type for certain applications is one of the key decisions you will need to make. Xponent is available in script counts and units. Xponent dollars are available, however, they are not calculated based on historical WAC pricing like DDD. The current WAC or manufacturer specified price is used for all current two-year data periods.

As mentioned earlier prescriptions vary in size. The Rx as a unit of measure is important for measuring the physician's action not the quantity of product dispensed. The quantity dispensed for two physicians with the same number of Rxs may vary. Prescribing smaller quantities and refilling more frequently increases script counts but the overall quantity may not exceed less frequently filled, larger quantity prescriptions. Retail Rxs are typically smaller than mail service scripts. The retail to mail service script-size ratio is an important dimension to calculate for products with significant mail service component. You can use it to normalize mail service prescriptions.

Use the quantity if you are interested in volume of product dispensed. When using quantity, keep in mind that Xponent does not provide pack units. Commonly, DDD is in pack units and Xponent in volume units. It is almost certain that analysts will be tempted to compare DDD retail units with Xponent quantity units. To avoid comparisons of incompatible DDD and Xponent units make sure to convert them first to the same basis. The complexity of these conversions depends on the composition of the product groups. Product groups with multiple brands, forms and strengths will be difficult if not impossible to convert.

DDD Retail – When using DDD and Xponent for the same market you will need to consider how to use the DDD retail sales. Showing DDD retail and Xponent in reports leads people to compare the two raising their level of anxiety when the two do not match. Sub-nationally, the two do not represent the same thing due to the 'traveling script' issue and the fact that DDD measures supply and Xponent measures demand.

TIP: Xponent represents the territory performance more accurately and should be used to measure territory performance in the retail market. In any case, avoid showing sales reps both the DDD ZIP retail sales and Xponent scripts at the same time.

For national level data, it is a given that DDD retail must be configured so that the retail sub-categories match those sub-categories included in Xponent to assure a fair comparison. Nationally, DDD retail and Xponent are expected to be close but not necessarily match. Sell-in vs. sell-out, physician alignment, projections and the DDD 4-4-5 calendar affect the comparisons.

Mail service and LTC Data – You will need to decide if and when to show a physician's mail service scripts in reports separately from retail and which applications benefit from the split. The split magnifies the already large data volume by a factor of almost two. Wherever possible, show combined retail and mail service activity to reduce the report size. The physician has little influence on where prescriptions are filled. Similar considerations apply to LTC scripts.

ZIP Level Data – For physician no-matches Xponent captures data at the ZIP code of the physician, the store or the patient. For each ZIP, therefore, there may be up to three separate data records per product group per record type. ZIP data should be included in applications when the total script activity must be demonstrated. The question here is whether there is any actionable value in the split of ZIP data by type. The split here has the potential of tripling the number of ZIP records. In most cases, you will be able to aggregate the ZIP's total activity to a single line of data.

TIP: One approach is to design your deliverables to include mail service split from retail and ZIP records split by type. You can then aggregate the sales in-house for your typical applications. If and when a special application requires split data you can always go back to your original deliverable for it.

Physician Demographics – The prescriber demographics in Xponent are provided by the AMA and other medical boards and very often conflict with other sources or information provided by the sales reps. Prescriber demographics are important because among other things they determine your territory composition; so you need to use the most reliable source available.

You must create a process for address overrides and whatever the source, it should include input from the sales force. Your sales reps have first hand information about a physician's address of practice. They have been there! Your reps are also aware of the physician's other office locations. Xponent provides a single address.

Ideally, you should start with a reliable third party source to obtain the physician demographics for a market and maintain it current going forward with input from the sales reps. For that you should look for newer demographic databases like IMS' HCPS. These databases, however, come with a premium over the cost of Xponent. Older databases that used input from manufacturer field forces, such as IMS' Consortium, are taking now the back seat. Xponent addresses can still be used for investigating new markets or as the default address for physicians you do no have any better information.

TIP: You should encourage the sales reps to participate actively in the maintenance of the physician addresses and provide other office locations for physicians. A good CRM system can aid this process greatly; however, bad implementations of CRM systems can result in chaotic situations of duplicate information. Use the IMS Prescriber Number as an 'anchor' to tie all of the physician demographic data. The Prescriber ID Number field is not unique unless used in combination with the Source ID and can potentially change if the source of demographic information changes.

Call Files - Call files are used in Xponent for address and territory overrides and apportioning. The problem with using call files is the slow implementation time and the fact that they duplicate physicians and, depending on apportioning method, the physician prescriptions in your source files. You must decide if the use of call files is appropriate for you. That will mainly depend on your capabilities to handle address overrides and apportioning in-house. Performing these tasks in-house allows you to maintain control of your processes and keeps your deliverables 'clean' from duplicate data.

Call files may be more appropriately used with weekly prescription data such as EarlyView to limit processing time and deliver data to the field faster. Once the call files are uploaded by the vendor, reports are generated and delivered seamlessly. The compromise is that uploading updated call files takes a few data cycles.

Apportioning – Xponent does not track prescriptions for physicians with multiple practices by location. Xponent credits a single territory allocating the full prescribing activity of the physician at the default address. Apportioning takes care of this problem by introducing one or more additional addresses for the physician and re-allocating his prescribing activity across all office locations. Your allocation options for apportioning are 100% apportioning or even split. In reality, the true contribution of each office location matches neither; however, for practical purposes the above methods are easy to implement.

Apportioning at 100% allows all reps calling on the physician to see the physician's full potential and place them in the right group of importance. This option duplicates total activity at the district level and above as each office location is credited the entire 100% of the prescriber's activity. For compensation purposes, depending on the structure of the plan, this option may overcompensate significantly. Even split apportioning credits all territories calling on the physician equal fractions of the physician's activity, even though most of the activity may be generated by a single territory. This can result in over or under compensation of territories. With even split, unless the rep knows how many ways the activity is split, he cannot calculate the physician's full potential.

TIP: *You may choose either method of apportioning or use both depending on the application. To be able to do that, however, you must keep the source data intact, which means you would apply the call file in house. In that case, you can apportion at any rate other than 100% or even split for certain physicians using factors from databases such as HCPS that weigh addresses based on actual script activity.*

Medco Rxs – Medco accounts for a large portion of the mail service prescriptions in Xponent. Medco data is no longer available at the prescriber level through the special agreements. Medco mail service prescriptions are included in Xponent now only at the ZIP level. However, you do have the option of breaking the data down by specialty within ZIP. This is important for specialty level data applications.

Volume of Data – The volume of the Xponent data depends on the number of prescribers in a given market, the selected options discussed in this section, and the new and total script measures. The volume is challenging when it comes to producing reports. You will need to think of ways to keep report sizes manageable.

One option is to control which physicians appear on the reports. While you are doing that, keep in perspective targeted physicians vs. the physician universe in the given geography. Lines of data with little value at the detail level can be suppressed and replaced by an 'All Other' summary line. Summary lines are important to get to the true total figures used for performance measures. Start by quantifying the data volume problem for your markets and consider options under which the data volume is not destructive but it is not limiting the rep's view of the bigger picture either.

Rounding – Xponent uses decimals for all data types including the Rx counts. That is due to the projections. You simply cannot accurately project and allocate a pharmacy's scripts to prescribers in whole numbers without overstating the results. Data deliverables should be setup with enough decimals to achieve the right precision. For the novice Xponent user, however, a physician having written 2.4 scripts is not an intuitive concept. Therefore, this issue should be given enough consideration before the implementation of a solution.

Data Quality

The vendor has implemented a number of controls to assure the Xponent data quality. Xponent in general requires fewer controls than DDD due to the fact that its history is static and it is projected; therefore, it does not have to account for suppliers and accounts with missing, replacement data, rejects, back data, interrupted data, changed ZIP codes, etc. The manufacturer here again must review the reports generated by the vendor's control systems and determine what action if any must be taken. Below is a list of data quality steps and reports available to the manufacturer.

Xponent Data Management Reports

The Xponent database management reports provide information on the sample make up and confidence levels of alignment geographies. They can help you identify territories with 'thin' sample data in terms of number of stores and physicians. Your action might be to redesign these territories. The vendor uses this information to recruit more stores in areas that are underrepresented in the sample. These reports should be reviewed by the manufacturer periodically and especially after territory re-alignments.

Territory Store Sampling Points – The report provides counts of sampled stores by type and size and the percent of pharmacies covered within the universe of a given territory. Look for territories with percent of sampled stores much below the national average or the immediately higher geography. The report also provides raw counts of NRx and TRx in the sample for a given geography.

Territory Prescriber Sampling Points – The report provides counts of physicians in the universe and counts of physicians with matched prescriptions within a given geography for a specific market. It also provides total number of prescriptions in the universe of the geography. Only part of the physician universe will prescribe a specific product. In fact, that number would vary by market and specialty; therefore, any comparison between sampled physicians vs. the universe is not particularly meaningful. You need to focus on the number of prescribers here. A low number may indicate that the territory is too small.

Confidence Intervals – The market share confidence interval table can be used as a reference to check the accuracy of the market share for a 'suspect' territory. It is based on the projected market share and the volume of the sample prescriptions in the geography. The actual market share lies within the projected market share plus or minus the sampling error with a confidence level of 95%.

The projected volume confidence interval table can be used as a reference to check the accuracy of the projected prescriptions for a territory or district. It is based on volume of projected prescriptions and the percent of stores sampled vs. the universe in a given geography. The actual prescriptions for the geography lie within the projected volume plus or minus the sampling error with a confidence level of 95%.

In both cases, the smaller the sample error is, the smaller the range of potential values and the more accurate the data. For large sales forces analyzing these reports is a long process. Refer to these reports when issues with certain territories arise. They can be used together with the sampling reports to further investigate territories with low sample data.

Data Investigations

Similarly to DDD, a data investigation process should exist to handle field requests and vendor responses. Data investigations may involve simpler inquiries on physician demographics and prescription volumes, and more complex ones related to trend and audit comparisons. Investigated data eventually impacts compensation and ultimately the sales reps. Especially with Xponent inquiries, understanding the nature of the problem is more critical than the fix itself. Xponent corrects only a few types of errors and if you are truly in need of a fix, you may have to make your own manual adjustments.

Physician demographic inquiries can be handled rather easily in Xponent by making changes to the doctor universe database. All address and territory inquiries are easy to investigate and fix in-house, as well, by simply overriding addresses and territories with the correct ones.

For volume inquiries, Xponent can fix certain problems on a going forward basis but makes infrequent changes to history; therefore, leaving most situations unchanged. Xponent treats some cases of misallocation of scripts to the wrong physician by correcting the physician's DEA number in the prescriber universe database. Other cases, such as when a physician's prescriptions are split between two prescribers with very similar names and low physician script volume are not dealt with. You can correct many of the above volume errors in-house by using physician cross-references to re-point the activity to the right physicians.

Call files add one more level of complexity when investigating data inquiries. You must first determine what the vendor reported versus what the call file overrode. Generally, processing the call file in-house affords you a clean dataset from the vendor. The advantage of making corrections in-house is the speed of execution.

Control Totals

The concepts of optimizing your data quality controls and data processing discussed in DDD are applicable here as well. Control totals similar to DDD are available in Xponent and can be used to automate these processes. Refer to DDD for a discussion on this topic.

Report Timing

Many of the concepts discussed in DDD are applicable to Xponent as well. One particular issue you will need to deal with, however, has to do with the fact that DDD and Xponent have different production schedules. This issue can be important enough to override any concerns of how fast the data is delivered.

Your first priority with your vendor should be to synchronize the production of your DDD and Xponent reports so that they are made available at the same time by speeding up the Xponent production. Then you should aim to further reduce the overall time it takes to get the data. It is preferable to produce all reports for the field at the same time rather than sending them out with a lag time of a week or more. Your data processing group appreciates that as well.

TIP: The worst case scenario is to have an asynchronous DDD and Xponent production by the vendor and a synchronous internal data processing so that DDD processing is delayed until Xponent production catches-up. In a situation like that you should process and deliver the two independently from each other. Avoid building processing dependencies in your systems that will prevent you from doing this.

Building Data Deliverables

See the DDD section discussion on data formats, frequency, media, SRA assignments, costs, time periods, market definitions and file codes. These concepts are substantially the same between DDD and Xponent. Following is a discussion of Xponent deliverable specific features:

- **File Formats** – With NGPS Xponent offers both weekly and monthly data with the ability to rollup weekly into monthly. Therefore, a single weekly data file is sufficient for reporting on either schedule. Certain weekly file formats incorporate a split-week feature that allows you to rollup data to monthly buckets either on the 4-4-5 or calendar month basis. Choosing a file format that supports the split week, even if you do not make immediate use of this feature, makes most sense for the system expandability point of view. For that matter, a weekly file format that also supports plan data offers additional advantages. Ultimately, however, as your products and markets are growing, a normalized delivery system like Xponent's WxDM should be your ideal solution.

- **Alignments** - Xponent does not place restrictions on competitor data levels of detail; all of the data is available at the prescriber and ZIP code level. Therefore, unlike DDD TCR reports, Xponent does not have to be pre-aligned. When you align data in-house, you do not have to time your changes with the submission of the alignments to the vendor. Last moment changes can be implemented and reflected in reports immediately.

- **Data Types** – Select from Rx or quantity based on your needs. Special dollar reports can also be produced. For unit reports, determine if factoring is necessary. See previous discussion on DDD vs. Xponent units.

- **Level of Data** – There is virtually no difference in the levels of data between own and competitor data in Xponent. Following along with the concepts discussed in DDD, you may want to build your deliverables at the prescriber and ZIP level and handle all aggregations in-house.

- **Rx Type** – Definitely include both NRx and TRx measures in your source files and use as needed.

- **Record Types** – Include retail, mail service and LTC data for a given market in the same deliverable split by type. This can triple the number of records but it is a very versatile option. You can then filter and aggregate data for your applications as needed.

- **File Codes** – Mirror Xponent file codes with DDD file codes to avoid discrepancies in the market definitions that produce incompatible results. Review and update periodically file codes with new products and product strengths.

XPONENT DATA APPLICATIONS

Xponent has several uses in applications involving prescription data. It is not by any means the most applicable product in all situations considering that the prescription family of products includes a number of other offerings. Xponent being more of a full version, it often offers too much detail or it is too costly for certain business cases. The abbreviated products of NPA® and Prescriber Profiler® work as well or better in those situations saving time and money. In other cases, EarlyView offers standard solutions without the time and effort overhead of dealing with complex and time-critical reporting. The following section discusses the other products in IMS' prescription family and the key applications of Xponent.

Xponent or Prescriber Profiler?

Prescriber Profiler can be thought of as an abbreviated version of Xponent. As the name implies, it profiles prescribers based on their script activity for a specific product, group of products or markets. It provides aggregate 12-month TRxs and physician deciles within each individual selected product and within the selected market. Currently it is based on retail pharmacy scripts only.

What makes Prescriber Profiler unique is its user friendliness, speed and the relatively low cost compared to Xponent. Prescriber Profiler is a web based system using an intuitive front-end interface through which the user enters the report parameters. Free summaries for submitted requests appear instantly and downloads of detailed data for a fee are normally available within a period of one to two days in standard Excel format files.

Prescriber Profiler can be tremendously useful in investigative analysis of existing and new markets. You can perform preliminary analysis of new markets looking into the number of prescribers, prescriber specialty make-up and the value of specific deciles, and at the same time retrieve a list of prescribers with their basic demographic information and script activity. For existing markets, you can profile the prescribing behavior of one or more key market specialties in other drug classes.

Prescriber Profiler allows you to limit your selection to a range of deciles as opposed to the entire list of prescribers. This option limits the volume of unnecessary data and controls the cost of the report which is a function of the number of downloaded prescribers. For that it offers a free summary cross-tab for previewing specialties and the number of prescribers in each decile.

Providing data that is a snapshot in time and in the absence of a historical perspective, Prescriber Profiler is not suitable for trending of any sort. Also, Prescriber Profiler is based solely on scripts and lacks totally the quantity and dollar measures. And until it includes mail service scripts you should consider its applicability in a market with high mail service component. These gaps must inevitably be filled by Xponent which is by far a more complete but costlier solution.

Xponent or EarlyView?

EarlyView belongs in the same family of prescription products as Xponent. Before NGPS, EarlyView was the closest thing to a weekly version of Xponent delivering physician level new and total units and scripts; however, with a major shortcoming. It was not certified for compensation applications and while sales reps were using it for targeting, monthly Xponent reports were still necessary for compensation. With NGPS and the streamlining of script projections EarlyView is more of a branded report than a separate product because it is no longer projected separately and can be produced out of the weekly Xponent. Because it is a by-product of Xponent it is now inherently suitable for compensation.

EarlyView was originally created to track the retail performance of a drug during the critical time around its launch. Soon, it was recognized for its versatility and speed in providing on-going targeting insight and sub-national level prescription trend-monitoring that became the reporting tool to the field. To address the speed of data delivery, IMS has created a production system that delivers script data to the field or the home office with a lag time of ten days from the close of the week. EarlyView produces detailed prescriber reports for territories, districts and regions as well as summary reports at the district level and above that can be delivered directly to the sales reps via email.

The field data is delivered in Excel files and is preformatted in a standard EarlyView design showing the physician demographics, the most recent 13-week script performance of the specified products and a cumulative script activity column. Additionally, a trend indicator evaluates the performance of each product in terms of up, down or static state. Built-in sorting capabilities allow the user to rearrange the information in meaningful ways. To make the reports actionable for the sales reps EarlyView uses cut-off thresholds limiting the number of prescribers in the field reports to the top 200 prescribers per territory, district or region. In that respect, EarlyView reports may not represent the total activity of a territory, district or region. The top prescribers are determined based on the volume of activity of the key product specified. Customarily, companies use abbreviated versions of their markets in EarlyView to reduce the amount of data and allow sales reps to identify the most important bits of information with ease. That often means compromising drug form and strength detail and showing only key competitor products on the field reports. District level data and above may include duplicates when a call file is used and physicians are assigned to more that one territory with 100% apportioning.

The original EarlyView Trend Files were intended for home-office use providing raw weekly prescription data. Trend files do not need to be setup like the field reports, therefore, they may not be limited to top prescribers, use the same product groups like the field reports or use a call file and apportioning. With NGPS the Trend Files are just another form of weekly Xponent reports and they could be redundant if you had another weekly Xponent deliverable.

The combination of a weekly Xponent file and a call file with apportioning information can provide the raw ingredients that make up EarlyView. Companies with the capabilities to rapidly and accurately process data can replicate the EarlyView reports in-house and deliver them to the field almost at the same speed as IMS. The advantage of this is that you can implement alignment changes almost instantly. IMS needs a few data periods to implement an updated call file. On the other hand, if this is not a significant consideration for the customer, then using the reliable, tested EarlyView report engine for the report production and distribution is probably the safest bet.

Xponent or NPA?

The National Prescription Audit (NPA) also belongs in the family of prescription data products of IMS HEALTH offering national level projected script activity. Similarly to NSP, it is more suitable for market research applications providing prescribing activity for any product in the market down to the strength and pack level. Because NPA offers data at higher levels of detail it is more economical product than Xponent. As such, it is typically subscribed for all markets and products, unlike Xponent which is subscribed for specific markets only.

The lowest level of detail in NPA is the prescriber specialty. Currently, however, the specialty is available only for retail pharmacy scripts with all other activity attributed to an unspecified specialty bucket. That is scheduled to change with NGPS and specialty of mail service and LTC scripts will be made available.

Previously projected using its own methodology, NPA now shares the common projection methodology with Xponent. In fact, the new methodology borrowed a key component of NPA's methodology; the census region projections that Xponent uses to reconcile the prescriber projections. A key difference between NPA and Xponent is that while projected mail service is optional in Xponent, it is standard in NPA. NPA does not have to deal with the unpredictability of the mail service store patterns that Xponent is subject to when projecting mail service at the national level. Clearly, because of the mail service projections, NPA can be more complete than Xponent and may offer a more accurate figure if you are looking for total overall script counts.

NPA offers the new and total script and unit data measures of Xponent. The dollar measure of NPA is based on the retail value of the scripts, however. That is the price used by the pharmacy when dispensing a script. Xponent on the other hand, with its limited dollar reporting capabilities, calculates dollars based on WAC which makes it more comparable to retail DDD sales. The retail price of a drug can be significantly higher than the WAC. Consequently, the NPA dollars can be much higher than the manufacturer's retail DDD sales of the product.

NPA provides a number of other measures not available in Xponent that include the average daily consumption, total and average days of therapy, average script size, average authorized refills, dispensed-as-written and substituted counts. The method of payment in weekly NPA breaks down scripts by payment type to Cash-Medicaid-Third Party for individual products or markets. Pharmacy cost and retail price are calculated pricing figures. The first provides the average pharmacy acquisition price for the script while the second the average selling price of the script or the cost to the patient. The retail price is calculated by diving the total retail dollars by the number of scripts.

NPA provides weekly and monthly updates with lag times of ten and seventeen days respectively. Additionally, the rather new NPA Advanced Weekly squeezes the timelines further to offer daily forecasts for predicting the current week's performance. Data is updated daily with data submissions from suppliers and is made available on the web.

For prescriber level detail in compensation, targeting, segmentation, etc., Xponent will always be the first choice. Even at the specialty level Xponent has the advantage of providing physician specialties for mail service and LTC scripts. NPA is the clear choice for investigating new markets for prescription trends and key prescribing specialties. NPA weekly and NPA Advanced Weekly will complement each other in situations with a certain degree of urgency for fresh trend data. That will likely be the case for very recent launches, and for unstable, liquid markets due to a key event or a highly competitive situation. The more fluid the market situation is, the more frequent the desired updates.

NOTE: NPA is used by Wall Street Analysts to monitor prescription trends and the performance of pharmaceutical products and companies. Monitoring what the analysts see through NPA allows the investor relations groups to prepare for their interactions with the analysts.

Prescriber Segmentation and Targeting

Prescription data is the main source of quantitative data for physician segmentation methods. As mentioned in the customer chapter, the simplest way to segment the customer is deciling based on sales; in this case deciling physicians based on number of total scripts.

Deciling treats all physicians in the same segment equally when in fact the physicians may behave very differently. Many of the physicians in the top decile for the whole market may never prescribe your product. As a result, putting maximum effort on those physicians will earn you the maximum negative ROI.

Segmentation is not as critical in markets with small physician specialties because the sales force often has enough capacity to cover every prescriber. If you have, for example, a total of five thousand potential target prescribers, and a sales force of fifty reps making a total of 80,000 calls a year (50 reps x 8 calls/day x 200 days), you can call every physician 16 times during the year. And while you may put a lot of unproductive effort on some, you have covered sufficiently your best targets. Reducing the number of reps is not always an option because below a threshold the size of the territory increases enough so that the rep spends more time traveling than selling.

On the other end of the spectrum, using deciling alone to select your targets out of a large number of prescribers is very risky. Not only you could put a lot of unproductive effort on the wrong physicians, but you also incur a huge opportunity cost because you did not put any or enough effort on others.

In that case you must take segmentation to the next level and look into the prescribing behavior of the physician. By analyzing past prescribing activity you can determine the physician's tendencies for brand loyalty or brand switching, concentrating activity on one or more products or spreading the activity between several brands.

If you are launching a new product, by analyzing the activity around periods of past product launches, you can determine if the physician is likely to be an early or late adopter, and whether they will be in the early or late majority of adopters. To build sales momentum, knowing the physician's prescribing behavior, you may want to concentrate on early adopters, switchers and spreaders first. This will likely upset the decile order with physicians moving up or down the list, but it is part of the optimization of your targeting.

While Xponent can reveal the physician's past prescribing behavior it does not provide reasons for that behavior. It is important to keep in mind that what may appear as a physician preference or choice may actually be the work of managed care or other alliance, such as a group practice or IDN that enforces a formulary. What might appear a cost-conscious physician may be a practitioner giving in on the pressure of plans for generic usage. In other cases, spreading of activity is the result of patients failing other therapies.

Ideally, the physician's affiliations should be analyzed to determine how his behavior is influenced. If formularies are an obstacle, the physician will remain a good target on paper but will not prescribe until you achieve a favorable status for your drug with the physician's top plans.

Up to this level segmentation can be completed relatively easy. Explaining, however, the physician's true behavior requires that you take segmentation to an even higher level by analyzing the physician's psychographic profile. The complexity here is that the physician psychographic data is not readily available but must be collected through primary research. Predictive models are used here to apply sample data collected to the universe of prescribers. This method tries to exploit clues about a physician's perceptions, values and traits that allow you to place him in a similar group of physicians. Some of the key areas that psychographic analysis focuses are sensitivity to cost, social interactions, adoptability to technology, perception to medical advancements, etc. This segmentation method is gaining a lot of popularity.

Physician demographics are applicable at any level of segmentation adding a new dimension to your analysis. At this point, having defined the segments with one or more of the above methods and creating a profile for each segment from its key characteristics, marketing develops the appropriate targeting messages for each segment.

Deployment and Alignment

Prescription data is one of the main data sources for deployment and alignment applications for markets with some retail component. The size of the sales force is partly determined by the number of targeted prescribers calculated through the physician segmentation exercise and the call frequencies required.

The non-retail component of the market affects the sales force structure and the total sales force size. Physician alignment is typically geographic based on the physician's ZIP code. However, there are two complicating factors; inaccuracies in AMA addresses and physician multiple office locations. Aligning a physician on the wrong address may place the physician in the wrong territory. While you can correct the prescriber's address and re-align them at a later time, you will disturb the balance of the territories. Similarly, adding second office locations after the alignment exercise is completed will add to the territory workload. These issues should be resolved prior to executing the alignment.

In markets you are operating in you must have a wealth of information on physician addresses and multiple office locations through field input captured by the company's CRM system. For new markets, vendors offer multiple ranked addresses and 'best address' databases for prescribers that can be used to correct AMA addresses and pick additional office locations. IMS' HCPS discussed earlier is one such database.

Quota and Compensation

Prescription data is very suitable for quota and compensation applications in the retail segment, primarily because it solves the 'traveling script' problem. Sales data like DDD favor territories with high concentration of pharmacies. Depending on the geographic dynamics, some pharmacies are 'pulling' business away from neighboring territories. Xponent 'pushes' back sales to the territory of the prescribing physician correcting the problem.

Territories where this situation happens typically have a wide gap between their DDD retail sales and prescription data with some territories having high pharmacy sell-in and low script count and vice versa. In this case, it is the prescription data that reflects accurately the sales activity while DDD shows a distorted view.

Territory alignment can artificially create the traveling script situation in several instances. In the case of physicians with multiple office locations, Xponent allocates all of the physician's activity to a single location. Depending on how you align the physician, you may be pulling scripts away from one territory and onto another, widening the gap between DDD and script data. Even when you apportion the activity equally, because the actual split of scripts is probably other than 50/50, you have a shift of scripts from one territory to another. Figure 55 demonstrates this case.

In the case of physicians with a single office location, aligning on the wrong physician address that happens to be outside the territory will shift scripts between territories. This is likely to happen early on when entering a new market or with physicians whose addresses have not yet been verified by the sales reps. Proper alignment and apportioning can solve the problem here.

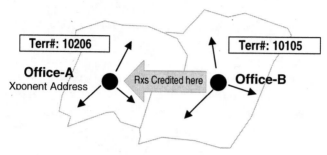

Figure 55. Multiple physician offices

With Xponent you can set your year-over-year growth, market share and commission script-based compensation plans like in DDD. Refer to the discussion in DDD for more information. In general, completeness is not an issue for retail pharmacies and LTC providers because the data is projected. Completeness is a problem with mail service pharmacies. See previous discussion on the topic.

Inaccuracies in script allocations to physicians are not a problem in quota and compensation applications as long as the prescriptions are allocated to other physicians within the territory. Accuracy is a problem, however, in situations where physicians are not in the sample or are underweighted in the sample and their prescriptions are partly projected to physicians aligned to an adjacent territory. See earlier discussion in the retail specialty pharmacy section. Because script history does not change or adjust like DDD, recalculating quota is not necessary with script plans, except for realignments and when there are new targets added to the territory.

The lack of history adjustments for new mail service data suppliers in Xponent, however, is rather problematic. The case can be well demonstrated in the following scenario where hypothetically we are using the pharmacy's DDD sell-in in a shared pool to compensate reps and in the middle of the compensation period the status of the pharmacy changes to reporting. Suddenly the DDD sell-in disappears because it is replaced with the ZIP level sell-out in DDD retail and the pool allocation is no longer feasible. On the Xponent side meanwhile, the account's current script activity starts to trickle-in. This data is incomplete and likely disproportionate to the quota the reps are credited with. Ideally, you need the full Xponent history to reallocate the appropriate quota to each territory and accurately calculate their current performance.

Other scenarios of handling non-reporting mail service pharmacies are likely to lead to the same problem, which incidentally occurs very frequently given the pace by which IMS signs up new mail service suppliers. IMS cites the unavailability of the data as a reason for not incorporating it in Xponent; however, the historical data exists in some kind of form in order to be brought into the DDD retail. This Xponent limitation is serious enough to warrant a solution even if that meant bringing the historical data in Xponent at the ZIP level.

TIP: You are almost better off bringing these suppliers into your deliverables at the start of a new quarter or the start of a new compensation period. Refer to recent DDD files for the sell-in of newly reporting mail service pharmacies.

Calculating Total Account Performance

Generally, DDD is used to evaluate the performance of non-retail accounts and Xponent is used to evaluate the prescription activity in the retail sector. However, in many cases the total account performance has both retail and non-retail components. A hospital, for example, may purchase a certain drug but may have prescriptions for the same drug filled in retail pharmacies for discharged patients. Therefore, a hospital's total performance should be:

Total Hospital$ = DDD Sales + Hospital Outflow Rxs

The hospital's Rxs in Xponent are captured under its DEA number, which can be used to cross-reference the hospital to DDD and its DDD sales. You can take this a step further and add prescriptions written by affiliated physicians to the hospital performance. This step requires a good physician-to-hospital affiliation list. The formula now changes to:

Total Hospital$ = DDD Sales + Hospital Outflow Rxs + Affiliated MD Rxs

Physician offices and clinics in general may or may not dispense drugs, dispense certain drugs but not others or partly dispense and partly fill scripts in retail pharmacies. It is possible to calculate the total performance of clinics and physician offices using physician-to-clinic and group-practice affiliations to integrate the account's DDD sales and prescription activity.

TIP: Earlier sources of physician affiliation data depended on association or organization membership information. They were at best of average-to-good quality. Newer sources use claims data extensively and are more reliable. The challenge with affiliation data is keeping it current. The combination of external database and sales force input is perhaps the best approach to maintaining good prescriber-to-account affiliations.

Effort and Result Analysis

The most insightful information you can derive from your prescription data perhaps is how the physician responds to your promotional efforts such as physician calling, speaker programs, sampling, symposia and special events. By overlaying script data from Xponent, call activity and other event data you can look for changes in the physician's prescribing behavior. You can identify the non-responsive physicians and redirect effort to others.

At the territory level, the analysis can identify those territories with low results-to-effort performance and try to troubleshoot potential problems or learn from high performance territories. You can improve your ROI by placing the right effort to the right targets.

You can also optimize your marketing messages to your segments using this kind of analysis. Custom messages are developed for each group from the segmentation exercise. You will not know how effective the messages are with the particular segment until you analyze the group's prescribing activity changes after the message was delivered. The messages can be varied until you get favorable responses.

TIP: *The key to efforts and results analysis is good input, which comes down to three things - type of event, date and participant or recipient. Again here, your CRM application is the key system for the collection of that information. Product milestones such as the release of a major study should be recorded on the timeline because these events can compound the impact.*

Chapter 7
Xponent
PlanTrak
Data

XPONENT® PLANTRAK™ DATA

Xponent PlanTrak is an extension of Xponent adding one more dimension to it - the payer of the prescription. It captures the level of reimbursement payers provide for each drug in your markets measured in number of scripts, quantity and dollars.

In our customer discussion, we placed the payer in the influencer tier because the payer does not play a direct role in the execution of the sales transactions being neither the seller nor the buyer, with the exception of the staff-model HMOs. The payer here can be any managed care or employer plan, Medicaid and Medicare. Cash-paying customer transactions that include uninsured, not-covered by a plan, or indemnity plan reimbursed cases are captured under the generic title 'Cash'.

Xponent PlanTrak captures the payer data at the physician level. Essentially, it takes a physician transaction in Xponent and breaks it down to several transactions, one for each plan having paid for at least one script. The similarities of Xponent and Xponent PlanTrak are such that you could practically bypass Xponent entirely and use Xponent PlanTrak for all purposes.

What is the Source of Xponent PlanTrak?

The source of the Xponent PlanTrak data is the same as that of Xponent. A large sample of retail pharmacy data is collected and used to project the remaining.

Essentially, the difference between the two comes down to one data element, the plan ID, derived from the sample data. It enables the breakdown of the script data in Xponent to the plan level. Mail service data is available in Xponent PlanTrak un-projected like in Xponent, with one caveat; plan level information for these scripts is not available. Plan data is not available for LTC scripts either.

What is the Importance of Xponent PlanTrak?

Xponent PlanTrak helps you explain certain physician prescribing behaviors that cannot otherwise be explained in Xponent. That is, why certain physicians do not respond to any targeting activities and for that matter, why others do at varying degrees.

Given the state of managed care, the physician's prescribing activity is influenced by their plan affiliations and subject to reimbursement limits imposed by the plans. A physician affiliated with plans having un-favorable formularies for your product will avoid prescribing it even if they think favorably about it. Xponent PlanTrak helps you identify the physician's plan affiliations, which combined with plan formulary data will allow you to identify the prescriber's limitations to prescribe your product. Realizing the constraints with these physicians you can work together with the corporate accounts team to overcome them.

Physicians receive influences from many plans by virtue of providing patient care for several of them. It is, however, the influence of those for which they prescribe most often that matter more. In many cases, influences from the dominant plans will work synergistically and there will be a spillover affect in the physician's overall activity. Physicians tend to extend their prescribing habits across all plans. Identifying and addressing formulary issues with dominant plans should be a priority.

Using Xponent PlanTrak and plan formulary data you can evaluate the physician's compliance with a plan's formulary. Logically, you would expect a physician to prescribe a product with a more favorable formulary status more often. That does not always happen and it will be particularly important to you when your product holds the most favorable status. Lastly, Xponent PlanTrak can help you identify differences in a physician's prescribing behavior for his cash, Medicaid and managed care reimbursed prescriptions.

TIP: Physician segmentation ideally should take into consideration physician-to-plan affiliations and plan formularies, although frequent changes in formularies could result in constant reconfiguration of your target lists.

XPONENT PLANTRAK PROJECTION

Before NGPS Xponent and Xponent PlanTrak were projected separately with Xponent PlanTrak projected from a subset of the Xponent sample data. The key characteristic of the projections were the different results they yielded in terms of total projected scripts for a prescriber. IMS justified the two methodologies based on the distinct objectives of the two products; the prescriber influence in the case of Xponent and the plan influence in the case of Xponent PlanTrak.

With NGPS both products are projected using the same methodology and the same sample producing the same value for a prescriber. This along with the availability of weekly data now changes drastically the logistics around data management and processing. The key improvement to Xponent PlanTrak as a result of NGPS is the enhanced process of identifying and projecting restricted managed care plans.

XPONENT vs. XPONENT PLANTRAK

What sets Xponent and Xponent PlanTrak apart is the customer. Both Xponent and Xponent PlanTrak measure physician performance, however, Xponent PlanTrak goes further to track a second type of customer; the payer. Xponent PlanTrak is applicable for all products and markets where managed care has some level of influence.

The managed care type of customer is defined hierarchically in Xponent PlanTrak. In the center of it is the payer. The payer is an organization with the financial responsibility of reimbursing the healthcare provider and therefore, of great importance. Payers were generally bucketed in three broad categories: cash, Medicaid and Third Party until Medicare Part D was introduced in January of 2006. Cash paying patients are payers with 100% out of pocket expense and account for a little more than 10% of all retail spend. Some of that activity may be reimbursed by an indemnity plan with a subsequent claim, nevertheless, this is considered cash business. The Medicaid bucket, with a little more than 15% of the retail spend includes spend only for directly reimbursed scripts as Medicaid signs ups a lot of patients with third party plans. In fact, all of Medicare Part D business is contracted to Third Party payers. The Third Party category includes all other payers with some level of cost control. That includes uninsured cash patients using discount cards.

To manage efficiently its business, especially when it operates over a large geographic area, the payer creates local coverage plans whose reach may be limited to part of a state or extend into several states. The plans are given various degrees of autonomy by the payer. Plans with greater levels of autonomy in benefit design are progressively more important to the manufacturer.

For the management of its drug benefit business, the payer assigns the responsibility to processors or PBMs. The difference of the two is in the level of service they provide to the payer with the PBM providing a more comprehensive suite of services. For this discussion we will use the term PBM to refer to both processors and PBMs. When the PBM's responsibility includes drug benefit design, the PBM is more important to the manufacturer. The PBM could be a business unit of the payer or an independent organization. A payer may use more than one PBM to service its plans; however, in Xponent PlanTrak there is a one-to-one relation between a plan and a PBM.

Independent PBM organizations serve more than one payer typically and supersede the payer in hierarchy. The vendor collects data on the payer-to-plan and payer-to-PBM relationships directly from the payers. The supplemental customer tables provided by the vendor depict these relationships so that you can navigate up and down the hierarchy. For example, you can identify the payer and the PBM of a given plan, or all of the affiliated plans and PBMs of a payer, or all the payers and their plans for a PBM.

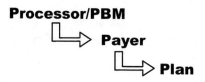

Figure 56. Customer hierarchy

Ideally, for every script in Xponent PlanTrak the vendor should identify the PBM, the payer and the plan. However, the level of difficulty for identifying the customer increases from the top of the hierarchy down. As a result, the PBM is visible in more Xponent PlanTrak transactions than the payer, which in turn is more visible than the plan.

The value of the data is higher when the PBM, payer and plan of the script are identified as opposed to identifying only the PBM and payer or just the PBM. This is particularly important for plans that make formulary decisions independently. Even in cases where the decisions are made by the payer or the PBM the granularity of the plan data is still relevant. IMS decodes approximately 60% of the data to the payer/plan level.

A PBM's activity is measured as the total activity of all the payers and plans it serves plus any of its activity not attributable to a payer. Similarly, a payer's activity is measured as the total activity of all its plans plus any of its activity not attributable to a plan. Payers and PBMs are identified by a 6-digit payer ID and plans by the parent payer ID plus a 4-digit plan ID.

PBMs have payer IDs starting with '7' with at least two plans underneath them. A plan ID of '0001' holds the PBMs activity not attributable to a specific payer/plan. A dummy plan ID of '9999' is created by default but it holds no data. Sometimes IMS is able to break down and bucket a PBM's activity by payer or plan without necessarily being able to identify them by name. In cases like that Xponent PlanTrak will isolate and attribute the activity to separate plans under the PBM. These plans are referred to as a PBM's 'Book of Business' and their plan numbers increment starting with "0002". Not all PBMs have 'Book of Business' plans in Xponent PlanTrak. The number of 'Book of Business' plans under a PBM depends on the PBM's size and volume of business with the plans it serves. The idea of the 'Book of Business' is that as the plan identity is eventually revealed their activity can be separated and stated under their own payer/plan ID.

Scripts matched to a specific plan are assigned to the plan's 10-digit payer/plan ID. Scripts with the payer identified but not the plan are assigned to an 'unspecified' bucket with the payer's 6-digit ID and a plan ID of '9999'. All other third party payer scripts not matched at any level are assigned a payer number of '888888' and plan number '0001'.

Cash-paid scripts are reported under the payer code '000001' and pure Medicaid under the payer code '000002'. Previously Medicaid data for all states was aggregated and reported under a single plan of '0001'. Now it is reported separately for each state with the same payer number and plan IDs assigned to each state starting with '0002'. Plan '9999' now holds any remaining data not attributable to a state.

Typically the plan information for mail service data is not known. As a result, all mail service scripts are assigned to a generic payer ID of '000581'. VA scripts filled in contracted retail pharmacies are captured under a single payer ID of '001027'. DOD scripts on the other hand are captured separately for each Tri-Care region. They have a payer ID of '000090' and plan IDs starting with '0001'. Under a new numbering scheme, Blue Cross and Blue Shield plans have now unique payer IDs. Unspecified Blue Cross and Blue Shield activity is captured under payer number '000030' and plan '9999'. To aggregate now Blue Cross and Blue Shield activity you must look for the abbreviation of "BC/BS" in the plan name.

Managed Medicaid data is reported under the third party payer/plan codes of payers contracted to serve Medicaid patients. Some third party payers have dedicated plans for their Medicaid business. These plans have a plan model type of 'MEDICAID'. For other payers their Medicaid business is practically indistinguishable from their third party business. Model type 'MEDICARE' is reserved for Managed Medicare plans.

The 'MGD MEDI' model type was originally intended for Managed Medicaid and Managed Medicare plans. With the introduction of 'MEDICAID' and 'MEDICARE' model types the use of the 'MGD MEDI' is now limited to plans that cannot be exclusively attributed to Managed Medicaid, Managed Medicare or 'CHIP' (Children's Health Insurance Program) plans.

Medicare Part D scripts are captured under plan model types 'MED PDP', 'MED ADV', 'MED ADVG', 'MED PDPG', 'MED SNP', 'MED SNPG' and 'MED UNSP'. Some Medicare Part B scripts are filled in retail pharmacies and reimbursed by the medical plan and are captured under model type 'MED B'. The approved Medicare cards used before Medicare Part D was introduced were phased out in May of 2006 and have a model type of "DISC MED".

General discount cards have a model type of 'DISC CRD'. Senior cards specifically designed for the elderly have a model type of 'SR CRD' and are not Medicare approved. All discount cards have unique payer/plan IDs. Pharmacy issued discount cards are usually good for select products from select manufacturers. Manufacturer issued discount cards are good for all or some of the manufacturer's products only. Even though discount card scripts are paid cash by the patient, they are attributed to Third Party due to the cost management. Voucher programs are captured under a single payer/plan ID of '001367' and have a plan type of "VOUCHER". Vouchers are issued by the manufacturer through the physicians or DTC programs and redeemed at the pharmacy by the patient.

Other special payer types include State Managed Care with a payer number of '555555' and State Assistance Programs with payer number of '666666'. State Managed Care plans are pharmacy benefit carve-outs for state operated plans. State Assistance Programs are Welfare and other state funded programs. Both have relatively low level of script activity. Their plan types are "MGD MEDI" and 'STATE ASST' respectively and they are captured under the Third Party bucket of the method of payment.

TIP: IMS provides documentation on model type definitions. The definitions change frequently. Make sure to obtain an updated copy periodically. Model types are useful for querying Xponent PlanTrak and creating custom versions of method of payment reports; for example, estimating government business by extracting its managed portion from the Third Party bucket.

NOTE: A distinction should be made between cash-paying and uninsured patients. Indemnity insurance patients usually fall in the 'Cash' category having to advance payment for drugs and get reimbursed at a later time. Third Party patients are not necessarily insured either. Uninsured patients fall in the 'Third Party' category when they use a drug discount card of any kind.

The Look of Xponent PlanTrak Data

The visible difference between Xponent and Xponent PlanTrak is in the plan level detail for the prescriber's retail pharmacy scripts. Figure 57 demonstrates an example of a prescriber's plan level data. In a typical case, there will be a data line for the prescriber's scripts paid by cash and one for the Medicaid reimbursed scripts, followed by several lines of third party plan scripts. The example below shows three third party plans including a PBM. That number can vary greatly depending on the physician's contracted relationships and his patient base.

0000120432	Dr. Joe Doe	prodA
❶	❷	❸
000001 0001	Cash	5 TRxs
000002 0001	Medicaid	10 TRxs
000123 0050	Plan1	20 TRxs
000456 0040	Plan2	13 TRxs
700021 0001	PBM3	10 TRxs

❶ A physician's plan-level transactions are reported at the 10-digit payer/plan codes

❷ Cash and typically Medicaid require a single transaction each while there are a number of third party plan transactions per physician in Xponent PlanTrak

❸ Using the same metrics as Xponent, each plan's activity is quantified individually

Figure 57. Plan data detail

XPONENT PLANTRAK DATA COMPLETENESS

The concepts discussed in the 'Xponent Data Completeness' section hold true with Xponent PlanTrak. There are, however, additional considerations with Xponent PlanTrak. The first relates to the availability of the data at the lowest level of detail, which is the physician-plan. To get to this level, the vendor must identify hierarchically the processor or PBM handling the transaction, the payer and the plan. The implication of this is that the breakdown of a physician's prescribing activity is not always a local plan but a payer or a PBM. This is not ideal for applications because the true value of local plans cannot be quantified.

Presently Xponent PlanTrak identifies the payer or plan for approximately 60% of the third party scripts. The great majority of the remaining 40% are reported as PBM scripts and a small portion of it generically as 'All Other Third Party".

Another consideration of data completeness is the availability of plan data for all 24 months of current data in the deliverables. Similarly to Xponent, Xponent PlanTrak does not adjust history. When a new plan code is identified for a plan previously reported as plan-unspecified, its scripts are reported from that point on leaving history unchanged. Therefore, the plan appears to have partial data when in reality the 'missing' data is aggregated with other plan-unidentified data. The vendor provides tables with the availability of plan data by month for the 24 months of current data.

XPONENT PLANTRAK DATA ACCURACY

The concepts of accuracy discussed back in Xponent are applicable to Xponent PlanTrak with an additional consideration for the plan specific data.

That is the reliability of using the script volume literally, given that data for certain plans in the sample is very 'thin' and when broken down by physician the numbers are very anemic. The vendor is using a three level rating system to indicate the data quality for each plan as shown below:

- V: The script volume is reliable
- S: The Market share is reliable but not the absolute script volume
- NR: Not Rated. The volume and market share are not reliable

Numerical sub-ratings of 1,2,3... further classify and limit the reliability of the data of 'V' and 'S' rated plans within levels of data detail such as physician, territory, product, market, etc. The vendor plan data ratings should be taken into consideration when using Xponent PlanTrak in data applications. Special attention should be given to applications like compensation with direct and immediate financial implications.

XPONENT PLANTRAK REPORTS

Xponent PlanTrak can only be mined adequately electronically so this discussion will focus on raw data files.

The Anatomy of the Xponent PlanTrak Record

The typical file layouts of Xponent and Xponent PlanTrak are almost identical, with Xponent PlanTrak having an additional field for the plan name. The level of detail for Xponent PlanTrak is physician by plan, with no restrictions for competitor data.

The figure below demonstrates a typical Xponent PlanTrak record:

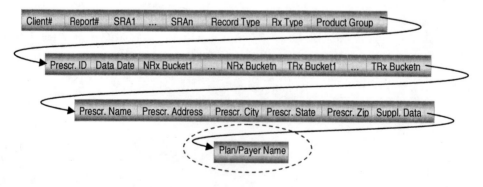

Figure 58. Anatomy of Xponent PlanTrak record

The plan/payer ID is added in one of the SRA fields. The payer is represented by a 6-digit code. Special payer numbers are reserved for the following categories of payers:

000001	Cash
000002	Medicaid
000003+	Managed Care Plans
555555	State Managed Care
666666	State Assistance Programs
700001+	Processors/PBMs
888888	All Other Third Party

A 4-digit sequence code is assigned to the plans. The special sequence code of '9999' is reserved for 'Unspecified' plan data. The payer and plan IDs provide the links to the supplemental payer/plan demographics provided by the vendor. For more information on the other data fields refer to the Xponent record discussion in the previous chapter.

PROCESSING XPONENT PLANTRAK DATA

Part of the Xponent PlanTrak data structure is almost identical to the Xponent data structure. That structure is extended using the payer/plan ID to include plan, payer and PBM demographics and plan data ratings provided by the vendor. Optionally, you can further extend the structure with physician-to-plan affiliations, additional plan demographic and formulary data provided by third party vendors or collected through the field staff.

The key to these extensions is the payer/plan ID supplied in one of the SRA fields. This is an IMS ID and external databases must provide the compatibility with it.

The diagram in figure 59 shows the basic Xponent PlanTrak data structures:

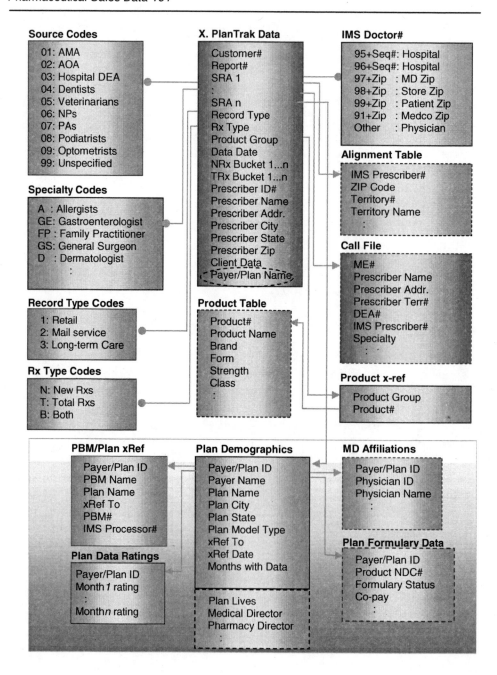

Source Codes

01: AMA
02: AOA
03: Hospital DEA
04: Dentists
05: Veterinarians
06: NPs
07: PAs
08: Podiatrists
09: Optometrists
99: Unspecified

Specialty Codes

A : Allergists
GE: Gastroenterologist
FP : Family Practitioner
GS: General Surgeon
D : Dermatologist
   :

Record Type Codes

1: Retail
2: Mail service
3: Long-term Care

Rx Type Codes

N: New Rxs
T: Total Rxs
B: Both

X. PlanTrak Data

Customer#
Report#
SRA 1
  :
SRA n
Record Type
Rx Type
Product Group
Data Date
NRx Bucket 1...n
TRx Bucket 1...n
Prescriber ID#
Prescriber Name
Prescriber Addr.
Prescriber City
Prescriber State
Prescriber Zip
Client Data
Payer/Plan Name

Product Table

Product#
Product Name
Brand
Form
Strength
Class
  :

IMS Doctor#

95+Seq#: Hospital
96+Seq#: Hospital
97+Zip : MD Zip
98+Zip : Store Zip
99+Zip : Patient Zip
91+Zip : Medco Zip
Other   : Physician

Alignment Table

IMS Prescriber#
ZIP Code
Territory#
Territory Name
  :

Call File

ME#
Prescriber Name
Prescriber Addr.
Prescriber Terr#
DEA#
IMS Prescriber#
Specialty
  :

Product x-ref

Product Group
Product#

PBM/Plan xRef

Payer/Plan ID
PBM Name
Plan Name
xRef To
PBM#
IMS Processor#

Plan Data Ratings

Payer/Plan ID
Month 1 rating
   :
Month n rating

Plan Demographics

Payer/Plan ID
Payer Name
Plan Name
Plan City
Plan State
Plan Model Type
xRef To
xRef Date
Months with Data

Plan Lives
Medical Director
Pharmacy Director
   :

MD Affiliations

Payer/Plan ID
Physician ID
Physician Name
   :

Plan Formulary Data

Payer/Plan ID
Product NDC#
Formulary Status
Co-pay
   :

Figure 59. Xponent PlanTrak data structures

You can align Xponent PlanTrak data geographically using ZIP-to-territory assignments. Physicians are aligned to territories based on the ZIP code of the address provided. You can override the default territory by explicitly assigning the physician to a territory. This can be accomplished by maintaining an exception file and assigning IMS Prescriber Numbers to territory numbers. These exceptions must be processed after the geographic alignment has been applied first. You can maintain a straight physician-to-territory alignment, however, the geographic layer provides a safety net for new prescribers that otherwise would fall into a default unassigned territory.

A physician can be aligned to more than one territory with the use of a call file, applied either by the vendor or the manufacturer. The additional addresses provided could be aligned to different territories.

Plans are handled typically by corporate account managers that call on the plans. You can assign plans to account managers at the payer or local plan level. That depends on the decision making process of the payer. When formulary decisions are made locally or regionally you will need to assign the local or regional plans to managers; otherwise, you will probably need to assign the payer and its plans as a whole to the manager. Plans operate across multiple territories and typically are not directly aligned to sales reps. You may instead attribute specific plan activity to sales reps through the physicians aligned to their territories.

Geographic alignment of accounts is possible based on the operating state of the plans; however, this alignment works better for small local plans. Aligning certain plans of payers operating in multiple states to managers geographically would be meaningless if the plans had no decision making authority.

MANAGING XPONENT PLANTRAK DATA

Implementing Xponent PlanTrak

The considerations for implementing Xponent PlanTrak are substantially the same as those of Xponent because of the similarities of the two products. For information on these considerations refer to the Xponent discussion. The following section discusses some additional considerations unique to Xponent PlanTrak.

NGPS, Xponent and Xponent PlanTrak

Before NGPS, perhaps the most challenging aspect of Xponent PlanTrak implementation was how to handle the Xponent and Xponent PlanTrak variance that the two projection methodologies produced and making it transparent to the users. With NGPS and the introduction of a common projection methodology for both products this is not an issue any longer. Instead, an opportunity has risen to change quite drastically the implementation of the two products.

First, the availability of weekly Xponent PlanTrakdata data provides the opportunity for weekly reporting now. Second, Xponent PlanTrak encompasses entirely Xponent being a broader product than Xponent. Without the valiances between the two products you can now produce Xponent straight out of an Xponent PlanTrak deliverable, therefore, allowing for the consolidation of multiple input data streams into one. Both options are worth pursuing given the importance of speedy data delivery to the field as well as the efficiencies gained from streamlining data processing.

Merged Plan Data

Plan mergers are common occurrence impacting your plan data. When two plans merge, Xponent PlanTrak captures and reports the consolidated activity of the two plans under the acquiring plan from the time of the merge forward. If for example, Plan-A acquires Plan-B, the activity of Plan-A after the merger will be the sum of the activities of Plan-A and Plan-B, while Plan-B ceases to have any new activity. In certain circumstances Plan-A and Plan-B result in an entirely new Plan-C.

Your decision here has to do with the pre-merger data, considering always the serious data volume issue and report sizes. Your choices are to keep the prescription history for the two plans separately as Plan-A and Plan-B, referred to by the vendor as the 'old view', or merge it as Plan A+B, referred to as the 'new view'. You can accomplish this either by setting up your data deliverables accordingly or in-house by record cross-referencing.

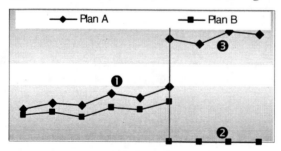

❶   Pre-merger Plan-A and Plan-B activity
❷   Acquired Plan-B shows no post-merger activity
❸   Acquiring Plan-A is credited with all post-merger activity

Figure 60. 'Old View' of merged plan data

In the first case, as shown in the figure above, the historical data for Plan-B is kept in a separate record until there is no activity for the last 24 months, at which time it drops off the dataset. This situation raises usually the question 'why the sudden drop in the Plan-B activity?', which can be answered by the higher activity of Plan-A.

In the second case, as shown in the figure below, the activity of Plan-B is removed from the data while the activity of Plan-A is adjusted higher to the sum of the activity of Plan-A and Plan-B. While this option works best in the long run, you must take the proper steps to explain the 'disappearance' of the acquired Plan-B.

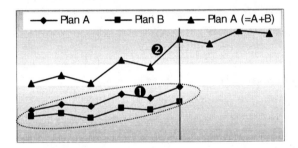

❶   Pre-merger Plan-A and Plan-B activity replaced with aggregate as Plan-A

❷   Acquiring Plan-A is credited with all pre and post-merger activity

Figure 61. 'New View' of merged plan data

In either of the above cases, given that all of the current activity is credited to Plan-A, if the two merging plans were assigned to different corporate account managers, they both must now be assigned to one. This may require certain adjustments to the compensation plans and goals of the corporate account managers involved. In the long run, there is no real benefit from showing the Plan-B record and the drawback with this option is that the extra record contributes to higher data volume.

TIP: Following up with the theme of getting the source data at the lowest level and rolling it up in-house as needed, you should consider getting Xponent PlanTrak with the pre-merger data split out and report it in consolidated form on reports using merged plan cross-references. This allows you to address field questions for pre-merger data.

Plan Data Volume

Xponent PlanTrak exaggerates an already big data volume problem with Xponent. Depending on your Xponent setup, you may have up to three records per product group for each physician for his retail, mail service and LTC Rxs. In Xponent PlanTrak each retail data record may be broken down to several plan records to capture the cash, Medicaid, Medicare and Third Party scripts.

In addition to the considerations for managing data volume, discussed in Xponent, you must consider limiting the transaction volume for plan data. Simply, low volume plans do not add significant insight about a physician's prescribing habits. Consolidating these records under an "All Other Plans' header can significantly reduce report space.

You can use number of records or script volume thresholds to accomplish this. For example, you can show individually only the physician's top five plans. Alternatively, you may show only plans whose total 12-month script volume exceeds some value. Given the territory differences, setting the script volume threshold can be challenging. Also, the way you determine the top five plans or the volume threshold is important. Using the market totals to rank the plans will surely give you different results than using your product totals. The top five plans based on market volume may force down the rank your top five plans. For territories, districts and regions the number of listed plans should be increased progressively to avoid excluding influential plans.

TIP: With electronic reports the volume of data and print volume issues go away; however, the issue of important and actionable information remains. You can provide the drill-down capability to reach very low levels of data but at higher levels you need to display only the essential information. You should not resort to information overload just because you have the capability. For example, strength level plan data is good but not critical when considering plan influences, since plans typically cover in their formularies entire brands.

Prescriber level data is valuable; however, broken down by plan the numbers could be so 'thin' that make trends almost meaningless. On the other hand, territory level data is most of the times suitable for trend analysis. When data for shorter data periods is anemic consider using longer time frames. Always check to see if trends hold true at higher levels of detail before drawing conclusions. A plan, for example, is not deemed important because it holds a high rank within a prescriber's activity unless it ranks high among plans at the territory level.

Plan Universe

Xponent PlanTrak does not require additional physician maintenance over Xponent, but it requires maintenance of the plan demographic data. The basic plan demographics are provided by the vendor. Whether it is part of your core customer master maintenance or a separate process, you must maintain the integrity of your plan data by accounting for plan demographic changes, merger cross-references, alignment to corporate account managers, etc.

Xponent PlanTrak uses a two-level plan definition; the payer nationally and the plan locally. The challenge for corporate account managers is the lack of a regional plan definition in Xponent PlanTrak for players with regional plans. To compensate for that, you can insert a regional plan layer and align the local plans to regional plans, with the regional plans connecting to the payer at the national level. You do not have to align every local plan to a regional one but only those actively managed by your corporate accounts group. This adds to the maintenance of your customer file but solves an important problem. New plans would need to be aligned to a regional plan or would be associated by default with the payer.

The figure below demonstrates the mapping of plans to regional plans and payers:

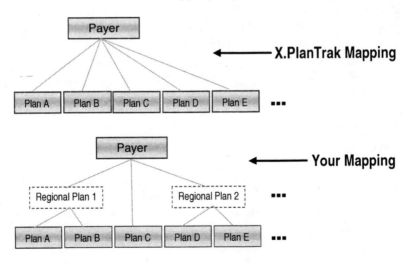

Figure 62. Regional plan alignment

XPONENT PLANTRAK APPLICATIONS

Xponent PlanTrak answers some very basic managed care related questions at the same time it provides some valuable insight to some key applications. Geographically, it helps you identify and understand plan influences from the solo physician practice to the territory and national levels. Plan data can be used to optimize structured applications such as targeting and compensation.

For the individual physician, Xponent PlanTrak identifies the plans paying for his patients' prescriptions for the manufacturer's own and competitor products. The business from each plan is quantified in number of scripts, volume units and dollar measures, which allow you to evaluate a plan's importance.

That by itself does not answer all of the questions but it is definitely a good start. Once you establish the influence of each plan, you need to determine the status of the drugs in your market with the formularies of the more influential plans. It is often this information that allows you to explain why some products perform better than others. Equally important is the co-pay amount for each product of each plan. The more formulary restrictions and the higher the co-pay, the more difficult it is to convince the physician to prescribe your product. A preferred status and low co-pay with a formulary, on the other hand, aids the sales process. The formulary and co-pay information is not available in Xponent PlanTrak. Formulary and co-pay information can be obtained from vendors, surveys or the sales reps and corporate account managers in the field.

The same analysis can be performed at the territory or higher levels to evaluate the impact of plans with restrictions. Ultimately, it becomes the job of the corporate accounts team to try to resolve reimbursement issues so that the sales reps achieve better pull-through results.

At the national level, the aggregate activity of Third Party plans, Medicaid and Cash gives you a complete payer-mix picture. Also, referred to as the method of payment, expressed in percentage terms, the data reveals the relative importance of the reimbursement types.

Targeting

Physician segmentation without consideration of managed care limitations assumes that 100% of the physician's business can be influenced. In reality, business from restricted plans is out of reach for products not in the formularies of these plans. Ideally, the estimated potential of a physician should reflect this and physicians should be segmented accordingly.

As the relative rank of physicians change, so does targeting. When the physician's ranking is lowered because of these influences, the physician now receives fewer calls and less effort. Instead, that effort goes to physicians with true potential for increasing business.

TIP: Formularies can change frequently, more so than any other variable in your segmentation. This could keep you in constant motion adjusting targeting. Allow the flexibility to make manual adjustments to the physician ranking or segment attributes.

At a more strategic level, regional and national plan influences can be evaluated using Xponent PlanTrak to create targeting lists for corporate account managers. Some of the measures considered in the segmentation of these plans include the Rx volume from Xponent PlanTrak, the geographic extend of the plan's influence and the number of lives covered by the plan.

Compensation

Strong plan influences can be more of a factor for a territory than others impacting the sales rep's ability to achieve his goals. This problem may be more pronounced in markets with more expensive drugs that are subject to higher plan restrictions. Compensation plans for territories could be adjusted for the restricted portion of the business.

Using Xponent PlanTrak in compensation applications should take into consideration the data condition of the plans included in the calculations. Some plans in Xponent PlanTrak often have less than desirable amounts of data and data reliability ratings. The vendor's supplemental tables on data completeness and reliability ratings should be used to determine the appropriateness of use of the plan data in compensation.

Glossary

Actual Acquisition Cost   The invoice price of a drug to a provider of care to patients. Required by some insurers with submissions of claims.

Acute Care   Care provided for the treatment of an immediate and severe episode of illness, the subsequent treatment of injuries related to an accident or other trauma, or during recovery from surgery. Acute care is usually provided in a hospital by specialized personnel using complex and sophisticated technical equipment and materials. Unlike chronic care, acute care is often necessary for only a short time.

Adjudication   The processing of claims according to contract.

Alignment   The process of dividing geographic areas or accounts into sales territories. Geographic assignments are typically done by ZIP code while accounts are explicitly assigned to the territory. The typical sales force hierarchy is territory-district-region.

Alternate Site Care   Refers to outpatient clinics, physicians' offices, nursing home facilities, home care, ambulatory infusion centers, outpatient surgery centers, urgent care centers, and certain other to hospital care sites.

Ambulatory Care   Also referred to as outpatient care it is health services provided without the patient being admitted for overnight stay at a hospital. It includes services of ambulatory care centers, hospital outpatient departments, physicians' offices and home health care.

Ancillary Services   Supplemental services, including laboratory, radiology, physical therapy, and inhalation therapy, that are provided in conjunction with medical or hospital care.

Average Wholesale Price (AWP)   The average cost of a non-discounted pharmaceutical product to pharmacies by wholesalers. The AWP is used by many public and private payers as the basis for reimbursing pharmaceuticals given in outpatient settings. AWP prices are published in references such as PriceChek and Red Book.

Benefit   A covered item such as a pharmaceutical, device, supply, service, or procedure by a private insurance plan or public health program.

Call   A visit or telephone contact made by a sales rep to a physician office, hospital or other site of care for the purpose of delivering promotional messages for one or more pharmaceutical products. The recipients of the messages are the physician, pharmacist, and other hospital staff.

CAM   Corporate Account Manager.

Capitation   A system for reimbursing healthcare providers with a fixed payment for every patient served, regardless of how many or few services the patient uses. Health maintenance organizations frequently use this system.

Carve outs   Types of services that are explicitly excluded from a subscriber's main health coverage plan. These benefits are often provided and managed by another group or insurer. Common examples include mental health, eye care, pharmacy, etc.

Case Management Method designed to accommodate the specific health services needs of an individual through a coordinated effort to achieve the desired health outcome in a cost effective manner. The process monitors and coordinates treatment for patients with specific diagnosis or requiring high-cost or extensive services. Case managers coordinate referrals to consultants, specialists, hospitals, ancillary providers and services. Case management is intended to ensure adequate care for the patient, continuity of services and accessibility, and to avoid misutilization of facilities and resources.

Centers for Medicare & Medicaid Services (CMS) Formerly the Health Care Financing Administration (HCFA). The federal government agency part of the Department of Health and Human Services which oversees the states' administrations of Medicaid, while directly administering Medicare.

Chain Pharmacy A chain of four or more stores bearing the same name, owned and/or operated by the same entity.

Chronic Care Care provided to individuals with long standing, persistent diseases or conditions.

Claim A demand for the payment of benefits made to the payer under the insurance contract. Claims are submitted manually or electronically.

CMS See Centers for Medicare & Medicaid Services.

Co-morbidities Diseases occurring at the same time.

Compliance-Drug The adherence of the patient to the dosing instructions of the physician.

Concomitance, Diagnosis Diagnoses that are reported by the patient together during the same visit.

Concomitance, Product Drugs in combination therapies used together to treat the same diagnosis.

Co-payment A specified flat amount paid by the insured or covered persons pay per unit of service with the rest of the cost paid by the insurer.

Co-promotion An arrangement based on which two or more companies jointly promote a single product.

Cost Per Call The average cost to the manufacturer for a sales rep's call to a physician or hospital.

CRM System Customer Relation Management System

DACON Abbreviation for Daily Average Consumption. A conversion factor used to convert units to days-of-therapy.

DDD Dollars The product of units sold and WAC or an alternative price selected by DDD clients.

DDD Price Most often the wholesaler acquisition cost. Alternatively a DDD client selected price for his direct sales and/or government depot sales.

DDD Units The quantity multiplied by the number of units in the package.

DEA Drug Enforcement Agency. Part of the Department of Justice. It regulates the use of control substances.

Diagnosis Related Groups (DRGs) A classification system that categorizes illness by diagnosis and treatment and used to pay a hospital or other inpatient provider for their services. The provider is paid a fixed set amount for each DRG regardless of the provider's actual cost. The group definitions are based on medical diagnosis, treatments, procedures, patient age and sex, presence or absence of significant co-morbidities or complications, discharge status, and other relevant criteria. The federal government uses DRGs to reimburse hospitals for care to Medicare subscribers.

Direct-to-Consumer (DTC) Promotional activities targeting directly the patient and include print ads, commercials, internet content, etc.

Discounted Fee-For-Service An agreed upon rate of reimbursement between a provider and a payer that is less than the provider's full fee. Providers accept the lower payment in exchange for volume of business.

Disease Management A process based on therapeutic guidelines that targets to improve the patient's total condition in order to prevent acute episodes.

Dispensed as Written Filled New Rxs as written by the physician without substitutions.

Double-Blinded Studies A method of researching outcomes by comparing the effects of a drug on a target to those of a placebo.

Drop Shipment A shipment directly from a manufacturer to a customer on the behalf of a wholesaler and billed by the wholesaler.

Drug Regimen Review Activities designed to guarantee that the patient receives the proper medications at the right time and in the right doses.

Drug Utilization Review (DUR) Also known as Drug Utilization Evaluation (DUE). The systematic review of drug use patterns for the purpose of reducing the cost of utilization, typically performed by a DUR committee. The review examines the number of prescriptions per patient per month and the average cost per prescription. DURs are commonly performed by MCOs, hospitals, and other payers for physicians, physician groups, medical specialties, retail pharmacies, employee groups and patients. DUR sanction or reward practitioners depending on performance.

Ethical Product A product requiring a written prescription, promoted primarily to physicians.

FDA Food and Drug Administration. It regulates the sale and manufacture of drugs.

Fee-for-Service Traditional method of payment for healthcare services where specific payment is made for specific services rendered. Patients may then seek reimbursement from a private insurer or the government.

Filled by Other Dispensed prescriptions with a product other than the one written by the physician.

Filled for Non-originator Dispensed prescriptions for a generically prescribed product by the physician.

Food Store Pharmacy A pharmacy located in a food store or supermarket.

Formulary List of approved drugs that will be reimbursed by the payer. Open formularies promote the use of generic and preferred drugs; Closed formularies reimburse only for approved drugs and require prior approval for use of other drugs.

Group Model HMO An HMO that contracts with one or more single or multi-specialty physician groups to provide a specified range of services to its patients. The medical group may serve non-HMO and it is usually paid with a capitation fee, that is, a fixed amount per patient. The group practice determines the compensation of the physician and may share profits.

Group Practice A group of physicians that engage in the coordinated practice of their profession in one or more group practice facilities, and who share common overhead expenses, medical and other records, and substantial portions of the equipment and the professional, technical, and administrative staffs. Group practices are formed primarily because of the need to lower costs and improve the ability to contract.

Health Care Finance Administration (HCFA) See CMS.

Health Maintenance Organization (HMO) A managed care organization that provides a specific range of inpatient and ambulatory services for a fixed fee. There are four basic models of HMOs: group model, independent practice association (IPA) model, network model, and staff-model.

Home Health Provider A healthcare entity that offers nursing, dietary, social, therapy and counseling services in the home of the patient.

Home Health Services Services and items furnished by a home health agency to an individual who is under the care of a physician. The services are provided in an individual's home on a visiting basis and include: nursing, physical therapy, dietary, counseling, and social services; physical, occupational, or speech therapy; part-time or intermittent skilled nursing care; medical social services, medical supplies and appliances and home health aid services. Services are provided under an established plan and reviewed periodically by a physician.

Home Infusion Therapy The provision of intravenous drugs and biologics in the home by a home health agencies and licensed pharmacies.

Hospice Health care facility providing medical care and counseling to terminally ill patients the last few months of their lives.

Hybrid/Mixed Model HMO An HMO that combines features of more than one principal HMO models.

ICD-9-CM Diagnosis Codes World Health Organization International Classification of Disease, 9th revision with clinical modification. Universal coding method used to document the incidence of disease, injury, mortality and illness.

ICD-9-CM Procedure Codes Supplement codes for therapy modes, surgery, radiology, laboratory, and other diagnostic procedures.

Incidence The number of new cases of disease, infection, or some other event over a period of time in reference to the population in which they occur.

Indemnity An insurance plan under which the insured person pays for the cost of care and is reimbursed for covered expenses.

Independent Pharmacy A pharmacy owned and/or operated independently, or a chain with fewer than four stores.

Independent Practice Association (IPA) Model HMO An HMO that contracts with individual physicians in private practice or physician groups. The physicians continue to practice independently and treat fee-for-service patients as well as HMO members. IPA physicians are paid by the HMO on either a capitation or a fee-for-service basis.

Indigent Patient Programs Manufacturer sponsored programs to provide free product to patients who are either uninsured or cannot afford to pay for drugs. They are also known as patient assistance programs.

Integrated Delivery System (IDS) A network of healthcare provider organizations usually including hospitals and physician groups, that provides a broad spectrum of services to a defined population and is held both clinically and fiscally accountable for the outcomes of the populations served. The IDS may incorporate healthcare plans in which case it is a mix of provider and payer.

Inventory The amount of merchandise physically "on hand" in drug warehouses at the end of the month.

IPA See Independent Practice Association.

Long Term Care (LTC) Healthcare delivered on a continuous basis to a patient for a period of 30 days or more by a hospital or other healthcare facility.

Mail service Pharmacy A pharmacy that dispenses prescription drugs through the mail or other parcel carrier.

Managed Care Healthcare systems and techniques used to control the use of healthcare services. Includes a review of medical necessity, incentives to use certain providers, and case management.

Managed Care Organization (MCO) A health plan that seeks to manage care. Generally, this involves contracting with healthcare providers to deliver healthcare services on a capitated basis.

Managed Care Plan A health plan that provides comprehensive care in a cost-effective manner. It has a defined system of selected providers that contract with the plan and enrollees have a financial incentive to use participating providers.

Mass Merchandiser A large discount store with several different lines of merchandise. Mass Merchandisers may or may not have a pharmacy department for prescription products.

Maximum Allowable Cost (MAC) A maximum amount that will be reimbursed for a given product or service, especially as it relates to prescription drugs.

Medicaid and some MCOs use it to manage costs for some generic and multi-source products.

Medicaid   Government entitlement program for the poor who are blind, aged, disabled or members of families with dependent children (AFDC). The program is federally aided but state-operated and administered and provides medical benefits for certain indigent or low-income persons in need of health and medical care. States set their own standards for qualification.

Medicare   A federal program providing health insurance for people at the age of 65 and older, and for disabled people of all ages. It is funded by the federal government and administered by the Centers for Medicare & Medicaid Services (CMS). Beneficiaries are responsible for deductibles and co-payments.

Medicare Part A   Covers hospitalization, nursing home care, hospice and the services of a home health agency. Medicare reimburses for hospital inpatient care based on DRGs and hospital outpatient care on a cost basis. Part A services are financed by the Medicare HI Trust Fund, which consists of Medicare tax payments.

Medicare Part B   Supplemental medical insurance which covers beneficiaries for physician services, medical supplies, and other outpatient treatment. Beneficiaries are responsible for monthly premiums, co-payments, deductibles, and balance billing. Part B services are financed by a combination of enrollee premiums and general tax revenues.

Medigap   A private insurance policy that supplements Medicare benefits by covering some costs not paid for by Medicare that include deductibles, co-payments and in many circumstances, services excluded by Medicare such as outpatient prescription drugs.

Method of Payment   Refers to the reimbursement breakdown of a drug by payment type.

Morbidity   The extend of disease, injury and disability in a defined population expressed in rates of incidence and prevalence.

Multi-Specialty Group   A group of physicians from different medical specialties who work in the same group practice.

National Drug Code (NDC)   Drug coding system, sort of a serial number for a drug. The components of the NDC number identify the manufacturer, product and pack size.

Network Model HMO   An HMO that contracts with single or multi-specialty groups as well as hospitals and other healthcare providers. Generally limited to large single or multi-specialty groups.

New Prescription   A prescription filled from a prescription slip presented for the first time at a specific pharmacy. Not necessarily the first prescription of a new therapy.

Nurse Practitioner   A registered nurse trained to provide primary care under the supervision of a physician but not necessarily under his presence. They practice in most healthcare settings and have limited prescribing authority under a protocol with the supervising physician.

Orphan Drug   A drug designed to treat a rare disease with a patient population of less than 200,000 individuals. Under the Orphan Drug Act of 1986, orphan drugs are granted seven years of market exclusivity from the time the product becomes commercially available, even if it exceeds the product's patent life. This economic incentive is intended to encourage manufacturers to develop products for the treatment of rare diseases.

Outcome   The result of medical or surgical intervention or non-intervention.

Outcome Measurement   System used to track clinical treatment and responses to that treatment, including measures of mortality, morbidity, and functional status.

Outcomes Management   Methods implemented by payers and providers for managing care in a way that would produce the best outcomes. Using a database of outcomes experience, providers know better which treatment modalities result in consistently better outcomes for patients. Outcomes management often results in the development of clinical protocols.

Outpatient Care   Also referred to as ambulatory care, it is care given to a patient who is not bedridden.

Over-the-Counter (OTC)   Drugs that do not require a prescription.

Patient Starts   The number of patients who received a prescription or a sample during a specified period of time.

Payer   An entity that pays for medical services and therapies. Usually an indemnity insurance, MCO, Medicare or Medicaid.

Payer Mix   The level of influence the payer types have in the reimbursement of a drug.

Payment Type   Refers to the method of payment of the prescription; cash, Medicaid, or third-party insurance.

PBM   Pharmacy Benefit Management Company. PBMs contract with healthcare plans to manage the pharmacy benefits of their members, from issuing pharmacy cards to full prescription adjudication.

Persistency   The adherence of the patient to the length of the drug treatment without lapses of significant length of time.

Pharmacoeconomic Studies   Research, usually sponsored by the manufacturer, to study the relationship between the cost of drugs and the clinical outcomes.

Physician Practice Management Company (PPM)   A company that offers management, administrative support and capital to member physician practices for a membership fee or part of the revenue.

Plan Of Action (POA)   A plan that outlines the promotional activities of the sales force for a specific time period.

Point-of-Service Plan   A health insurance benefits program in which subscribers can select between different delivery systems (i.e., HMO, PPO and fee-for-service). Also known as open-ended HMOs or PPOs, these plans allow members to see physicians outside of the network at a higher fee to the member.

Preferred Drug Drug formulary status that refers to all mandatory dispensing of generics and all drugs designated as maximum allowable cost drugs.

Preferred Provider Organization (PPO) A healthcare plan that contracts with healthcare providers who furnish medical care at discounted rates in exchange of a certain volume of patients. Enrollees select their provider from a predefined list of providers and may incur out-of-pocket expenses for covered services received outside the PPO if the outside charge exceeds the PPO payment rate.

Preferred Providers Contracted physicians, hospitals, and other to provide health services to patients covered by a particular health plan.

Preferred/Restricted Drug Any preferred drug that has prescribing limitations that affect reimbursement. These limitations may include prescriber specialty, patient age, indications, diagnoses, etc.

Prevalence The number of cases of disease, infection or other occurring at a particular point in time in relation to the population size from which it was drawn.

Primary Care Physician (PCP) A family practitioner, general internist, pediatrician, obstetrician who provides basic care and coordinates the referrals to specialists.

Prior Authorization A process requiring a healthcare provider to obtain approval prior to providing the patient certain services and procedures. Reserved usually for services that are either expensive or likely to be overused or abused.

Prior Authorization Required Drug Drugs that require prior approval from the plan before they are prescribed.

Private Managed Care Includes HMOs, IPAs, POSs, PPOs, EPOs, and prescription card programs.

Processors Organizations contracted with managed care plans to provide prescription benefits to enrollees.

Provider A physician, nurse, pharmacist, hospital, group practice, nursing home, pharmacy or any individual or group of individuals that provides a healthcare service. A health plan, managed care company or insurance carrier is not a healthcare provider. Those entities are called payers. A provider may create or manage health plans, in which case, the provider is also a payer. A payer can be provider if the payer owns or manages providers, as with some staff-model HMOs.

Public Managed Care Includes all Medicaid prescription-reimbursement programs.

Refill Prescription A dispensed prescription filled using the same number as the original prescription.

Reimbursement Payments received by providers or patients for benefits covered under an insurance plan.

Restricted Drug   An approved drug in the formulary that has prescribing limitations that affect reimbursement. The limitations may include prescriber specialty, patient age, indications, diagnoses, etc.

Sell-In   Term to describe the direct and indirect sales into an account or stated another way purchases made by the account.

Sell-Out   Term to describe the distribution of merchandise out of an account which equates to sales of the account.

Share of Voice   The total promotional spend of a product that includes detailing, sampling and professional journal advertising divided by the total promotional spend for the select market.

Skilled Nursing Facility (SNF)   A facility that provides 24-hour nursing care, physical, occupational and speech therapies, and other services. SNFs are either freestanding or part of a hospital. They cater patients with reduced physical and/or mental capacities.

Solo Practice   A physician that practices alone without sharing of expenses and revenues with other physicians.

Staff-model HMO   An HMO that owns its medical facilities and the health services are provided by physicians who are salaried employees of the HMO. Physicians in these HMOs treat only members of the HMO and have no private fee-for-service practices. Staff-model HMOs are the most restrictive both in terms of physician practice style and patient choice.

Substituted for Originator Product   Dispensed New Rxs where the product was substituted for another specified by the physician.

Surgi-Emergi Center   Non-hospital affiliated health facility that provides short-term care for minor medical emergencies or procedures needing immediate treatment; also called urgent center, urgi-center or free standing emergency medical service center.

Third-Party Administrator (TPA)   An independent organization that provides administrative services including claims processing and underwriting for other entities, such as insurance companies or employers. A TPA is either an insurance company or simply an organization with expertise and capability to administer all or a portion of the claims process. TPAs are utilized by insurance companies, self-insured employers and hospitals or provider organizations desiring to set up their own health plans for outsourcing certain responsibilities such as claims, utilization reviews or membership functions.

Third Party Payer   A public or private organization that pays for health or medical expenses on behalf of beneficiaries or recipients. Beneficiaries pay a premium for such coverage in all private and in some public programs; the payer organization then pays bills on the individual's behalf. These payments are referred to as third-party payments. The three parties involved are the individual receiving the service (first party), the provider of the service (second party), and the organization paying for it (third party).

Total Prescriptions (TRx) The sum of both New and Refill prescriptions.

Traveling Script A prescription written in one geographic area and filled in another.

Treatment Protocol Specific guidelines to treat specific symptoms of a disease.

Un-Managed Care Health services paid in cash and may include traditional indemnity insurance plans that reimburse cash payment, and non-insured healthcare.

Uniform System of Classification (USC) System for the classification of drugs designed by IMS Health.

Units Various measures of product quantities expressed in number of pieces in a package, number of pieces in a pack unit, number of potency units, etc.

Utilization Use of services and supplies expressed in terms of patterns or rates of use of a single service or type of service such as hospital care, physician visits, prescription drugs, etc.

Utilization Review The process of evaluating the necessity, appropriateness, and efficiency of the use of healthcare services, procedures, and resources. Utilization Review is one of the primary tools utilized by Integrated Delivery Systems, Managed Care Organizations and health plans to control over-utilization, reduce costs and manage care. Review can be performed either prospectively through prior-authorization, or retrospectively, for the appropriateness of hospital admissions, diagnostic tests, drug therapies, length of a stay, and discharge practices. Utilization Review looks for cases falling outside established norms by the use of protocols, benchmarks or data from an aggregate set of cases. Managed care organizations will sometimes refuse payment for services which do not meet their standards.

Withdrawals Merchandise distribution as sales out of a re-seller.

Index